Enjoy!
Jeanne Weisgal

Dinner *for* Eight

Healthy Cooking for the Kosher Gourmet

Jeanne N. Weisgal

Maxrom Press/Baltimore

Jeanne N. Weisgal
DINNER FOR EIGHT
Healthy Cooking for the Kosher Gourmet
P.O.Box 5636, Baltimore, MD 21210

Copyright © 1996 by Jeanne N. Weisgal and Maxrom Press

ISBN 0-930339-04-5
Library of Congress
#96-061659

Printed in U.S.A., 1996 by Ed Early Printing Co., Inc.

Introducing Jeanne N. Weisgal . . .

In her lifetime, Jeanne Weisgal has done just about everything: public school teacher, drama teacher, ACLU activist, political campaign manager, theatrical consultant and business owner — each job taken on and managed while married and raising five children. And throughout this varied career, a fascination with the very best recipe has always been a focal point.

This love of both the preparation and enjoyment of quality meals was a legacy from her father, Hirsh de La Viez. Growing up in Washington, D.C., the two would escape into the basement where a second kitchen was located; there to experiment, concoct, test, taste, test again, and eventually, savor the end results. This early culinary training became a mainstay of Jeanne's life.

Wherever she went, which included Baltimore through the first half of her married life, and later Israel, and whatever she did (see that long list of jobs at the beginning), cooking would remain a constant. Meetings of every ilk were invariably held around a table laden with an abundance of food, all tasty, appealing and interesting. Each of her children, at one point or another, was inveigled into acting as her sous chef, doing the preliminary preparation for the wide variety of dishes she produced (and later, the cleaning up). And as she traveled and experienced other cultures and cuisines, the diversity of comestibles appearing at meal time grew.

Jeanne imbued in her children this same love of food. Her first cookbook arose out of a desire to pass on those familiar and loved dishes to her progeny. But, since her home was usually a confluence of visitors from around the world, requests for "a copy of that recipe" were rife. Hence the first volume.

This second cookbook reflects the changing requirements of an aging baby-boomer population, now concerned with food that is at the same time both delicious and healthy. Since the two are so rarely synonymous, the array of recipes that follows is very welcome. Revel in familiar dishes as well as new ones to tempt your palate. So eat hearty. I promise you a pleasure far beyond your expectations.

Written by Margit B. Weisgal
Number one offspring and author of SHOW AND SELL

■

This book is dedicated to
Lois and Philip Macht
without whose love and encouragement
it would not have seen the light of day.
And to the memory of
Freddie Weisgal, husband and friend.

■

■

— IN APPRECIATION —

Thanks are due the "Tuesday Night Groups" who were my tasters and testers, whose patience and tolerance were unlimited, through thick and thin and crunchy, thank you, you know who you are. Also thanks to my children Margit, Samuel, Aran, Becky and David, real and adopted, who looked forward to every meal with anticipation and especially to son Lawrence, whose telephone calls and listening ear were a constant source of encouragement and comfort. Thanks to all the people who gave me recipes that I adapted and adopted for this book. These people have all been acknowledged on the various recipes. Thank you Marjorie Moch for editorial advice. Thanks also to the residents of 4401 who made me their in-house Gourmet and Food Guru.

■

TABLE OF CONTENTS

A Few Helpful Words About Using This Book

1. Read through the recipe completely for clarity before starting. This is also important for ingredients on your shopping list.

2. The order of ingredients is listed in order of use.

3. All servings are generous enough for hungry people; no need to worry about running out of food.

4. When recipe says "salt to taste", it is because there is no way to tell how salty your beef or chicken or vegetable broth is until you taste it or if your salt intake is restricted.

5. The book is written for the busy entertainer and is full of methods for preparing in advance.

6. All measurements in recipes are given in U.S. customary and in metric units; temperatures in Fahrenheit and in Celsius; tablespoons and teaspoons in standard measuring spoons, level unless otherwise stated; cups based on 8 ounces [225 milliliters] each. Absolute accuracy is important only in cake recipes or where specifically stated.

7. See measurement charts for equivalents used in this book.

8. On each recipe and in the index, "m" for meat, "d" for dairy, "p" for pareve is indicated.

9. Recipes calling for beef, chicken or vegetable broth can be made with homemade broth, canned, dry soup powder, bouillion cubes or the Israeli produced pareve beef or chicken flavored soup mix.

10. Where possible, I have indicated which foods can be frozen.

11. I always serve some kind of fresh fruit, either mixed in a salad or by itself, i.e. strawberries, pineapple, as an extra dessert for those whose sugar intake is restricted.

12. For larger dinner parties or a buffet, add an extra course or two or three, depending on the number of people invited.

13. If the size of ingredients, i.e. eggs, garlic cloves, vegetables, etc. is important, I have so indicated.

14. I use only extra virgin olive oil as indicated in recipes.

15. I use the following ingredients exclusively: fresh mushrooms, freshly ground pepper, freshly ground nutmeg and mace, fresh flat leaf [Italian] parsley, fresh dill and pareve margarine.

16. Generally speaking, the weight given in the recipe is the weight to buy, unless otherwise stated, i.e. shelled peas=weight after cleaning.

17. If fresh herbs are available or preferred rather than dried, as indicated in recipe, triple the amount indicated in the recipe.

A Few Important Utensils to Use in the Preparation and the Serving of Meals for Entertaining

1. Three large covered casseroles or attractive Dutch oven type pots, suitable for serving: 2 ½ quart [2 ¼ liter], 3 ½ quart [3 liter], and 6 quart [5 ½ liter]; also souffle and or casserole dishes.

2. Two au gratin or attractive baking pans: about 13 x 10 ½ x 3 inches [32 ½ x 27 x 7 ½ centimeters] and 12 ½ x 9 x 2 inches [32 x 23 x 5 centimeters] suitable for serving.

3. A set of graduated saucepans and fry pans with lids. I prefer non stick, which are readily available.

4. Kettles with lids for soups: 5 quart [4 ½ liter], 8 quart [8 liter], 12 quart [11 ½ liter]. I prefer non stick.

5. Pepper mills for black and white peppercorns and salt dispensers. A shaker for garlic granules.

6. A mixer with different beaters, especially the dough hook, and 2 bowls is a great help to me, a blender and a meat grinder or food mill are essential, a food processor is essential, I have found a mini processor indispensible for things such as chopping garlic, small amounts of parsley, etc. and an electric hand mixer.

7. Kitchen tools which are important for me are a set of graduated measuring spoons, a set of graduated measuring cups, a set of

wooden spoons of different sizes, two metal mixing spoons, wire whisks of different sizes, rubber and hard plastic spatulas, a broad flat knife, a slotted spoon, two heavy forks for meats, kitchen scissors for snipping chives, parsley, etc., a poultry shears for cutting up chickens, ducks and game hens, sharp rotary type vegetable peelers, pastry brushes, a flexible pancake turner [broad spatula], two or three colanders, a garlic press, tongs, flour sifter, rolling pin, cleaver, potato masher, funnels, a candy thermometer, an egg beater, a mortar and pestle, a set of glass mixing bowls of various sizes, a ginger grater, a steamer basket, a bamboo steamer, timers, kitchen scales, cutting boards, a can opener, a cork screw, heat diffusers, a pastry cutter, pastry bags with various tips, a ricer, a rubber hammer, an egg slicer for slicing fresh mushrooms, vertical roasting cones for chickens, a cherry pitter for seeding olives, a knife sharpener.

8. A spaetze maker is a great inexpensive gadget for tiny dumplings.

9. I have found an electric slicing machine to be a great help to me for slicing meats and breads.

10. A Foley grater strains and extracts all the essences of vegetables and fruits.

11. A mandoline is an inexpensive gadget consisting of a flat board with a flexible knife across the middle, for thinly slicing apples, cucumbers, carrots, onions and potatoes.

12. Strainers of all sizes are useful.

13. I use only 11 inch [28 centimeter] pie and quiche pans but two 9 inch [23 centimeter] pie pans will replace each one for pies and quiches.

14. A set of three 9 inch [23 centimeter] and three 8 inch [20 centimeter] cake pans, a set of four 5 x 9 inch [12 $\frac{1}{2}$ x 23 centimeter] and four 4 x 8 inch [10 x 20 centimeter] bread loaf pans, 9 x 13 inch [23 x 33 centimeter] and a 17 $\frac{1}{4}$ x 11 $\frac{3}{8}$ [34 x 43 $\frac{1}{4}$ centimeter] baking pans, a 10 inch [25 centimeter] tube form, a fish mold, a gelatin mold, two jelly roll pans, two cookie sheets, two cake racks for cooling, one or two fluted tube pans [kugel forms], tiny muffin tins, regular muffin tins, an open roasting pan with a rack, a heavy roasting pan with a lid are essential baking equipment for me.

15. Sharp knives of all sizes are, of course, in constant use.

16. Coffee pots of different sizes and a coffee grinder are an important part of entertaining.

17. Also essential are large wooden salad bowls, and all kinds of serving platters, trays and bowls.

A Few Helpful Hints

1. Adding a bit of lemon juice, placing the avocado pit in center, and covering tightly with plastic wrap, will keep your avocado salad from turning black.

2. To quick soak and de-gas dry beans, place beans in a large pot, cover beans with about 10 times the amount of water, bring water to a boil, boil for 2 minutes, cover pot and let sit, off heat for 1 hour. Drain and discard water. Directions in the recipe are the same as for overnight soaking.

3. If necessary destring celery with a rotary type vegetable peeler.

4. Skim froth from soups with a Chinese screen skimmer.

5. Save and freeze the necks, feet, wing tips and carcass of chickens to make homemade Chicken Broth [see Index].

6. Grate quanities of Parmesan cheese and freeze in small packets. Do the same with any dried-up cheeses.

7. A wire whisk will keep out or remove lumps from bechamel, cream and cheese sauces.

8. To peel tomatoes, pour boiling water over fresh tomatoes in a bowl. Let them sit in the water for a minute or so and the skin will easily slip off. Do the same for peaches.

9. To coddle an egg, place a raw egg in boiling water, turn off the heat and set the timer for required number of minutes.

10. Keep all knives sharp for easier preparation.

11. Lightly mash a garlic clove with the side of a cleaver or a small hammer and it will be easy to peel.

12. Chop a quanity of peeled garlic cloves in a mini processor and keep in a small jar in your fridge for convenience.

13. Put a bay leaf or hot pepper in your flour, cornmeal, sesame seed, noodle container, dried mushrooms, etc. to keep out bugs or if you have room, store in your freezer.

14. Putting a bay leaf in the water when cooking cauliflower will help eliminate the odor.

15. To core apples and pears, cut fruit in half and use a melon baller to scoop out core and seeds.

16. Freeze juiced lemon halves to have peel on hand for those recipes calling for lemon peel.

17. Rubbing your hands with juiced lemon halves will help remove the odors of fish, onion, garlic, etc.

18. After using cheese cloth, wash well with soapy water and hang to dry, it can be used many times.

19. To blanch a vegetable, plunge the vegetable into a pot of boiling water for the number of minutes indicated in recipe, drain and cool quickly under cold running water and drain again.

20. If food begins to stick to bottom of pot, let the pot sit off heat for 15 to 20 minutes, stir well from bottom of pot and the food will easily unstick.

21. To clean copper, make a paste of salt and white vinegar and rub copper pieces to shine like new.

22. Before measuring honey or corn syrup, spray container or coat with oil and honey or corn syrup will slide out of measuring container easily.

23. Freeze celery tops with leaves, diced, in batches for soups.

24. Remove odor and taste from oil by frying sliced, unpeeled potatoes in the oil.

APPETIZERS AND FIRST COURSES

Antipasto [m or d]

I love to make and arrange an antipasto. It someimes takes me an hour or more as I ponder what to include and the placement of each ingredient. I serve this buffet style with cocktails and skip the salad course. I use a very large platter on which I place items from the following list. I try to select a variety and use enough so that everyone will have a taste of each item. I can't give you exact measurements just an overall picture of what is interesting to have. I use about 12 items [more or less], and garnish the platter [or tray] with olives, pickles, and/or radishes, and place everything on a bed of shredded lettuce. Stand some bread sticks in a large glass to accompany.

sliced and halved tomatoes or cherry tomatoes
sliced red onion or Vidalia
sliced Provolone or Mozzarella, rolled, or Feta cheese
sliced dry salami or turkey sausage
rolled anchovies
sardines or smoked mackeral
smoked salmon
Tuna Salad [see Index] or chunked canned tuna
whole tiny green onions
artichoke hearts, marinated in Caesar Salad Dressing [see Index]
tiny whole carrots, either Pickled [see Index] or raw
celery sticks
cucumber sticks or Cucumber Salad [see Index]
hearts of palm
asparagus, cold, freshly cooked or canned
sliced avocado, sprinkled with lemon juice

Place different ingredients grouped according to kind and arranged according to color, so that your platter resembles a painter's palette. Be artistic and enjoy.

15

Avocado Salad [p] [Guacamole]

This is actually more of an appetizer dip than a salad. A bit zippy in taste, I serve this with baked corn chips or tortilla chips. If you add the tomatoes [see option], the dip is different in taste, but equally good. This dish freezes well, but do not add tomatoes until thawed and just before serving.

Makes about 5 cups [1.2 liters]

3 pounds [1.4 kilos] avocados, well ripened [see Note] [about 5 or 6]
18 ounces [500 grams] sweet onions, chopped finely [Vidalias]
4 ½ tablespoons lime juice
1 tablespoon salt, or to taste
6 to 8 large garlic cloves, minced
1 to 2 teaspoons chili powder, to taste
fresh black pepper, to taste
optional: 2 pounds [900 grams] fresh tomatoes, peeled, seeded, chopped finely

Carefully peel avocados, reserving pits. Coarsely chop avocados in a food processor [or mash with a silver fork]. Add the rest of the ingredients, except tomatoes, and pulse or work with a fork until combined. Taste for seasoning. Place salad in containers and put in the pits. Cover tightly with plastic wrap and refrigerate for at least 1 hour to develop the flavor. Freeze in convenient-sized containers, without the pits. Add tomatoes just before serving.

Note: To ripen avocados, wrap in newspaper and leave at room temperature until soft.

Caponata [p]

This is an Italian ratatouille growing in popularity over the years; it makes a wonderful relish, a good addition to an antipasto and is a delicious side dish. It keeps well in the fridge for about a month or you can preserve [can] it in small jelly jars, easier to do than you think. [See Index.]

Makes about 12 cups [2.7 liters]

2 pounds [900 grams] eggplant, unpeeled, cut into ¹/₂ inch [1 centimeter] cubes
salt, for sprinkling
olive oil cooking spray
1 ¹/₂ tablespoons extra virgin olive oil
1 pound [450 grams] onions, quartered, sliced thickly
5 garlic cloves, chopped
10 ounces [290 grams] celery, sliced diagonally
7 ounces [200 grams] pimiento stuffed olives
7 ounces [200 grams] brine-cured black olives, seeded
1 ³/₄ ounces [45 grams] capers, drained
3 - 14 ¹/₂ ounce [410 gram] cans diced tomatoes, undrained
2 ¹/₂ tablespoons sugar
5 tablespoons red wine vinegar
1 tablespoon dried basil
1 tablespoon dried oregano
salt, to taste
fresh black pepper, to taste

Sprinkle eggplant cubes liberally with salt and let drain in a colander for 30 minutes. Rinse and drain well. Set aside.

In a well sprayed 5 quart [5 liter] kettle, add olive oil and heat until hot. Saute onions and garlic until golden, stirring frequently. Add celery, tomatoes and eggplant and bring to a simmer. Simmer for 15 minutes, stirring occasionally.

Add the rest of the ingredients and simmer until eggplant is well softened, about 1 ¹/₂ to 2 hours.

Let cool and place in jars, cover and refrigerate. If you wish to preserve the Caponata, process in a water bath for 15 minutes.

Chopped Herring [p]

I like the sweet and sour flavor of chopped herring as an appetizer. Serve with thin slices of 3 Stage Rye Bread [see Index].

Makes about 5 ½ cups [1.3 liters]

13 ½ ounces [380 grams] Matjes herring filets
19 ounces [525 grams] onions, peeled
12 ½ ounces [350 grams] tart apples, peeled, cored
10 eggs, hard boiled, 6 yolks discarded
4 to 6 tablespoons matzo meal
2 tablespoons cider vinegar
sugar, to taste

Drain any oil from herring. In a food processor, finely chop onions. Add herring and pulse until chopped and combined with onions. Transfer onions and herring to a mixing bowl. Without washing processor, chop apples and then add eggs and chop together. Add this mixture to mixing bowl. Add the rest of the ingredients and mix well to combine. Cover and refrigerate at least 1 hour to develop the flavors. The herring can be prepared a week or so in advance.

Roasted Garlic Crostini [p]

This simple, quickly put together appetizer is a great last minute dish to have in our repertoire. It contains ingredients usually on hand, either in the fridge or freezer.

Makes 12 to 18 crostini, depending on desired thickness

olive oil cooking spray

1 loaf Italian bread, cut diagonally into 12 to 18 slices

about 12 to 18 teaspoons Roasted Garlic [see Index]

optional: 12 to 24 anchovy filets, about 2 cans, drained

Lightly toast both sides of each slice of bread. Lightly spray one side of each slice of bread. Spread about 1 teaspoon garlic on sprayed side of each slice. If desired, lay 1 to 1 ½ anchovy filets on top of garlic. This part can be done ahead of time, if desired.

Warm crostini in a preheated 300°F. [150°C.] oven for 10 minutes and serve.

Dough for Zviha or Pizza [p]

Halil el Khatib, who was our houseman in Jerusalem for 14 years, lived in Bethlehem with his wife, Jamilla, who cooked for a school, and his 3 children. Jamilla made zviha for me many times and kindly gave me her recipe. Zviha is an Arab pizza, served as an appetizer. It is made in small 4 inch [10 centimeter] rounds. This dough is also terrific for pizza. I make the dough in a jiffy in the food processor. I often make this dough when I have time and after the first rising, divide it in half, wrap it in plastic wrap and freeze it. Let thaw covered.

Makes about 22 to 24 zviha rounds or 2 large pizzas

1 package yeast

¹/₄ cup [55 milliliters] lukewarm water

¹/₂ teaspoon sugar

5 cups [700 grams] all purpose unbleached flour

2 teaspoons salt

1 ¹/₄ cup [300 milliliters] lukewarm water, approximately

¹/₈ cup - 2 tablespoons extra virgin olive oil

1 recipe Meat for Zviha [see Index] or 1 recipe Topping for Pizza
  [see Index]

Proof yeast with ¹/₄ cup [55 milliliters] water and sugar in a large measuring cup, for 10 minutes.

Place flour and salt in food processor and pulse to aerate. Add 1 1/4 cup [300 milliliters] water and oil to yeast mixture. Run processor and add liquid mixture through feed tube slowly. Continue to run machine until dough comes together in a ball. If necessary add a few more drops of water until dough comes together. Turn dough out onto a lightly floured surface and knead a bit. Place dough in a bowl, cover with plasic wrap and let rise in a warm place until doubled, about 1 1/2 hours.

Punch down dough and turn out onto a lightly floured surface. Divide dough into 22 to 24 equal pieces for zviha about 1 1/2 ounces [46 grams] each or into 2 parts for pizza.

For zviha, roll each piece into a ball and press or roll each ball into a round about 4 inches [10 centimeters]. Place rounds on 2 baking sheets and let rise for 30 minutes, covered with plastic wrap.

Divide meat for zviha among rounds, about 2 heaping tablespoons each and sprinkle each with pine nuts. Bake in a preheated 425°F. [220° C.] oven for 20 to 25 minutes. Serve hot or warm.

For pizza, roll each piece into a 14 inch [35 centimeter] round or into a rectangle 16 x 11 inches (40 x 27 centimeters)and top with topping of choice. Bake in a preheated 450°F. [230°C.] oven for 15 minutes until crust is brown.

The baked zviha and baked pizza can be frozen. No need to thaw to reheat for serving. The uncooked dough can be frozen after the first rising well wrapped in plastic wrap.

Gefilte Fish *[p]*

I learned to make gefilte fish from my father-in-law, Abba Weisgal. In Jerusalem we would pick out the carp swimming in a tank in the super market. He would start by fileting the fish himself. He had a special wooden bowl with a wooden handled chopper and he would prepare everything by hand. I can remember it would take him all morning so it was a dish only for special occasions. With the food processor and a good fishmonger to filet the fish, this is no longer a labor-intensive dish. Gefilte fish is traditional holiday fare in our family. Serve the gefilte fish with either or both of the 2 Horseradishes [see Index]. Gefilte fish is delish. The cooked fish balls can be frozen, [see Note]. We like to think of this as "religious fish mousse."

Makes about 25 balls

5 $\frac{1}{2}$ pounds [2 $\frac{1}{2}$ kilos] mixed fish: carp, white fish, pike, fileted, reserve bones, heads and skin of fish, weight after cleaning
1 $\frac{1}{2}$ pounds [680 grams] onions, peeled, cut up
14 ounces [400 grams] carrots, peeled, cut up
1 cup [225 milliliters] frozen egg substitute, thawed
$\frac{1}{2}$ cup [70 grams] matzo meal
$\frac{1}{2}$ cup [110 milliliters] water
3 $\frac{1}{2}$ tablespoons salt, or to taste
1 $\frac{1}{2}$ teaspoons fresh white pepper

Broth
bones, heads, skin of fish
18 ounces [500 grams] onions, sliced
14 ounces [400 grams] carrots, peeled, sliced
11 to 12 cups [2 $\frac{1}{2}$ to 2 $\frac{3}{4}$ liters] cold water
2 teaspoons salt
$\frac{1}{2}$ teaspoon fresh white pepper
1 teaspoon sugar

Using the pulse action, finely chop fish filets, onions and carrots in a food processor, in batches, transferring as chopped to a large mixing bowl. Add egg substitute, matzo meal, water, salt and pepper. Mix thoroughly until well combined.

In a 12 quart [12 liter] kettle, place bones, heads and skin of fish on the bottom. With moistened hands, form fish mixture into ovals using about 1/2 cup [110 milliliters] of fish. Place ovals carefully in kettle in layers, dividing each layer with a layer of onion and carrot slices.

Carefully and slowly, pour in cold water to barely covering fish balls. Bring quickly to a boil. Add salt, pepper and sugar. Simmer covered, for 2 hours. After 1 hour, taste broth and correct the seasoning. Let fish cool in the kettle, in the broth, uncovered.

Transfer balls carefully with a spoon and a fork, to 2 au gratin or large deep platters. Pick out carrot slices and arrange decoratively on balls. Strain broth over balls. Place heads in a separate bowl with some of the broth, [some people, for instance, my daughter Aran and my father-in-law, think this is the best part of the fish]. Cover fish with plastic film and refrigerate for 6 hours to overnight before serving. The fish lasts for 1 week.

Note: If you want to freeze the fish: freeze in the broth, in batches well covered. Thaw uncovered the day before using. Place in a pot and bring slowly to a boil. Simmer covered for 5 minutes. Cool fish in the broth, uncovered. Transfer to containers and refrigerate, covered with plastic film, overnight before serving.

Eggplant Salad [p]

A K A Baba Ghanoush is a delicious "first", best served with plain or toasted pita. The Israelis claim that there are 26 or more ways to serve eggplant. This versatile vegetable can be served hot or cold, from appetizer to main course.

Makes about 2 ½ cups [560 milliliters]

2 pounds [900 grams] eggplant
salt, for sprinkling
¾ cup [175 milliliters] red wine vinegar
¼ cup [55 milliliters] extra virgin olive oil
2 tablespoons Dijon mustard
1 ounce [30 grams] fresh parsley leaves, chopped finely
2 teaspoons minced garlic, about 2 large cloves
2 tablespoons tchina paste, drained of oil
¼ Preserved Lemon [see Index], rinsed, seeded, cut into small pieces
1 ½ tablespoons lemon juice, from preserved lemons or fresh juice
salt, to taste
fresh black pepper, to taste

Cut eggplants in half lengthwise. Score cut side in a diamond pattern. Sprinkle salt on cut side of eggplant and drain upside down on paper towels for 30 minutes. Wipe dry.

Place eggplants, cut side up, on a foil-lined open baking sheet. Whisk vinegar, oil and mustard until well combined. Pour dressing over eggplants. Turn eggplants cut side down. Bake in a preheated 400° F. [205°C.] oven for 15 minutes. Turn cut side up and bake an additional 15 minutes. Remove eggplants from oven and let sit until they can be handled. Reserve pan juices.

Peel eggplants and let drain in a colander for 1 hour. Remove root end and in a food processor, puree eggplant pulp together with lemon. Add the rest of the ingredients and pulse until combined. Add enough of reserved pan juices to obtain desired consistency, if necessary. Taste and correct the seasoning. Let sit at least 1 hour, refrigerated, to develop the flavor. The salad can be frozen.

Herring In Cream Sauce [d]

This hors' d'oeuvre is creamy and delicious; no one will suspect the absence of sour cream.

Makes 1 ½ quarts [1 ½ liters]

32 ounces [900 grams] no-fat plain yogurt, without food starch, gums or gelatin
8 ounces [225 grams] onions, sliced thinly, halved
1 ½ cups [350 milliliters] skim milk, approximately
a 32 ounce [900 gram] jar herring in wine sauce, juices reserved, cut into bite-size pieces
½ cup [110 milliliters] red wine, approximately, to taste

If you have a yogurt funnel, follow directions for use; if not, place a paper coffee filter in cone assembly of a coffee maker, or in a strainer, fill it with yogurt and let drain, in the fridge, lightly covered with film, for 8 to 12 hours. Discard the whey [liquid.]

Soak onion slices in milk to cover, for 8 to 12 hours. Drain and discard milk. Do not rinse onions.

In a large bowl, combine yogurt with onions and herring. Add wine and mix well. Add as much of reserved herring juices to make a good consistency.

Let herring mixture sit, refrigerated, stirring occasionally, for 2 to 4 hours. Taste, add more wine and/or juice, if necessary. Pack into a jar and refrigerate. The herring lasts easily for a month in the fridge.

Serve with thin slices of 3 Stage Rye Bread [see Index.]

Houmous [p]

Houmous is a basic part of Israeli and Middle Eastern cuisine. I always serve houmous and Tchina [see Index] together because for me, you can't have one without the other. Delish, and easy to fix.

Makes 2 ½ cups [560 milliliters]

a 20 ounce [570 gram] can chick peas, drained parially
½ cup [110 milliliters] tchina paste, drained of oil
fresh black pepper, to taste
salt, to taste
¾ to 1 teaspoon ground cumin, to taste
4 tablespoons minced garlic, about 6 cloves
2 tablespoons chopped fresh parsley leaves
3 to 4 tablespoons lemon juice, to taste
1 tablespoon extra virgin olive oil

Put aside about 12 chick peas. Put the rest of the chick peas in a food processor and process until peas are ground to a paste. Add the rest of the ingredients and process until well combined and mixed. Taste and correct the seasoning. Place houmous in a dish with reserved chick peas nestled on top. Refrigerate, covered, until ready to serve. Houmous can be made 2 days ahead of time.

Meat for Zviha [m]

This is a turkey meat filling for the Arab pizzas, Zviha [see Index]. In the original recipe, beef was used and still can be, but ground turkey has a lot less fat and has a softer texture that I like for this dish.

Enough for 22 to 24 zvihas

olive oil cooking spray

1 teaspoon extra virgin olive oil

10 $\frac{1}{2}$ ounces [300 grams] onions, chopped finely

1 tablespoon chopped garlic

1 pound [450 grams] ground turkey

a 14 $\frac{1}{2}$ ounce [420 gram] can diced or chopped tomatoes

an 8 ounce [225 gram] can tomato sauce

1 teaspoon cider vinegar

1 $\frac{1}{2}$ teaspoons lemon juice

1 $\frac{1}{2}$ tablespoons minced parsley leaves

1 teaspoon salt

fresh black pepper, to taste

2 ounces [55 grams] pine nuts

1 recipe Dough for Zviha [see Index], formed into rounds

In a sprayed non-stick saucepan, heat oil until hot. Add onions and garlic and saute until browning. Add meat and saute, breaking up lumps until meat is no longer pink. Add the rest of the ingredients, except pine nuts, and cook covered, over low heat, stirring occasionally, for 1 hour.

Place about 2 heaping tablespoons on each zviha round and sprinkle each zviha with pine nuts.

Olive Salad *[p]*

I never met a person who didn't like olives. This savory dish is good served with crackers or toast. It is the base for a Muffuletta Sandwich [see Index] or a cream cheese and olive sandwich. It keeps well in the fridge for weeks.

Makes about 1 quart [1 liter]

4 ¹/₂ ounces [125 grams] black olives, seeded
5 ounces [135 grams] green pimiento stuffed olives
a 4 ounce [110 gram] jar sliced pimientos, drained
1 tablespoon chopped garlic
4 pepperoncini peppers, stems and seeds removed, about 40 grams
2 anchovy filets
1 ¹/₂ tablespoons capers
2 tablespoons extra virgin olive oil
¹/₄ cup [55 milliliters] red wine vinegar
1 ¹/₂ teaspoons dried oregano
fresh black pepper, to taste

Lightly chop or pulse all the ingredients in a food processor, scraping down as needed, to desired consistency. Let sit several hours to overnight before using.

Pesto Topping For Pizza [d]

I am not a lover of pizza, but this pizza is gourmet food. I would eat it any time. I like to have a casual pizza, pasta and salad party. People seemed to enjoy the informality.

Makes 1 pizza [can be doubled or tripled]

¹/₂ recipe Dough For Pizza [see Index]

olive oil cooking spray

4 ounces [110 grams] Pesto [see Index]

a 2 ounce [60 gram] can flat anchovies, drained

5 ¹/₂ ounces [150 grams] fresh Mozzarella cheese, sliced into thin strips

8 ounces [220 grams] fresh tomatoes, halved, sliced thinly

fresh black pepper, for sprinkling

garlic granules, for sprinkling

Roll out pizza dough into a rectangle 16 x 11 inches [40 x 27 centimeters] and place on a sprayed jelly roll pan. Bake pizza dough in a preheated 425°F. [220°C.] oven for 5 minutes.

Spread pesto thinly over entire dough using all. Lay anchovies in a diagonal pattern in rows over pesto. Place Mozzarella strips between anchovy rows. Lay tomato slices on top of Mozzarella. Sprinkle entire pizza with black pepper and garlic, to taste.

Bake pizza in a preheated 425°F. [220°C.] oven for 8 to 10 minutes, until crust is browned and cheese is melted.

Cut into squares to serve.

Pita Pizzas [d]

These delicious little pizzas are a charming and appealing appetizer. I always make them ahead of time, sometimes freezing them until the day of the dinner.

Makes 8 pizzas, 32 slices

4 - 7 inch [18 centimeter] pitas, split horizontally into 8 rounds
1 recipe Tomato Sauce for Pizzas [see Index]
10 $\frac{1}{2}$ ounces [300 grams] part skim milk Mozzarella cheese, shredded
3 ounces [100 grams] grated Parmesan cheese
8 anchovies, drained, rinsed
16 brine cured black olives, seeded

Lay pita halves on 1 or 2 baking pans in one layer. Divide tomato sauce among rounds about $\frac{1}{4}$ cup measure for each, spreading almost to the edge. Mix cheeses together and divide among pita rounds, about $\frac{1}{2}$ cup measure each, spreading evenly over tomato sauce.

Cut anchovies in half and place decoratively on 4 pita rounds. Cut olives in half and place decoratively on 4 pita rounds.

[If pizzas are to be frozen, bake them in a preheated 400°F. [205° C.] oven for 7 minutes. Cool completely before wrapping for freezing.]

Just before serving, cut each pizza into 4 wedges and bake in a preheated 450°F. [230°C.] oven for 15 to 20 minutes until bubbly.

If pizzas are frozen, no need to thaw, just cut into 4 segments and bake for only 10 minutes.

Quesadillas *[d]*

I love these tasty appetizers. They are easy to make and can be made several hours ahead of time. I first tasted similar quesadillas at a local restaurant, The Ambassador, and have successfully copied them using low fat ingredients.

Serves 8

10 tablespoons no-fat sour cream substitute
10 flour tortillas
10 ounces [285 grams] smoked salmon [I buy ends and pieces]
dried dill weed, for sprinkling
butter-flavored cooking spray
a 2 ounce [60 gram] jar salmon roe caviar

Spread 2 tablespoons sour cream on one side of each of 5 of the tortillas. Place about 2 ounces [55 grams] smoked salmon on top of sour cream. Sprinkle dill over top. Sandwich the other 5 tortillas on top. Lightly spray each tortilla on both sides with butter-flavored spray. In a sprayed non-stick frypan, fry tortilla sandwiches lightly on each side until tortillas are speckled with brown. Quarter each quesadilla and add a dab of $1/4$ teaspoon caviar on the point of each triangle of each quarter. Serve either hot or at room temperature.

These can be prepared several hours in advance. Let sit at room temperature, covered with plastic wrap. If desired, reheat in the microwave or serve at room temperature.

Red Pepper Salad [Turkish Salad] [p]

This spicy, fiery salad is a typical Middle Eastern Arab dish. When our friend, Hashem, had a tiny restaurant in the Old City of Jerusalem, the whole family would go to eat wonderful Palestinian meals. If I wanted a recipe, Hashem would invite me into the kitchen to watch the preparation. Then I would go home and try to duplicate it. This is one of those recipes. Hashem later opened the wildly sucessful Philadelphia Restaurant in East Jerusalem. We took many of our friends there for fabulous food. [This was before all the troubles began. I hope Hashem fared well.]

Makes about 1 ½ quarts [1 ½ liters]

18 ounces [500 grams] sweet red bell peppers, seeded
4 ounces [110 grams] hot red peppers, not seeded
2 pounds [900 grams] onions, cut into chunks
2 to 4 large garlic cloves, minced, to taste
a 12 ounce [340 gram] can tomato paste
3 tablespoons lemon juice
1 tablespoon extra virgin olive oil
1 tablespoon salt, or to taste
fresh black pepper, to taste

In a food processor, finely chop sweet and hot peppers. Add onions and pulse until onions are chopped finely and mixture is well combined. Transfer to a bowl. Add the rest of the ingredients and mix thoroughly. Chill at least one hour to develop the flavors. Store, covered in jars, in the fridge for up to 3 weeks.

Salmon Mousse [d]

I always hope for leftovers of this dish, so that I can have some for lunch [or for breakfast on a bagel] the next day. I thank Neilson Andrews, the daughter of one of my neighbors, for sharing this recipe.

Makes a 3 cup [700 milliliter] mold

18 $^{1}/_{2}$ ounces [525 grams] canned red salmon [a 14 $^{3}/_{4}$ ounce and a 3 $^{1}/_{4}$ ounce can] reserve juices

1 $^{1}/_{2}$ envelopes unflavored gelatin

4 tablespoons no-fat sour cream substitute

4 tablespoons low fat mayonaisse

1 egg white

1 teaspoon dried dill weed

vegetable cooking spray

no-fat sour cream substitute, to "ice" the mousse

dried dill weed, for sprinkling

Remove and discard skin and bones from salmon. Skim fat from salmon juices. Measure juices and add water, if needed, to make $^{1}/_{2}$ cup [110 milliliters]. Pour juices into a small saucepan. Sprinkle gelatin over salmon juices, to soften. Heat until gelatin is melted.

Place salmon, sour cream, mayonaisse, egg white and dill in a food processor. Pulse until mixture is smooth. Add gelatin mixture and mix until well combined. Scrape mixture into a sprayed 3 cup [700 milliliter] mold, and cover with plastic wrap. [I use a small glass mixing bowl.] Refrigerate until mousse is firm, several hours to overnight.

Loosen sides of mousse with a thin knife. Unmold mousse onto a serving plate. "Ice" mousse with a thin layer of sour cream and sprinkle all over with dill weed.

Serve with thin slices of 3-Stage Rye Bread [see Index] or crackers.

Salmon Spread [d]

This is a delicious spread to serve with bagel chips, crackers or thin slices of 3-Stage Rye Bread [see Index].

Serves 8

$^1/_2$ pound [225 grams] no-fat cream cheese, softened

$^1/_2$ pound [225 grams] low fat cream cheese, softened

2 to 4 tablespoons no-fat plain yogurt

2 tablespoons low fat mayonaisse

2 tablespoons Worcestershire sauce

8 drops Tabasco sauce

$^1/_4$ teaspoon garlic granules

2 - 6 $^3/_4$ ounce [190 gram] cans chunk salmon, drained

3 $^1/_2$ ounces [100 grams] slivered almonds, divided

fresh black pepper, to taste

Combine cream cheeses with yogurt, mayonaisse, Worcestershire, Tabasco, and garlic granules. Add salmon and mix until well combined. Toast half of the almonds and add to salmon mixture. Add pepper to taste. Pour mixture into a small oven safe serving dish. Sprinkle the rest of the almonds over top. The spread can be prepared ahead of time up to this point. It can be frozen or refrigerated for a day or two.

Bake salmon spread in a preheated 375°F. [190°C.] oven for 15 minutes and serve. The spread can be served warm or at room temperature.

Sardine Spread [p]

There are so many people who do not like sardines, that I hesitated about including this recipe. But for those of us who like sardines, this spread is so good that I decided that everyone should have the chance to decide. The spread is quick and easy to do. It is delicious served with thin slices of 3 Stage Rye Bread [see Index] or with crackers or crudities.

Makes about 2 ½ cups [560 milliliters]

3 - 3 ¾ ounce [106 gram] cans Bristling sardines in olive oil, drained well, rinsed lightly
juice of ½ lemon, about 1 ½ to 2 tablespoons
6 ½ ounces [185 grams] Vidalia onions, minced, 2 small onions
2 tablespooons Horseradish [see Index] or bottled
2 tablespoons Dijon mustard
2 tablespoons Worcestershire sauce
2 to 3 teaspoons chopped garlic
1 teaspoon lite soy sauce
fresh black pepper, to taste [I like lots]
Tabasco sauce, to taste

Mash sardines with a fork and transfer to a small mixing bowl. Add the rest of the ingredients, mixing and mashing until well combined. Cover and refrigerate for 2 hours to develop the flavor. Serve in a bowl surrounded by bread, crackers and/or crudities. The spread can be made 3 days ahead of time and kept refrigerated.

Stuffed Mushrooms [d]

These can be prepared the day before or early in the morning of the day of your dinner. They are not difficult to fix and are pleasing to most people. I like them a lot and they are very low in fat.

Makes 16 to 20, serving 8 people

about 2 pounds [900 grams] stuffing mushrooms [large ones]
butter flavored cooking spray
1 ounce [28 grams] margarine
6 ounces [175 grams] onions, chopped finely
1 teaspoon dried thyme
½ teaspoon fresh black pepper
1 tablespoon lemon juice
3 ½ ounces [100 grams] blue cheese, crumbled
salt, to taste

Pick out 16 to 20 of the nicest and largest mushrooms. Remove stems and reserve. Wipe caps with a damp paper towel. Heat a sprayed non-stick fry pan and add margarine. Brown caps on each side for 2 minutes. Transfer to paper towels, cap side up, to drain and cool.

Wash the rest of the mushrooms and stems and chop finely. Saute chopped mushrooms, onions and thyme in same fry pan, resprayed, until tender and all moisture is evaporated. Turn off heat, add pepper, lemon juice and blue cheese. Mix until cheese is melted and add salt to taste. Let cool.

Turn mushrooms cap side down and divide and mound cheese mixture among them. Place in one layer, stuffing side up, in a sprayed au gratin or baking pan. This part can be prepared ahead of time. Refrigerate until continuing.

Just before serving, place mushrooms in a preheated 375°F. [190° C.] oven for 10 to 15 minutes, until hot and bubbly.

Tabouli [p]

Tabouli is part of my Middle East collection of appetizers. It is crunchy and full of different tastes on the palate. I like to serve this with Tchina [see Index] and Houmous [see Index] as part of an appetizer array or serve it as a side dish or salad. Serve with toasted pita triangles.

Makes 3 cups [700 milliliters] serving 8 easily

1 cup [170 grams] bulgur [cracked wheat]

water, for soaking

$1/4$ cup [20 grams] fresh parsley leaves, chopped

$1/4$ cup [20 grams] fresh mint leaves, chopped

$1/2$ cup [65 grams] green onions, including green, sliced thinly

9 ounces [250 grams] fresh tomatoes, peeled, seeded, diced finely

1 $1/2$ tablespoons extra virgin olive oil

1 $1/2$ tablespoons lemon juice

2 large garlic cloves, minced

salt, to taste

fresh black pepper, to taste

lettuce leaves, to garnish, if desired

Rinse bulgur well. Place in a bowl, cover with cold water and let soak for 1 hour. Drain well.

In a medium bowl, combine bulgur with the rest of the ingredients, adding salt and pepper to taste. Serve in a bowl lined with lettuce leaves, if desired.

Tapenade [p]

A delicious appetizer to serve with drinks. Place toasted pita triangles or thin slices of homemade 3 Stage Rye Bread [see Index], toasted, around a bowl of Tapenade. I first tasted this dish at Tapas Bars in Spain. The Spaniards have made the serving of appetizers an Art form.

Makes 1 ½ cups [350 milliliters]

2 large garlic cloves

5 ounces [135 grams] Spanish green salad olives, drained

6 ounces [175 grams] pitted black olives, drained

a 2 ounce [55 gram] can flat anchovies with oil

1 tablespoon capers, drained

1 ½ teaspoons lemon juice

pinch cayenne pepper

1 tablespoon extra virgin olive oil

Drop garlic cloves through feed tube of a running food processor and run until garlic is chopped finely. Add the rest of the ingredients and pulse until chopped fairly finely but still a bit chunky.

The tapenade keeps for a week or so, refrigerated.

Tchina *[p]*

Tchina is an important part of Middle Eastern cuisine. I serve it as an appetizer with toasted pita triangles. It also makes a delicious sauce with fish and meat. The tchina paste is a base for other dips and side dishes, ie: Baba Ganoush and Houmous [see Index]. Before using, I drain almost all the oil from the top of the jar.

Makes 2 ½ cups [560 milliliters]

I cup [225 milliliters] tchina paste, drained of oil
1 cup [225 milliliters] ice water
2 tablespoons plus 1 teaspoon minced garlic, about 4 cloves
4 tablespoons minced fresh parsley leaves
4 tablespoons lemon juice
½ teaspoon fresh black pepper
salt, to taste, about ¾ teaspoon
optional: 1 tablespoon extra virgin olive oil

Combine all the ingredients in a blender and blend until well mixed. Add oil if desired. Refrigerate, covered, until ready to serve. Tchina can be prepared 2 days in advance.

Yogurt Cheese [d]

Yogurt cheese has become an essential ingredient in low or no-fat dairy recipes throughout the book. I have used it in place of cream cheese, or mayonaisse, or sour cream, etc. I like the taste of it plain and think it is worthwhile exploring its many uses.

16 ounces [450 grams] yogurt yields about 8 ounces [225grams] yogurt cheese

I use only no-fat plain yogurt. Do NOT use yogurt that contains food starch, gums or gelatins as these ingredients prevent the whey from dripping away.

If you have a yogurt funnel, follow the directions for use; if not, place a paper coffee filter in cone assembly of a coffee maker or in a strainer, place over a glass or a measuring cup. Spoon in yogurt and let it drip, lightly covered with film, in the fridge for 8 to 12 hours for most recipes. Discard whey [liquid]. Use it plain or:

Mix cheese with snipped dill, snipped chives, snipped garlic chives, salt to taste and\or other finely chopped herbs.

If you want a firmer cheese, let it drip up to 24 hours, covered, in the fridge.

CREPES, QUICHE, SOUFFLES AND TIMBALES

Corn Pudding *[d or p]*

This dramatic pudding is really a souffle. It will appeal to all corn lovers. You will receive applause when you serve this to your guests at the table. Don't be squeamish, it is a simple dish to prepare, and it is foolproof.

Serves 8 to 10

3 pounds [1.35 kilos] corn, fresh, frozen or canned, drained, reserve liquid
1 ½ tablespoons sugar
3 tablespoons cornstarch
couple grinds fresh white pepper
1 ounce [30 grams] margarine
1 ½ cups [350 milliliters] evaporated skim milk or corn liquid plus pareve chicken flavored soup, from the mix, to make 1 ½ cups (350 milliliters) liquid
2 egg yolks
salt, to taste
8 egg whites, room temperature
vegetable cooking spray

Mash corn with a potato masher or lightly crush in a food processor.

In a large saucepan, combine all the ingredients, except egg whites. Bring to a boil over low heat and cook, stirring almost constantly, until it is thickened. Remove from heat and cool. This part can be prepared ahead of time. Cover and set aside until about 1 hour before serving.

Quickly beat egg whites until stiff. Fold whites into corn mixture gently but thoroughly. Pour mixture into a sprayed 3 quart [3 liter] casserole or souffle dish, suitable for serving. Bake in a preheated 350°F. [175°C.] oven for 1 hour to 1 hour and 10 minutes, until pudding is well puffed and brown. Serve immediately.

Blintzes [d]

Blintzes are one of the first things that I learned to cook after I got married. My father, Hirsh de LaViez, taught me this recipe [with some modifications] that he had learned from my maternal grandmother, Elizabeth Brown Mesirow. These are not sweet blintzes as is the custom on the Russian side of our family. If your taste runs to sweet, I have included some optional ingredients.

Makes 24 to 26 blintzes

Pancakes [crepes]

³/₄ cup [175 milliliters] frozen egg substitute, thawed

2 to 2 ¹/₂ cups [450 to 560 milliliters] water

2 cups t280 grams] all purpose unbleached flour

¹/₂ teaspoon salt

1 teaspoon baking powder

butter flavored cooking spray

1 teaspoon margarine

Filling

1 ¹/₂ pounds [680 grams] low fat cottage cheese, drained

3 egg whites

¹/₂ teaspoon salt

1 teaspoon sugar

optional:

2 teaspoons sugar mixed with

¹/₂ teaspoon ground cinnamon

3 ¹/₂ ounces [150 grams] white raisins

butter flavored cooking spray

3 teaspoons margarine

Apple Sauce [see Index] or no-fat sour cream or no-fat yogurt,
  to garnish

With a wire whisk, beat egg substitute with 2 cups water. Add dry ingredients gradually and whisk well. The consistency should be that of light cream. Add more water, if necessary.

Over medium high heat, heat a 6 to 7 inch [15 to 17 centimeter] sprayed non-stick crepe pan and add 1 teaspoon margarine. Remove from heat, half fill a ¼ cup measure [2 tablespoons] with batter and pour into center of pan, tilting pan quickly so that batter covers bottom of pan, making a thin pancake. Return pan to heat and when pancake begins to pull away from sides of pan, remove it from pan, cooking on one side only. Stack pancakes on a plate as they are cooked, keeping them covered with a towel. Continue making pancakes until all batter is used, reserving 2 tablespoons for sealing blintzes. Cool completely.

Combine cottage, egg whites, salt and sugar for the filling [plus the optional ingredients, if desired].

On cooked side of each cooled pancake, place 1 ½ to 2 tablespoons of filling close to one edge. Fold over edge to enclose filling. Fold in each side and roll to enclose completely. Use reserved batter to seal blintze. Continue filling each pancake in the same way, laying them seam side down on the towel.

When all the blintzes are filled, either freeze blintzes unfried or fry slowly in a sprayed non-stick fry pan with 1 teaspoon margarine added, turning only once, until they are browned on each side, respraying and adding 1 teaspoon margarine as necessary. If frozen, no need to thaw before frying.

Serve hot with the garnish of your choice.

Chicken Filling for Crepes [m]

Poach a couple of chicken breasts or use chicken from making chicken soup or left over roast chicken. These are easy to make and can be frozen either before or after filling the crepes.

Enough for 24 to 28 crepes

olive oil cooking spray
14 ounces [400 grams] onions, chopped finely
1 tablespoon extra virgin olive oil
1 pound [450 grams] fresh mushrooms, chopped
4 tablespoons all purpose unbleached flour
1 $^1/_2$ cups [350 milliliters] hot Chicken Broth [see Index] or canned
1 teaspoon salt
$^1/_2$ teaspoon fresh white pepper
1 pound [450 grams] cooked chicken, chopped finely
1 ounce [28 grams] margarine
4 tablespoons all purpose unbleached flour
1 $^1/_2$ cups [350 milliliters] hot Chicken Broth [see Index] or canned
3 tablespoons snipped fresh dill
2 tablespoons Dijon mustard
salt, to taste
fresh white pepper, to taste
1 recipe prepared Crepes For Meat or Vegetable Filling [see Index]

In a sprayed large fry pan or Dutch oven, saute onions in oil until well softened. Add mushrooms and saute until tender. Sprinkle 4 tablespoons flour over mixture and mix well. Add 1 1/2 cups [350 milliliters] hot broth, stirring constantly and cook mixture until thick and smooth. Remove from heat, add salt, pepper and chicken. Mix well and set aside to cool.

In a sprayed saucepan, melt margarine. Add 4 tablespoons flour and whisk until smooth. Add 1 1/2 cups [350 milliliters] hot broth in a stream, whisking constantly until sauce is thick and smooth. Let simmer for 5 minutes. Add dill, mustard, salt and pepper and mix well. Set aside this topping.

Divide cooled chicken mixture among cooled crepes, about 1 heaping tablespoon for each. Roll crepes and place, seam side down, in 1 or 2 sprayed au gratin pans, suitable for serving. Divide topping among filled crepes, spreading some on top of each.

The filled crepes can be covered and refrigerated until about 1/2 hour before serving or can be frozen, well wrapped, for later.

Bake crepes in a preheated 375°F. [190°C.] oven for 15 to 18 minutes, until hot and bubbly.

Special Quiche, David [d]

By special request from my adopted grandson, David Eislesberg, I include this lightened version of a very delicious quiche. This is a wonderful luncheon main dish or a very special appetizer.

Makes an 11 to 13 inch [28 to 32 ½ centimeter] quiche

olive oil cooking spray

2 tablespoons extra virgin olive oil

1 ½ pounds [680 grams] onions, sliced thinly

2 leeks, white and light green parts, sliced thinly, after cleaning
about 7 ounces [200 grams]

12 ½ ounces [350 grams] fresh mushrooms, sliced

5 tablespoons pareve dry onion soup mix

1 cup [225 milliliters] evaporated skim milk

½ cup [110 milliliters] skim milk

½ cup [110 milliliters] frozen egg substitute, thawed

1 whole egg

salt, to taste

fresh white pepper, to taste

10 ounces [300 grams] part-skim milk Mozzarella cheese, shredded

1 single Pie Crust [see Index], baked, cooled

In a sprayed Dutch oven, in oil, saute onions and leeks until lightly colored. Add mushrooms and saute until mushrooms are tender and all moisture has evaporated. Drain on paper towels and set aside.

With a wire whisk, combine soup mix, milks, egg substitute, egg, salt and pepper. Spread onion mushroom mixture evenly over pie crust. Sprinkle cheese in a layer over this. Carefully pour custard mixture over cheese.

Place quiche on a foil lined baking sheet and bake in a preheated 350°F. [175°C.] oven for 30 to 40 minutes, until custard is firm.

Slice into wedges to serve warm or at room temperature.

The quiche can be frozen, wrapped in foil still in quiche pan. Thaw and if desired, reheat in a 300°F. [150°C.] oven for 15 minutes.

Crepes For Meat or Vegetable Filling [p]

Crepes are a lovely addition to any meal. I sometimes make different kinds and use them as the centerpiece of my meal. They are very easy to make and can be made a day or two ahead of time or weeks ahead and frozen.

1 ¼ cups [175 grams] all purpose unbleached flour
1 cup [225 milliliters] frozen egg substitute, thawed
1 ½ tablespoons [20 grams] margarine, melted or vegetable oil
1 teaspoon salt
1 ⅓ cups [325 milliliters] beer [not dark], room temperature
water [optional]
vegetable cooking spray
a bit of margarine or vegetable oil

Whisk together flour, egg, margarine, salt and beer until well combined. Cover and let sit at room temperature for at least 1 hour. Stir before using. The batter should be the consistency of light cream. If it gets too thick, add a few drops of water.

Spray a 6 to 7 inch [15 to 17 centimeter] non-stick crepe pan and heat until hot. Add a bit of margarine, pouring off any excess. Remove from heat, stir batter and half fill a ¼ cup measure [about 2 tablespoons] with batter and pour into center of pan, tilting pan quickly so that batter covers bottom of pan, making a thin pancake. Return pan to heat and with a flat, thin flexible knife, loosen edges of crepe. Let crepe brown lightly and turn to other side to brown, just a few seconds. Transfer crepe to a kitchen towel. Continue making crepes until all batter is used, keeping crepes covered with towel. Cool completely before filling with filling of choice [see Index].

If crepes are made ahead, store, wrapped in plastic wrap for a few days or freeze for later use.

Keep crepe pan hot and if necessary, add a bit more margarine. I find that if pan is well seasoned, margarine is needed only with the first crepe.

Mushroom Filling for Crepes [d]

This filling makes a fabulous crepe dish. It definitely has an assertive mushroom flavor which will please all mushroom and crepe lovers.

Enough for 24 to 28 crepes

1 pound [450 grams] fresh Portobello mushrooms, halved, sliced thinly

³/₄ pound [350 grams] fresh button mushrooms, sliced

8 ounces [225 grams] onions, chopped finely

butter flavored cooking spray

1 ounce [30 grams] margarine

3 tablespoons lemon juice

1 teaspoon salt

¹/₄ teaspoon dried thyme

¹/₄ teaspoon fresh white pepper

8 ounces [225 grams] evaporated skim milk

2 ounces [55 grams] margarine

4 tablespoons all purpose unbleached flour

1 ¹/₂ cups [350 milliliters] hot skim milk

7 ounces [200 grams] part-skim milk Mozzarella cheese, shredded

salt to taste

fresh white pepper, to taste

a good pinch ground cayenne pepper

1 recipe prepared Crepes For Meat or Vegetable Filling [see Index]

Saute mushrooms and onions in a well sprayed Dutch oven, with 1 ounce margaine added, until mushrooms are tender and all moisture is evaporated. Add lemon juice, salt, thyme, pepper and evaporated milk. Cook, stirring, over high heat, until slightly thickened. Transfer mixture to a bowl and let cool.

In a sprayed saucepan, melt margarine and add flour and whisk until smooth. Add hot milk all at once, whisking constantly. Cook, whisking, until sauce is thick and smooth. Simmer sauce for 2 minutes. Add cheese and stir until cheese is melted. Remove from heat and add salt, pepper and cayenne. Set aside.

Divide cooled mushroom mixture among cooled crepes, about 2 tablespoons for each. Roll crepes and place, seam side down, in 1 or 2 sprayed au gratin pans, suitable for serving. Divide cheese sauce among filled crepes, spreading some on each crepe.

The filled crepes can be covered with film and refrigerated until about $1/2$ hour before serving or can be frozen, well wrapped in foil, for later.

Bake in a preheated 375°F. [190°C.] oven for 15 to 18 minutes, until hot and bubbly.

Mushroom Quiche [d]

We can take advantage of the availability of the many new mushrooms on the market. I particularly like the Portobello mushrooms. They are large, meaty and delicious. I have mixed them here with regular culti-vated button mushrooms. The result is a very successful melange in this quiche.

Makes an 11 to 13 inch [28 to 32 $^1/_2$ centimeter] quiche

olive oil cooking spray
1 $^1/_2$ tablespoons extra virgin olive oil
10 $^1/_2$ ounces [300 grams] onions, minced
1 pound [450 grams] fresh Portobello mushrooms, halved, sliced thinly
1 pound [450 grams] fresh button mushrooms, sliced
3 tablespoons lemon juice
1 teaspoon dried thyme
salt, to taste
fresh white pepper, to taste
1 cup [225 grams] evaporated skim milk
$^3/_4$ cup [175 milliliters] frozen egg substitute, thawed
1 whole egg
10 $^1/_2$ ounces [300 grams] part-skim milk Mozzarella cheese, shredded

1 single Pie Crust [see Index], baked, cooled

In a sprayed Dutch oven or fry pan, saute, in oil, onions and mushrooms, until mushrooms are tender and all moisture has evaporated. Add lemon juice, thyme, salt and pepper. Drain on paper towels and set aside.

With a wire whisk, combine milk, egg substitute and egg.

Spread mushroom mixture evenly over pie crust. Sprinkle cheese in a layer over mushrooms. Carefully pour custard mixture over cheese.

Place quiche on a foil lined baking sheet and bake in a preheated 350°F. [175°C.] oven for 30 to 40 minutes, until custard is firm.

Slice into wedges to serve warm or at room temperature.

The quiche can be frozen, wrapped in foil, still in quiche pan. Thaw and if desired, reheat in a 300°F. [150°C.] oven for 15 minutes.

Mushroom Pie [d]

This quick and easy savory pie is very quiche-like without a lot of cheese. This pie will please anyone who likes mushrooms. It is suitable served as an appetizer or as a light supper or lunch.

Makes an 11 inch [28 centimeter] pie

1 ³/₄ pounds [800 grams] fresh mushrooms, sliced
9 ounces [250 grams] onions, chopped finely
butter flavored cooking spray
2 ounces [55 grams] margarine or light vegetable oil
3 tablespoons lemon juice
1 teaspoon salt
¹/₂ teaspoon dried thyme
a few grinds fresh white pepper
1 cup [130 grams] Bisquick, regular or low fat
¹/₂ cup [55 grams] grated Parmesan cheese
3 tablespoons chopped fresh parsley leaves
1 teaspoon chopped garlic
a 4 ounce [110 gram] container apple sauce
³/₄ cup [175 milliliters] frozen egg substitute, thawed
1 whole egg

Saute mushrooms and onions in a sprayed Dutch oven with margarine or oil added, until well softened. Add lemon juice, salt, thyme and pepper and saute until all moisture is evaporated. Set aside to cool.

In a mixing bowl, combine Bisquick, Parmesan, parsley and garlic. Add apple sauce and eggs and mix well. Add cooled mushroom mixture and mix well.

Pour mixture into a well sprayed quiche or pie pan. Place pan on a foil lined baking sheet and bake in a preheated 350°F. [175°C.] oven for 40 to 45 minutes until golden brown and custard is done.

Slice into wedges to serve.

Mushroom Timbale [d]

This unusual side dish is an interesting way to eat mushrooms. It can be prepared early in the day and baked just before serving or it can be baked ahead and rewarmed for dinner.

Serves 8

1 pound [450 grams] mushrooms, halved, sliced
3 ounces [90 grams] celery, chopped
2 ounces [55 grams] onions, chopped
1 ½ ounces [40 grams] margarine
9 ounces [250 grams] evaporated skim milk
2 cups [450 milliliters] vegetable broth or pareve chicken flavored soup, from the mix
1 cup [225 milliliters] frozen egg substitute, thawed
4 whole eggs
1 teaspoon salt, or to taste
fresh white pepper, to taste
1 teaspoon sweet paprika
pinch dried thyme
2 tablespoons chopped fresh parsley leaves
vegetable cooking spray

Saute mushrooms, celery and onion in margarine, over medium heat until tender, about 15 minutes. Drain and set aside.

Whisk the rest of the ingredients until well mixed and add mushroom mixture and combine well. Pour mixture into a well sprayed 2 ½ quart [2 ¼ liter] souffle dish or casserole.

Place dish or casserole on a folded towel in a deep baking pan. Pour hot water into pan half way up the sides of the casserole. Bake in a preheated 375°F. [190°C.] oven for 1 hour 10 minutes to 1 hour 20 minutes, until custard tests done.

Serve from the casserole. Or cool on a rack and rewarm in a medium oven or in a microwave.

Spinach Timbale [d]

A timbale is first cousin to a souffle. You can be more flexible with time as a timbale can wait in the oven for a short time before serving. Most of the preparations can be done ahead of time.

Serves 8

1 tablespoon [$^1/_2$ ounce - 15 grams] margarine
2 tablespoons all purpose unbleached flour
1 cup [225 milliliters] hot skim milk
$^1/_2$ cup [55 grams] grated Parmesan cheese
1 $^3/_4$ pounds [800 grams] fresh or frozen spinach, cooked, chopped, squeezed of all liquid
$^3/_4$ cup [175 milliliters] frozen egg substitute, thawed
4 tablespoons vegetable broth or pareve chicken flavored soup, from the mix
salt, to taste
fresh white pepper, to taste
pinch ground nutmeg
pinch ground cayenne pepper
vegetable cooking spray

Melt margarine in a saucepan. Add flour and whisk until smooth. Add hot milk all at once, whisking constantly. When sauce is thick and smooth, add Parmesan and mix well. Remove from heat. Add spinach, eggs, broth and seasonings and combine well. Pour mixture into a sprayed 2 $^1/_2$ quart [2 $^1/_4$ liter] casserole or souffle dish, suitable for serving.

Place casserole on a folded kitchen towel in a deep baking pan. Pour enough hot water into pan to reach half way up sides of casserole. Bake in a preheated 350°F. [175°C.] oven for 30 to 45 minutes, until timbale tests done as with any custard.

The timbale can be prepared ahead of time and baked just before serving.

Zucchini Pie [d]

This delicious quiche-like pie is wonderful served as the main dish at a light supper or cut into thin wedges, as an appetizer. I thank my friend Florence Caplan for this recipe, it is special.

Makes an 11 inch [28 centimeter] pie

1 cup [130 grams] Bisquick, regular or low fat
¹/₂ cup [55 grams] grated Parmesan cheese
3 tablespoons chopped fresh parsley leaves
2 tablespoons snipped fresh dill or 1 ³/₄ teaspoons dried dillweed
1 teaspoon chopped garlic
¹/₂ teaspoon salt
¹/₄ teaspoon dried oregano
¹/₄ teaspoon fresh white pepper
a 4 ounce [110 gram] container apple sauce
³/₄ cup [175 milliliters] frozen egg subsitute, thawed
1 whole egg
12 ¹/₂ ounces [350 grams] zucchini, trimmed, sliced thinly [3 cups]
2 ¹/₂ ounces [75 grams] sliced green onion [¹/₂ cup]
pareve butter flavored cooking spray

In a large mixing bowl, place Bisquick, Parmesan, parsley, dill, garlic, salt, oregano and pepper and mix. Add apple sauce and eggs and mix. Fold in and mix with a large fork, zucchini and onions.

Pour mixture into a well sprayed 11 inch [28 centimeter] quiche or pie pan. Place pan on a foil lined baking sheet and bake in a preheated 350°F. [175°C.] oven for 40 to 45 minutes, until golden.

The pie can be eaten warm or at room temperature. It can be re-heated in a slow oven or it can be frozen well wrapped in foil. Thaw before rewarming.

DRINKS

Bloody Marys *[p]*

These Bloody Marys for a crowd are wonderful and spicy and tingly on the tongue. It definitely makes life easier for the host, to have a pitcher of drinks ready for guests when they walk through the door. These are seasonless, great all year round.

Each recipe makes 6 to 8 drinks

4 $\frac{1}{2}$ cups [1 liter] tomato juice
1 cup [225 milliliters] vodka
1 $\frac{1}{2}$ tablespoons Worcestershire sauce
$\frac{1}{4}$ teaspoon Tabasco sauce, or to taste
1 teaspoon salt
4 teaspoons lemon juice
$\frac{1}{4}$ teaspoon fresh black pepper
celery ribs, to garnish, washed and trimmed

Combine all the ingredients in a large pitcher and mix well. Taste and correct the seasoning. Serve in tall glasses over ice cubes and garnish with a rib of celery.

Coffee Flavored Liqueur [Kahlua] [p]

This is an inexpensive recipe to use when this ingredient is called for in recipes.

Makes about 1 ½ quarts [1 ½ liters]

2 cups [425 grams] sugar
2 cups [450 milliliters] water
10 teaspoons dry instant coffee
1 fifth vodka [any kind will do]

In a saucepan, over low heat, dissolve sugar in water. Add coffee and stir until coffee dissolves. Remove from heat and let cool. Add vodka and mix well. Pour into bottles and store, almost indefinitely.

Margaritas [p]

Margaritas are one of my favorite drinks. I am amazed by the number of people who love them, even people who don't drink any whiskey at all. Margaritas are a very refreshing drink to serve at a chili dinner, it seems to cool the palate.

Each recipe makes 4 drinks

12 ounces [340 milliliters] Tequilla
6 ounces [175 milliliters] orange flavored liqueur
8 ounces [225 milliliters] fresh lime juice
5.5 ounces [150 milliliters] pineapple juice
salt, to taste

Combine all the ingredients, except salt, in a pitcher. Dampen the rim of glasses and dip rims in salt, if desired. Pour mixture over ice cubes in salt-rimmed glasses. This recipe can be doubled or tripled.

Sangria *[p]*

I find that my friends don't drink as much hard liquor as they used to. It makes a nice change to prepare a pitcher of Sangrias to serve either before or during dinner. This is a lovely refreshing drink, especially suitable for a Spanish meal but equally nice to serve on a summer's evening.

Each recipe makes 8 servings

1 bottle dry red wine [750 milliliters]
¹/₄ cup [55 milliliters] brandy
¹/₄ cup [55 milliliters] orange flavored liqueur
¹/₄ cup [55 milliliters] lemon juice
¹/₂ cup [110 milliliters] orange juice
2 tablespoons sugar or equivalent sugar substitute
assorted fruit, sliced thinly, oranges, lemons, strawberries, kiwi
1 cup [225 milliliters] soda water, iced

Combine all the ingredients, except soda water and refrigerate until serving time. Just before serving in a punch bowl or large pitcher, add soda water. Serve over ice cubes, if desired.

Whiskey Sours *[p]*

A pitcher of frosty whiskey sours is delicious at a summer's eve party. These are easy to make and are definite crowd pleasers.

Each recipe makes 8 to 10 drinks

18 ounces [1/2 liter] whiskey; bourbon, blended whiskey or brandy
a 7 ounce [200 gram] can frozen lemonade mix, thawed, undiluted
3 ¹/₂ ounces [100 grams] scant ¹/₂ cup lemon juice
¹/₄ teaspoon Angostura bitters
oranges, sliced thinly, seeded, halved, to garnish

Combine and stir well, whiskey, lemonade, lemon juice and bitters in a large pitcher. Pour over ice cubes in short glasses and garnish with orange halves.

SOUPS

Asparagus Soup [m or p or d]

I save all the ends of asparagus [in the freezer] that are broken off and thrown away, for this soup. Not only is the soup delicious, making it will make you feel virtuous. Freeze the extra soup. This light soup is suitable for almost any meal.

Makes about 18 cups [4 liters]

4 ¹/₂ pounds [2 kilos] ends of asparagus
1 ³/₄ pounds [800 grams] onions, cut into large dice
9 ounces [250 grams] celery, with leaves, sliced thickly
³/₄ teaspoon dried thyme
salt, to taste
fresh white pepper, to taste
12 cups [2.7 liters] pareve chicken flavored soup, from the mix or Chicken Broth [see Index] or canned
9 ounces [250 grams] fresh or frozen asparagus spears, cooked, to garnish
optional: no-fat plain yogurt, to taste

In an 8 quart [8 liter] kettle, place aparagus ends, onions, celery, thyme, salt, pepper and soup. Bring to a simmer, skimming the froth as it rises. Simmer soup for 50 minutes.

Remove solids with a slotted spoon and puree in a food processor. Put vegetable puree mixed with broth through a Foley grater to remove all fibrous and tough parts. [This takes a while.] Return strained and pureed soup to kettle. Cut cooked aparagus spears into 1 inch [2 ¹/₂ centimeter] pieces and add to soup. Reheat and serve, with yogurt, if desired.

Avgolemone Soup *[Lemon and Egg] [m or p]*

I like this lightly piquant soup. You must be careful not to let it boil or it will curdle. Although the soup is Greek in origin, try it with an Italian meal. This is an unusual and delicious soup suitable for many dinners.

Makes about 10 cups [2.25 liters]

7 ¹/₂ cups [1.6 liters] cold Chicken Broth [see Index] or
    pareve chicken flavored soup, from the mix

¹/₃ cup [75 milliliters] lemon juice

1 cup [225 milliliters] frozen egg substitute, thawed

2 eggs

pinch ground nutmeg

1 to 3 teaspoons salt, to taste

fresh white pepper, to taste

1 cup [175 grams] cooked white rice

In a saucepan, whisk all the ingredients together, except rice, until well combined. Place pan over low heat and bring slowly almost to a simmer, whisking almost constantly. DO NOT LET BOIL. When soup is hot, add rice, and while stirring constantly, bring barely to a simmer.
    Serve.

Cold Avocado Soup *[m or p]*

The velvety texture of this heavenly summer soup is very inviting. I like to make this refreshing icy soup, its flavor appeals to me greatly.

Makes about 10 cups [2.25 liters]

2 to 2 ¼ pounds [900 grams to 1 kilo] avocados, very ripe [seeNote]

11 ½ ounces [335 grams] onions, minced

4 large garlic cloves, minced

6 cups [1.4 liters] cold Chicken Broth [see Index] or canned or pareve chicken flavored soup, from the mix

⅓ cup [75 milliliters] fresh lime juice

1 teaspoon salt, or to taste

1 teaspoon chili powder

½ teaspoon fresh black pepper, to taste

Peel avocados and cut into chunks. Combine and puree all ingredients in a food processor. Chill at least 3 hours and serve icy cold.

Note: To ripen avocados, wrap each one in newspaper and leave at room temperature until soft.

Bean Soup [m]

This is a fabulous bean soup, the kind I remember from my past. It is thick and smoky with lots of taste. I dedicate this soup to my bean fanciers. This soup gets better every day.

Makes 24 cups [5.5 liters]

1 pound [450 grams] dry navy beans, picked over for stones
1 pound [450 grams] dry baby lima beans, picked over for stones
water, for de-gassing
12 ¹/₂ ounces [350 grams] beef marrow bones
5 ¹/₂ ounces [150 grams] celery, chopped
11 ¹/₂ ounces [325 grams] onions, quartered, sliced
7 ounces [200 grams] carrots, peeled, chopped
11 ¹/₂ ounces [325 grams] smoked turkey wings
a 14 ¹/₂ ounce [400 gram] can diced tomatoes
12 cups [2.7 liters] water
fresh black pepper, to taste
1 hot pepper, pricked
14 ounces [400 grams] smoked turkey sausages, cut into bite size
1 tablespoon salt, to taste

Place beans in a large kettle with 30 cups [6.67 liters] of water. Bring to a boil, boil for 2 minutes, cover, and let sit for 1 hour. Drain and discard water [this de-gasses beans and quick soaks them].

Place beans in an 8 quart [8 liter] kettle and add the rest of the ingredients, except sausages and salt. Bring to a boil, skimming the froth as it rises. Simmer, covered, for 2 to 4 hours, depending on age of beans, until beans are very soft, stirring occasionally.

Cover sausages with cold water in a medium saucepan and bring to a boil. Boil for 10 minutes, drain and discard water.

Remove and discard bones. Remove wings from soup, dice any meat, discard bones and return meat to kettle. Add sausages and salt. Partially cover and simmer an additional 30 minutes, stirring occasionally.

Taste and correct the seasoning and serve.

Beef Stock *[m]*

I use to walk into the kitchen of Katy's Restaurant in Jerusalem and watch her chef, Omran, make the most marvelous beef stock, from which he made demi glace' for use in all their sauces. He would use huge beef marrow bones, that I took home for the dogs. A good rich stock is the base for many soups, sauces, and gravies. Demi glace' is a very reduced stock that is used as a seasoning to make very rich soups and sauces. This stock is very rich and can be frozen in batches for convenience.

Makes 18 cups [4 liters]

about 1 $^7/_8$ pounds [850 grams] veal bones
2 very large beef marrow bones
1 beef foot, about 1 $^1/_3$ pounds [610 grams], sliced
2 $^1/_2$ pounds [1.16 kilos] beef shanks with bones
water
2 large bay leaves
handful of parsley stems
9 ounces [250 grams] celery root, peeled, cut into chunks or celery tops, sliced, or both
9 ounces [250 grams] onions, unpeeled, quartered, stuck with
4 whole cloves
carrot tops, if available, washed well
18 ounces [500 grams] carrots, unpeeled, cut into large hunks
9 ounces [250 grams] parsnips, unpeeled, cut into large hunks
2 - 14 $^1/_2$ ounce [420 gram] cans diced tomatoes with juice
5 sprigs fresh dill
$^1/_2$ tablespoon whole black peppercorns, lightly crushed
24 cups [5 $^1/_2$ liters] water

In a large kettle, place bones, foot, beef shanks and enough water to cover by about 2 inches [5 centimeters]. Bring water to a rolling boil and boil for 2 minutes. Discard water, rinse off bones and meat and wash out kettle.

Place bones, foot, meat and the rest of the ingredients back in kettle. Bring to a boil, skimming the froth as it rises. Cover kettle and simmer for about 4 hours, stirring occasionally. Strain stock. Reserve meat for another use. Discard bones and vegetables [or save for the dog]. Cool stock and refrigerate overnight.

Skim fat from stock and store in containers in freezer.

Carrot Soup [m or p]

This creamy [with no cream] light slightly sweet soup is lovely to serve at a summer dinner or anytime for that matter. Delicious.

Makes 11 to 12 cups [2.5 to 2.7 liters]

2 pounds [900 grams] carrots, peeled, sliced thinly
2 ounces [60 grams] margarine
2 ounces [60 grams] preserved ginger, rinsed if sugared, chopped
12 ounces [340 grams] potatoes, peeled, sliced thinly
10 cups [2.25 liters] Chicken Broth [see Index] or pareve chicken flavored soup, from the mix
5 fresh parsley stalks, with leaves
1 ¹/₂ teaspoons ground ginger
salt, to taste
fresh white pepper, to taste
2 tablespoons chopped fresh parsley leaves, to garnish

In a 4 ¹/₂ quart [4 liter] pot, saute carrots in margarine over medium heat, stirring frequently, about 20 minutes. When nice and brown and syrupy, add the rest of the ingredients, except parsley leaves. Bring to a boil and simmer, covered, for about 30 minutes, until carrots and potatoes are very tender.

Puree entire mixture in a blender or food processor. Return soup to pot to reheat or refrigerate for a few days or freeze for longer storage.

Garnish hot soup with parsley and serve.

Black Bean Soup [m]

Every culture seems to have a black bean soup. I think all of them are delicious. This is my version, a special request from my friend Philip Macht. This soup freezes well.

Makes about 12 cups [2.7 liters]

1 ¹/₂ pounds [680 grams] dry black beans [turtle beans]
water, for de-gassing
18 ounces [500 grams] onions, chopped coarsely
6 large garlic cloves, chopped
6 ¹/₂ ounces [180 grams] celery, chopped
8 ounces [225 grams] carrots, chopped
10 cups [2.25 liters] tongue broth or Chicken Broth [see Index] or canned
19 ounces [550 grams] beef bones
9 ounces [250 grams] smoked turkey wings
a 14 to 16 ounce [400 to 450 gram] can tomatoes, cut up
3 bay leaves
1 ¹/₂ tablespoons cocoa, sifted
¹/₂ teaspoon ground cumin
good pinch ground cloves
salt, to taste
coarsely ground fresh black pepper, to taste

In a very large kettle, combine beans with about 20 cups [4.5 liters] water. Bring to a boil, boil for 2 minutes, cover and let sit for 1 hour. Drain and discard the water [this de-gasses beans and quick soaks them].

In an 8 quart [8 liter] kettle, combine beans with the rest of the ingredients except salt and pepper, and bring to a boil, skimming the froth as it rises. Simmer, covered, stirring occaionally, until beans are very soft, 2 to 4 hours, depending on age of beans. Pick out and discard bones, wings and bay leaves. Add salt and pepper, to taste. Reheat and serve.

Bone Soup [m]

If you are a bone lover, if you love a thick gelatinous meaty flavor, then this is the soup for you. As with most soups, preparation is easy and it tastes better the second [or third] day.

Makes about 20 cups [4.5 liters]

4 $^1/_2$ pounds [2.25 kilos] beef feet, cut up
12 cups [2.7 liters] water
4 $^1/_2$ ounces [130 grams] celery with leaves, chopped
6 $^1/_2$ ounces [185 grams] leeks, sliced thinly
12 $^1/_2$ ounces [350 grams] onions, chopped
12 $^1/_2$ ounces [350 grams] carrots, chopped
a 28 ounce [800 gram] can tomatoes, chopped
1 $^1/_2$ tablespoons chopped garlic
1 large hot pepper, pricked
6 cups [1.4 liters] Beef Stock [see Index] or canned
2 tablespoons salt, or to taste
1 $^1/_2$ teaspoons fresh black pepper
2 teaspoons dried thyme
2 to 2 $^1/_2$ teaspoons chili powder, to taste

Rinse bones well. Place bones and water in a 10 quart [10 liter] kettle and bring to a boil, skimming froth as it rises. Add the rest of the ingredients. Cover and simmer for 4 hours.

Transfer bones to a cutting board and cut meat and gristle into bite size pieces. Return to kettle. Discard bones. Remove and discard hot pepper. Taste and correct the seasoning. Refrigerate soup overnight.

Skim and discard fat from soup, reheat and serve.

The soup freezes well.

Broccoli Soup [m or p]

This is an interesting way to serve broccoli, it is quite delicious. I think you'll enjoy this. It is equally good hot or cold.

Makes about 12 cups [2.7 liters]

2 ¹/₄ pounds [1 kilo] broccoli, before trimming or 1 ³/₄ pounds [800 grams] frozen broccoli
10 cups [2 ¹/₄ liters] Chicken Broth [see Index] or pareve chicken flavored soup, from the mix, or canned
2 garlic cloves, minced
1 teaspoon dried thyme
salt, to taste
¹/₂ teaspoon fresh white pepper
pinch ground bay leaf
pinch ground nutmeg
handful fresh parsley leaves, chopped
¹/₂ cup [110 milliliters] frozen egg substitute, thawed
2 tablespoons lemon juice

Cut florets off broccoli and peel stalks. Separate florets and cut stalks into pieces.

In a 4 ¹/₂ quart [4 liter] pot, place all the ingredients, except egg substitute and lemon juice. Bring to a boil and simmer, covered, until broccoli is very tender, about 40 minutes.

Drain off broth through a strainer and reserve. Puree solids and return to pot together with reserved broth.

Beat egg substitute in a bowl with lemon juice. Add a ladle or two of hot soup to egg mixture, to warm mixture. Add egg mixture to soup, whisking constantly, and bring soup to a simmer.

Serve the soup hot or icy cold.

Cabbage Borscht *[p or d]*

This is a hearty winter soup with lots of flavor, one of my favorites, and very easy to make. This is another tasty, wonderful vegetarian dish.

Makes about 18 cups [4 liters]

1 tablespoons chopped garlic
12 ounces [340 grams] onions, sliced thinly
1 ³/₄ pounds [800 grams] cabbage, shredded
1 ¹/₂ pounds [680 grams] potatoes, peeled, cut into small dice
a 1 pound [450 gram] can sliced beets, chopped, including juice
a 1 pound [450 gram] can pickled beets, chopped, including juice
a 14 ¹/₂ ounce [410 gram] can diced tomatoes
12 ounces [340 grams] celery, chopped finely
12 ounces [340 grams] carrots, chopped finely
2 pounds [900 grams] fresh sauerkraut, rinsed, drained
12 cups [2.7 liters] pareve beef flavored soup, from the mix
3 tablespoons pareve beef flavored soup powder
1 bunch fresh dill leaves, snipped finely
4 tablespoons red wine vinegar
2 tablespoons brown sugar
1 tablespoon lite soy sauce
1 tablespoon sweet Hungarian paprika
¹/₂ teaspoon ground cinnamon
¹/₂ teaspoon ground caraway
¹/₂ teaspoon ground bay leaf
1 teaspoon hot Hungarian paprika
salt, to taste
fresh black pepper, to taste
optional: no-fat plain yogurt, to garnish

Place all the ingredients, except yogurt, in a 10 quart [10 liter] kettle, mix well and bring to a simmer. Simmer over low heat for about 2 hours, stirring occasionally.

Serve with yogurt, if desired.

The soup freezes well.

Chicken Broth [m]

I save and freeze the necks, wing tips and gizzards from all the chickens I use. I buy backs and bones and some extra gizzards from the market to enrich the pot. Use in any recipe calling for Chicken Broth. The broth can be frozen in batches.

Makes about 18 cups [4 liters]

4 ¹/₂ pounds [2 kilos] chicken pieces, necks, backs, wing tips, gizzards and bones [from a leftover chicken, maybe]
3 to 4 large veal or beef marrow bones
18 cups [4 liters] water, twice
9 ounces [250 grams] onions, peeled, halved lengthwise
10 ¹/₂ ounces [300 grams] carrots, cut into hunks
7 ounces [200 grams] celery with leaves, cut into hunks
7 ounces [200 grams] parsnips, cut into hunks
6 full sprigs fresh dill
salt, to taste
fresh white pepper, to taste

Place chicken pieces, bones and 18 cups [4 liters] water into an 8 quart [8 liter] kettle and bring to a rolling boil. Boil 5 minutes and throw out water. Rinse chicken pieces and bones, wash kettle and start again.

Place chicken pieces, bones and 18 cups [4 liters] water back into kettle along with the rest of the ingredients. Bring to a boil, skimming the froth as it rises. Cover and let simmer for 3 hours. Cool slightly and strain broth through a fine strainer. Discard solids. Chill and skim fat.

Place in convenient containers and freeze.

Chicken Soup [m]

This is the old-fashioned kind that is sure to cure what ails you. At the first sign of a sniffle from anyone in the family, I make this soup. Freeze the extra. [One should always have chicken soup on hand.]

Makes about 20 cups [4.45 liters]

3 ½ to 4 pounds [1 ½ to 2 kilos] chicken, cleaned, whole
3 large meaty marrow or knuckle beef bones
1 pound [450 grams] gizzards, cleaned, halved
18 cups [4 liters] cold water, twice
9 ounces [250 grams] onions, quartered lengthwise
7 ounces [200 grams] celery with leaves, sliced thinly
10 ½ ounces [300 grams] carrots, peeled, chopped
9 ounces [250 grams] parsnips, peeled, sliced thickly
6 full sprigs fresh dill, tied with a string
salt, to taste
fresh white pepper, to taste

In an 8 quart [8 liter] kettle, place chicken, bones, gizzards and water. Bring to a boil, boil 5 minutes and throw away water. Rinse meats and bones and wash kettle and start again.

Place chicken, bones, gizzards and water back in kettle. Bring to a boil, skimming the froth as it rises. Add the rest of the ingredients. Cover and simmer for 2 ½ to 3 hours, until chicken is tender. Remove chicken and reserve for another use [Chicken Salad [see Index]]. Remove bones and dill and discard. Let soup cool and skim fat. [Or chill overnight and skim fat.]

Reheat soup and serve with Matzo Balls [see Index], noodles, or Dumplings [see Index].

The soup keeps for days, if brought to a boil every couple days, cooled quickly and refrigerated. If you freeze soup, strain out vegetables, they do not freeze well.

Fresh Corn Soup *[m or p]*

I make this soup with fresh corn just picked. There are roadside trucks nearby that bring in corn from various farms. In the winter months, frozen corn is an adequate substitute. I prefer white corn to yellow. This is a quick and easy soup which I think is delicious.

Makes 14 cups [3 liters]

10 to 11 ears corn or 3 pounds [1.35 kilos] corn kernels [10 cups]

10 cups [2.25 liters] Chicken Broth [see Index] or canned or vegetable broth or pareve chicken flavored soup, from the mix

6 tablespoons instant mashed potatoes flakes

1 1/2 teaspoons dried thyme

1/2 teaspoon celery seed

salt, to taste

fresh white pepper, to taste

Cut corn off ears and with the back of a knife scrape ears to extract all milk from cobs. Lightly crush corn in a food processor, pulsing 10 to 15 times. [Or mash with a potato masher.]

Place broth in a 5 1/2 quart [5 liter] kettle and add corn. Bring to a simmer and add the rest of the ingredients, stirring. Simmer for 20 minutes, stirring occasionally.

Serve. The soup freezes well.

Cold Cucumber Yogurt Soup [d]

Everyone seems to like this soup, which I serve on hot summer evenings. It is easy to make, with ingredients readily available and can be whipped up quickly, just allowing time to chill thoroughly.

Makes 10 cups [2.25 liters]

2 ¼ pounds [1 kilo] English [seedless] or Kirby cucumbers, peeled, seeded if necessary, sliced thickly
9 ½ ounces [275 grams] onions, chopped coarsely
6 cups [1.4 liters] pareve chicken flavored soup, from the mix
2 large handfuls fresh mint leaves, 2 cups [24 grams]
3 garlic cloves, sliced
salt, to taste
fresh white pepper, to taste
1 ½ to 2 cups [350 to 450 grams] no-fat plain yogurt
extra mint leaves, sliced, to garnish

In a 4 quart [4 liter] kettle, place all the ingredients, except yogurt. Bring to a boil and simmer, covered, for 30 minutes. Cool slightly and puree in a blender or food processor. Taste and correct the seasoning. Cool and chill soup completely.

When soup is cold, add yogurt and mix well. Chill soup for several hours, stirring occasionally.

Garnish each bowl or cup with a few mint shreds and serve the soup icy cold.

Garlic Soup *[p]*

The garlic soup in my first cookbook was full of eggs and cream. Tabu in a healthy cookbook. But I love garlic and garlic soup sounds like the ideal way to eat lots of garlic in a tasty vehicle. If you like garlic, try this lovely velvety soup.

Makes about 12 cups [2.7 liters]

12 ounces [330 grams] peeled garlic cloves, trimmed [2 cups, about 76 cloves]
20 ounces [550 grams] potatoes, peeled, chopped coarsely
20 ounces [550 grams] carrots, peeled, chopped coarsely
11 ¹/₂ ounces [325 grams] leeks, white and tender light green parts only, cleaned well, chopped coarsely, 2 fat leeks
4 cups [900 milliliters] vegetable broth or pareve chicken flavored soup, from the mix
6 cups [1.4 liters] water
salt, to taste
fresh white pepper, to taste

In a 5 quart [5 liter] kettle, combine all the ingredients and bring to a boil. Cover and simmer until vegetables are very soft and tender, about 2 hours, stirring occasionally. Cool soup slightly and puree in a food processor.

Return soup to a simmer, taste and correct the seasoning and serve. The soup can be made 4 or 5 days ahead of time and can be frozen.

Gaspacho [p]

This is a lovely refreshing cold soup. I call it my "salad in a soup bowl". This soup is by special request from my daughter, Becky Weisgal-Lavon. It's her favorite.

Makes about 12 cups [2.7 liters]

2 ¹/₄ pounds [1 kilo] fresh tomatoes, peeled, seeded
7 ounces [200 grams] celery with leaves
9 ounces [250 grams] green peppers, seeded, membranes removed
18 ounces [500 grams] cucumbers, peeled, seeded or Kirby or English, seeded if necessary
6 large garlic cloves, peeled
large handful fresh parsley leaves
large handful fresh basil leaves
1 ¹/₂ teaspoons salt, to taste
1 teaspoon fresh white pepper
1 teaspoon dried thyme
¹/₂ teaspoon chili powder
6 drops Tabasco sauce, to taste
2 to 4 tablespoons Worcestershire sauce, to taste
3 ¹/₂ to 5 cups [830 to 1.2 liters] tomato juice
2 tablespoons extra virgin olive oil
10 ¹/₂ ounces [300 grams] onions, peeled, chopped finely

Dice finely, by HAND, tomatoes, celery, peppers and cucumbers. Set aside.

In a food processor, drop garlic through feed tube into running processor and run until chopped finely. Add parsley, basil, salt, pepper, thyme, chili powder, Tabasco, Worcestershire, 3 ¹/₂ cups [830 grams] juice and oil. Process until smooth. Pour contents of processor into a bowl or large pitcher and add diced and chopped vegetables. Thin soup with more juice, if desired.

Serve the soup icy cold in bowls or mugs.

Goulash Soup [m]

We have many Hungarians living in Israel and it seems that they are all good cooks. This hearty soup, with an Hungarian flavor, is my daughter Margit Weisgal's favorite. I had never tasted this soup before I moved to Israel, where it is well known. It is a welcome addition on a winter's night.

Makes about 14 cups [3 liters]

olive oil cooking spray
14 ounces [400 grams] onions, chopped coarsely
5 ounces [140 grams] green bell peppers, cored, seeded, cut into large dice
2 to 2 $^1/_2$ pounds [1 kilo] boneless veal, well trimmed of fat, cut into bite size cubes
10 cups [2 $^1/_2$ liters] water
4 large meaty veal marrow bones
a 14 to 16 ounce [400 to 450 gram] can diced tomatoes, with juice
1 tablespoon salt, to taste
$^1/_2$ teaspoon fresh black pepper
$^1/_2$ teaspoon ground caraway
2 tablespoons sweet Hungarian paprika
1 tablespoon hot Hungarian paprika
2 cups [450 milliliters] vegetable juice
6 $^1/_2$ ounces [185 grams] carrots, peeled, chopped
1 $^1/_2$ pounds [680 grams] potatoes, peeled, cut into small dice
1 recipe cooked Nuckerl [see Index] or Spaetzle [see Index]

In an 8 quart [8 liter] well sprayed kettle, saute onions and peppers until soft. Add meat and saute until browning. Add bones and water and bring to a boil, skimming the froth as it rises. Add tomatoes and seasonings. Simmer, covered, for 1 $^1/_2$ hours, stirring occasionally.

Add vegetable juice, carrots and potatoes. Simmer, covered, an additional hour, stirring occasionally. Taste and correct the seasoning.

Add nuckerl or spaetzle and simmer for 5 minutes and serve.

The soup freezes well BUT do not add nuckerl or spaetzle until after thawing the soup as they do not freeze well.

Green Pea Soup *[m or d or p]*

I like green peas, fresh or frozen. This light pleasant soup is good either hot or cold, garnished with yogurt or not. It is a suitable accompaniment to many meals and is a satisfying light lunch. As with most soups, it can be made ahead.

Makes about 12 cups [2.7 liters]

8 ounces [225 grams] leeks, white and light green parts, sliced thinly, 2 leeks
10 ¹/₂ ounces [300 grams] head lettuce, shredded thinly [Iceberg]
2 garlic cloves, minced
1 tablespoon margarine
12 cups [2.7 liters] hot Chicken Broth [see Index] or pareve chicken flavored soup, from the mix, or vegetable broth
28 ounces [800 grams] shelled peas, 6 ¹/₄ cups, fresh or frozen
2 tablespoons lemon juice
1 teaspoon salt or to taste
1 teaspoon dried thyme or 1 tablespoon fresh thyme leaves
¹/₂ teaspoon fresh white pepper
pinch ground bay leaf
optional: no-fat plain yogurt, to garnish

In a 5 quart [5 liter] kettle, saute leeks, lettuce and garlic, in margarine, over medium heat, until well softened, about 20 minutes. Add ¹/₂ of hot broth and simmer mixture for 10 minutes. Let mixture cool slightly and puree in a blender or processor and return it to pot. Add the rest of the ingredients, except yogurt, and simmer for 20 minutes, stirring occasionally.

Serve hot or cold, with a dollop of yogurt in each bowl, if desired.

Lentil or Split Pea Soup [m]

This is a thick, hearty, comforting soup. It has a velvety, smoky flavor. Delicious served on a stormy winter's day. Wonderful reheated and easily frozen for another time. I like to serve this soup on New Year's Eve.

Makes about 18 cups [4 liters]

olive oil cooking spray
20 ounces [560 grams] onions, chopped
4 ounces [110 grams] celery, chopped
5 1/2 ounces [150 grams] carrots, chopped
2 large garlic cloves, chopped
1 tablespoon vegetable oil
5 cups [1.2 liters] Beef Stock [see Index] or canned [see Note]
5 cups [1.2 liters] Chicken Broth [see Index] or canned
8 ounces [220 grams] smoked turkey wings
1 1/2 pounds [680 grams] lentils or green or yellow split peas or both
2 - 14 1/2 ounce [400 gram] cans diced tomatoes, with juice
1 to 3 teaspoons salt, to taste
1/2 teaspoon fresh black pepper
1/4 teaspoon ground bay leaf
3/4 teaspoon dried thyme
1/4 teaspoon ground cloves
11 1/2 ounces [325 grams] smoked turkey sausage, sliced thinly into bite size pieces
Note: 3 large beef marrow bones, if using canned soup

In a well sprayed 8 quart [8 liter] kettle, saute onions, celery, carrots and garlic in oil until well softened, about 15 to 20 minutes. Add the rest of the ingredients, except sausages, and bring to a boil. Simmer, covered, for 1 1/2 to 2 hours until legumes are soft. Remove and discard turkey skin and bones and cut meat into small pieces. Add sausages and simmer for an additional 30 minutes and serve.

The soup can be made 3 or 4 days ahead and can be frozen.

Onion Soup *[p or d]*

This all time favorite soup is easy to make and liked by most people. This superb soup can stand on its own or can be luxurious with the optional cheese extra.

Makes about 10 cups [2.25 liters]

olive oil cooking spray

3 1/3 pounds [1 1/2 kilos] onions, sliced thinly

2 1/2 ounces [75 grams] margarine or 5 tablespoons extra virgin olive oil

1 tablespoon chopped garlic

1 to 1 1/2 teaspoons salt, to taste

1 1/2 teaspoons sugar

fresh black pepper, to taste

9 cups [2 liters] hot pareve beef soup, from the mix

optional extra:

French or Italian Bread [see Index], sliced 3/4 inch [2 centimeters] thick

6 ounces [175 grams] Swiss cheese, shredded

2/3 cup [70 grams] grated Parmesan cheese

extra grated Parmesan cheese, to garnish

In a sprayed wide Dutch oven, saute onions in margarine or oil over medium high heat for 10 minutes, stirring frequently. Add garlic, salt, sugar and pepper and cook, stirring frequently, over medium heat until onions are evenly golden brown, about 45 minutes.

Add hot soup and simmer, partly covered, for 1 hour, stirring occasionally.

Serve as is or:

Toast bread slices. Mix cheeses and mound some on each slice of toast. Place toast slices on a baking sheet and place under a preheated broiler just until cheeses melt. Ladle soup into bowls and float a piece of toast on top in each bowl. Pass extra Parmesan cheese.

Mock Oxtail Soup *[m]*

I use short ribs to make this soup. They are a lovely sweet meat. They are also full of fat so follow directions carefully to melt away most of the fat. Make this soup a day ahead so that the rest of the fat can be skimmed from the top of the soup. This is a favorite soup of my friends, the Machts.

Makes about 26 cups [5.8 liters]

about 5 ¹/₂ pounds [2.5 kilos] short ribs
salt, for sprinkling
fresh black pepper, for sprinkling
12 cups [2.7 liters] beef broth, canned, homemade or from the mix
12 cups [2.7 liters] water
1 pound [450 grams] onions, chopped
9 ounces [250 grams] leeks, chopped, tough green discarded
18 ounces [500 grams] cabbage, chopped
11 ¹/₂ ounces [325 grams] carrots, chopped
7 ounces [200 grams] celery, chopped
an 8 ounce [225 gram] can tomato paste
1 tablespoon chopped garlic
1 bay leaf
1 teaspoon dried marjoram
1 teaspoon dried basil
1 teaspoon dried thyme
1 teaspoon ground turmeric
1 teaspoon ground allspice
1 teaspoon curry powder
1 teaspoon dry mustard
2 tablespoons Worcestershire sauce
2 tablespoons chopped parsley leaves
1 tablespoon chili powder
salt, to taste
fresh black pepper, to taste

78

Trim as much fat as possible from short ribs. Sprinkle on all sides with salt and pepper. Place ribs on a rack in a foil lined baking pan and bake in a preheated 450°F. [230°C.] oven for 45 minutes. Most of the fat will drain away. Discard fat.

Transfer ribs to a 10 quart [10 liter] kettle and add broth and water. Bring to a boil, skimming the froth as it rises. Add the rest of the ingredients and simmer soup for 2 hours, covered, stirring occasionally. Uncover and simmer an additional 30 minutes. Let cool. Fish out meat and bones. Discard bones, cut meat into bite size. Discard bay leaf. Chill and skim off fat.

The soup can be made several days ahead of time and can be frozen.

Pumpkin Soup [d]

This is a delicious, different soup, made in a jiffy. It has a sweet taste and is smooth on the tongue.

Makes about 15 cups [3.37 liters]

2 - 29 ounce [820 gram] cans pumpkin puree

3 cups [700 milliliters] strong pareve chicken flavored soup, from the mix

2 cups [450 milliliters] water

5 cups [900 milliliters] skim milk

3 tablespoons brown sugar

1 tablespoon salt, to taste

$1/4$ teaspoon ground ginger

$1/8$ teaspoon fresh white pepper

pinch ground cinnamon

Combine all the ingredients in a 5 quart [5 liter] saucepan and bring to a simmer, stirring frequently. Simmer for 15 minutes, stirring frequently. Thin soup with more water, if desired.

Serve. The soup freezes well.

Potato, Leek & Mushroom Soup *[m or p]*

The ingredients in this soup marry beautifully to make a lovely velvety soup. This soup keeps well and is so good, I've made sure that there is plenty for leftovers.

Makes about 18 cups [4 liters]

1 ounce [30 grams] dried porcini mushrooms
1 ½ cups hot water
olive oil cooking spray
1 tablespoon extra virgin olive oil
2 ribs celery, 4 ½ ounces [125 grams], sliced
4 fat leeks, 1 ¾ pounds [800 grams], tough green leaves discarded, washed well, sliced
1 bunch green onions, about 3 ounces [90 grams], sliced
1 medium onion, 6 ounces [175 grams], chopped coarsely
1 tablespoon chopped garlic
3 pounds [1.3 kilos] potatoes, peeled, cut into large dice
14 cups [3 liters] defatted Chicken Broth [see Index] or pareve chicken flavored soup, from the mix
¼ teaspoon dried thyme
¼ teaspoon dried marjoram
¼ teaspoon celery seed
1 tablespoon Worcestershire sauce
salt, to taste
fresh white pepper, to taste

Soak mushrooms in hot water for 30 minutes. Remove mushrooms with a slotted spoon and set aside. Strain soaking liquid to add to soup.

In a sprayed 8 quart [8 liter] kettle, in olive oil, saute, over medium heat, celery, leeks, green onions, onions and garlic, until vegetables are very soft, stirring occasionally, about 10 minutes. Add the rest of the ingredients, including mushroom liquid, and bring to a simmer. Simmer soup for about 2 hours, until potatoes are very soft.

Chop soup coarsely in a food processor using pulsing action. Reheat to serve. The soup freezes well.

Tomato Celery Soup *[p]*

This is a simple and interesting soup. The flavors are intense and different. The soup can be made smooth or slightly chunky.

Makes about 15 cups [3.37 liters]

olive oil cooking spray
1 tablespoon extra virgin olive oil
1 $1/3$ pounds [600 grams] celery with leaves and root, chopped, about 1 large bunch
1 $3/4$ pounds [800 grams] onions, chopped
2 tablespoons chopped garlic
2 - 28 ounce [800 gram] cans crushed tomatoes
6 cups [1.4 liters] water
2 teaspoons fresh thyme leaves or $1/2$ teaspoon dried thyme
2 teaspoons fresh basil leaves, chopped or $1/2$ teaspoon dried basil
2 teaspoons fresh tarragon leaves or $1/2$ teaspoon dried tarragon
salt, to taste
fresh white pepper, to taste
sugar, to taste

In a sprayed 8 quart [8 liter] non stick kettle, add oil and heat until hot. Add celery, onions and garlic and saute over high heat until vegetables are well softened, about 15 minutes.

Add tomatoes and water and bring to a simmer. Simmer for 1 hour, stirring occasionally. Add thyme, basil, tarragon, salt, pepper and sugar. Simmer an additional 15 minutes.

For a smooth texture, put mixture through a Foley food mill or a coarse strainer, pressing well to extract all the essence. Or for a chunky soup, put into a food processor and pulse until desired texture.

The soup can be made several days ahead of time and can be frozen.

Tomato Consomme [m]

Twice a year, when I travel to California, I work at Meals on Wheels of Sonoma County. I make Beef Stock [see Index] and Chicken [or Turkey] Broth [see Index], enough to last until I am next expected. My friend, Susan Weeks, who heads the organization, devised this simple recipe, using my beef stock. It is delicious and a favorite of many friends.

Makes about 12 cups [2.7 liters]

5 ¾ cups [1.37 liters] Beef Stock [see Index]

5 ¾ cups [1.37 liters] tomato juice

2 teaspoons lemon-pepper

½ teaspoon dried oregano

3 tablespoons dry Sherry

1 tablespoon lemon juice

1 teaspoon Worcestershire sauce

Tabasco, to taste

dry beef soup powder or bouillion, to taste, about 1 tablespoon

sugar, to taste

Combine all the ingredients, mix well and bring to a boil. Simmer for 20 minutes and serve. The soup freezes well.

If desired, serve this soup with Spaetzle [see Index] or Nuckerl [see Index].

Turkey Barley Soup [m]

It is almost worth buying a turkey for the leftovers, including and especially turkey barley soup and Turkey Gumbo [see Index]. This is a particular favorite with our family. It is warming, healthful and very delicious. Everyone likes this soup.

Makes about 16 cups [3.6 liters]

carcass and bones from a Roast Turkey [see Index]
wing tips and necks from turkeys and/or chickens [from the freezer]
3 cups [700 milliliters] Chicken Broth [see Index] or canned
3 cups [700 milliliters] Beef Stock [see Index] or canned
6 cups [1.4 liters] water
1 pound [450 grams] onions, chopped coarsely
11 ounces [320 grams] carrots, chopped
10 $^1/_2$ ounces [300 grams] celery, with leaves, diced small
2 teaspoons salt, or to taste
$^1/_2$ teaspoon fresh black pepper, or to taste
1 $^1/_2$ cups [315 grams] pearl barley, rinsed

In an 8 quart [8 liter] kettle, place carcass, bones, broth, stock and water. Bring to a boil, skimming the froth as it rises. Add the rest of the ingredients, except barley. Cover and simmer for 2 hours. Remove and discard bones and skin.

Add barley, taste and correct the seasoning. Simmer an additional 1 to 1 $^1/_2$ hours, until barley is very tender.

The soup can be made 3 or 4 days ahead and can be frozen.

Vegetable Beef Soup [m]

I have a friend, Harriet Rosenthal, who requested an old fashioned vegetable soup like the kind that she remembered from childhood. So I made her this soup. She says it makes her want to cook again. This is almost a whole meal soup. With a salad and bread, it is perfect light dinner fare.

Makes about 20 cups [4.45 liters]

18 cups Beef Stock [see Index] or canned [see Note]
meat from the stock or 1 shin of beef, trimmed
20 ounces [580 grams] green cabbage, shredded
10 ounces [290 grams] parsnips, peeled, chopped
12 ¹/₂ ounces [350 grams] carrots, peeled, chopped
optional: carrot top leaves, chopped, delicious
10 ounces [290 grams] frozen baby lima beans
9 ounces [250 grams] celery with leaves, sliced
10 ounces [290 grams] frozen cut green beans
10 ounces [290 grams] onions, diced
10 ounces [290 grams] frozen corn
3 ¹/₂ ounces [100 grams] leeks, cleaned, sliced
10 ounces [290 grams] frozen peas
12 ¹/₂ ounces [350 grams] turnips, peeled, quartered, sliced
1 to 2 teaspoons dried sweet basil
1 teaspoon dried marjoram
salt, to taste
fresh black pepper, to taste

Combine all the ingredients in a large soup kettle. Bring to a boil, skimming the froth as it rises. Lower heat and simmer for 2 hours. Fish out meat and cut into small dice.

The soup freezes beautifully.

Note: If you use canned beef broth instead of Beef Stock [see Index], replace 4 cups of the stock with cut up canned tomatoes.

Zucchini Soup *[d or p]*

Zucchini is one of the most versatile vegetables we have. It is available all year round, quick to cook, marries well with any number of herbs and spices and can be prepared in many different ways. This is just one of them. This soup is equally good hot or cold, garnished with yogurt or not and it can be made in a jiffy.

Makes 10 cups [2.25 liters]

2 ¼ pounds [1 kilo] zucchini, unpeeled, sliced thickly
12 ounces [340 grams] onions, chopped coarsely
large handful fresh dill sprigs
8 cups [1.8 liters] pareve chicken flavored soup, from the mix
salt, to taste
fresh white pepper, to taste
optional: no-fat plain yogurt, to garnish

In a 4 quart [4 liter] kettle, place all the ingredients, except yogurt. Bring to a boil and simmer, covered, until squash and onions are very tender, about 30 minutes. Cool slightly.

Puree entire mixture in a blender or food processor and return soup to pot. Bring to a simmer, stirring occasionally.

Serve the soup hot or cold, garnished with yogurt, if desired. The soup freezes well.

Vegetarian Minestrone *[p or d]*

Each time I make this soup I vary the vegetables. I like it sometimes with zucchini squash, eggplant or okra and sometimes with tiny macaroni.

Makes about 20 cups [4.45 liters]

$^1/_2$ **pound [225 grams] dried navy or pea beans**	
10 cups [2.25 liters] water, for de-gassing	
18 cups [4 liters] well flavored pareve broth, chicken, beef or vegetable	
a 14 $^1/_2$ ounce [410 gram] can stewed tomatoes	
10 ounces [285 grams] cabbage, shredded	
13 ounces [375 grams] carrots, quartered, cut into 2 inch [5 centimeter] pieces	
7 ounces [200 grams] kolrabi, peeled, diced	
9 $^1/_2$ ounces [275 grams] parsnips, peeled, quartered, cut into 2 inch [5 centimeter] pieces	
8 ounces [225 grams] leeks, cleaned, sliced	
5 $^1/_2$ ounces [150 grams] fennel, sliced, including some tops	
14 ounces [400 grams] frozen corn	
11 $^1/_2$ ounces [325 grams] frozen cut green beans	

10 $\frac{1}{2}$ ounces [300 grams] frozen peas

9 ounces [250 grams] frozen mixed vegetables

optional: 1 pound [450 grams] sunchokes [Jerusalem artichokes], peeled, diced

$\frac{1}{4}$ cup [55 milliliters] fresh basil leaves, sliced

2 teaspoons dried oregano

salt, to taste

fresh black pepper, to taste

optional: Parmesan cheese, for sprinkling or Pesto [see Index] to garnish, or cooked with Parmesan cheese rind

Place beans and water in a kettle. Bring to a boil and boil for 2 minutes. Cover and let sit for 1 hour. Drain and discard water. This de-gasses beans.

Place beans in a large kettle and add broth. Bring to a boil, skimming the froth as it rises. Cover and simmer beans until they are almost tender. This can take from 1 to 3 hours depending on age of beans.

Add the rest of the ingredients, except cheese, and simmer for 1 $\frac{1}{2}$ hours. Add salt and pepper to taste.

Sprinkle each serving with Parmesan or add a bit of pesto to each bowl, if desired.

The soup freezes well.

SALADS

Blue Cheese Dressing [d]

This dressing is delicious over Spinach Salad [see Index] and with plain hearts of lettuce. It also makes a good dip with crudities.

Makes about 2 ½ cups [560 milliliters]

16 ounces [450 grams] no-fat plain yogurt, without gelatin
5 tablespoons low fat mayonaisse
1 tablespoon Dijon mustard
1 teaspoon garlic granules
1 teaspoon Worcestershire sauce
6 ½ ounces [185 grams] blue cheese, crumbled or diced finely

Place yogurt in a yogurt funnel or in a paper coffee filter inside a strainer and let drain for 2 hours. Discard whey.

Combine all the ingredients in a covered jar. Refrigerate for up to 3 weeks.

Caesar Salad [d]

I love Caesar salad. I make this almost every day for myself for dinner or sometimes for lunch. I serve this often to guests. You'll like the new ingredient.

Serves 8 salad lovers

2 large heads Romaine lettuce, each about 18 ounces [500 grams]
1 small head radiccio lettuce, sliced finely
¾ to 1 ⅓ cups [75 to 150 grams] freshly grated Parmesan cheese [Reggiano], to taste
fresh black pepper, to taste

88

4 ounces [110 grams] pine nuts

¹/₂ recipe Caesar Salad Dressing [see Index]

1 cup [90 grams] croutons

Early in the day, wash Romaine. Shake out water, lay lettuce leaves on kitchen towels. Roll up towels, slide into a plastic bag and refrigerate several hours.

About ¹/₂ hour before serving, tear lettuce leaves into bite size pieces into a large salad bowl. Mix with radiccio slices and Parmesan. Grind lots of fresh pepper all over salad. Lightly toast pine nuts in a dry skillet for about 45 seconds and add to salad. Just before serving, dress the salad and toss well.

Serve in individual salad bowls and pass the croutons.

Caesar Salad Dressing [p]

This is my every day dressing from Caesar Salad [see Index] to Greek Salad [see Index] to Mixed Vegetable Salad [see Index] to Italian Salad [see Index]. It is my best vinaigrette dressing.

Makes enough for 2 big salads for 8 people [or maybe more]

³/₄ cup [175 milliliters] extra virgin olive oil

¹/₂ cup [110 milliliters] red wine vinegar

¹/₈ cup [28 milliliters] rice wine vinegar

1 can anchovies, with the oil, cut into small pieces

1 to 3 tablespoons chopped garlic, to taste

a 4 minute coddled egg [see Note]

Place all the ingredients in a screw-top jar. Shake well to mix. Pour over salad just before serving. The dressing lasts at least a week, maybe three. Shake well just before serving.

The dressing can be varied by adding dried herbs; basil, dill, oregano, etc., or by adding 1 ¹/₂ tablespoons Dijon mustard.

Note: To coddle an egg: bring a small pot of water to a boil, add an egg, turn off heat, and let egg sit in the water the stated length of time.

Cauliflower Salad [d]

This different salad is redolent of basil. It has nice textures and interesting flavors. It is quickly and easily put together and can be prepared a day or two ahead of time.

Serves 8

about a 1 3/4 pound [820 gram] fresh white cauliflower
14 ounces [400 grams] seedless or Kirby cucumbers
3 1/2 ounces [100 grams] green onions, including green, sliced
5 tablespoons Pesto [see Index]
1/4 cup [55 milliliters] red wine vinegar
salt, to taste
fresh black pepper, to taste

Remove cauliflower leaves [reserve for soup] and cut out the core. Separate into florets and slice into bite size pieces. Bring a kettle of salted water to a boil, add cauliflower, cover and cook for 5 minutes ONLY from the time cauliflower is added to kettle. Drain immediately, refresh under cold running water, drain again and place in a bowl.

Quarter cucumbers lengthwise and slice crosswise. Add to cauliflower in bowl. Add sliced green onions.

Combine pesto and vinegar. Pour over salad ingredients in bowl and mix carefully with a large fork. Add salt and pepper to taste. Chill at least one hour to develop the flavor.

Cauliflower Yogurt Salad [d]

This is a simple refreshing salad, taking advantage of no-fat yogurt. After draining, the yogurt becomes very creamy and mixed with the other ingredients, is very delicious.

Serves 8

12 ounces [340 grams] no-fat plain yogurt
about 2 pounds [900 grams] fresh white cauliflower
3 ¹/₂ ounces [100 grams] green onions, including green, sliced, about 1 bunch
2 tablespoons Dijon mustard
¹/₂ to 1 teaspoon salt, to taste
fresh white pepper, to taste
garlic granules, to taste

Drain yogurt in a yogurt funnel or paper coffee filter for 1 hour.

Remove cauliflower leaves [reserve for soup] and cut out core. Separate into florets and slice into bite size. Bring a kettle of salted water to a boil. Add cauliflower, cover and cook for 5 minutes ONLY from the time cauliflower is added to kettle. Drain immediately, refresh under cold running water and drain again and place in a bowl. Add green onions.

Combine drained yogurt, mustard, salt, pepper and garlic in a small bowl. Add yogurt mixture to cauliflower and mix with a large fork to combine well.

Refrigerate covered for 4 hours to overnight and serve.

Chicken Salad [m]

Because skinless and boneless chicken parts are so available, it is easy to make this salad often during the summer season. It is a lovely dish for a light supper or for luncheon. I love to serve sandwiches at a casual meal and chicken salad on Sour Dough Italian or Rye Bread [see Index] is delicious.

Serves 8

4 cups [900 grams] defatted Chicken Broth [see Index] or canned
18 ounces [490 grams] skinless, boneless thighs
18 ounces [490 grams] skinless, boneless breasts
12 ¹/₂ ounces [350 grams] celery, diced finely
12 ¹/₂ ounces [350 grams] mild, sweet onions, chopped [Vidalias]
1 teaspoon salt, to taste
¹/₂ teaspoon fresh black pepper, to taste
¹/₄ teaspoon garlic granules
¹/₂ teaspoon celery seed
¹/₄ cup [4 tablespoons] snipped fresh dill or 1 ¹/₂ tablespoons dried dillweed
³/₄ to 1 cup [175 to 225 grams] reduced fat mayonaisse
lettuce leaves, tomato wedges, to garnish

In a saucepan with chicken broth add thighs and breasts. Bring to a boil, lower the heat and simmer for 3 minutes. Turn off heat, cover and let chicken cool in broth. Remove chicken from broth, remove all fat and cut into dice. Strain and reserve broth for another use, it can be frozen.

Combine chicken with the rest of the ingredients and mix thoroughly. Chill at least 3 hours to develop the flavors. Taste and correct the seasoning.

Serve just slightly chilled or at room temperature, on a bed of lettuce leaves, garnished with tomato wedges.

Cole Slaw [d]

When our family traveled all over the United States in a trailer, we enjoyed sampling the different cuisines of wherever we happened to be. We would shop for what we thought of as exotic foods and prepare them in our kitchen or outside over the fire or on a grill. On one trip when we were passing through Kansas on a very long day's drive, we stopped at a Hotel-Restaurant that we saw advertised on the road. They touted "family style" dinners and as we were very tired, we looked forward to a relaxed dinner. Indeed the tables were large and families sat together with other families and the food was brought in on large platters and passed around. You could take as much as you wanted. They had a cole slaw that I dreamed about but could never duplicate. Thumbing through a magazine one day, I came across an article by Jane and Michael Stern containing the recipe for the cole slaw from the Brookville Hotel in Kansas. This is my low fat version of the slaw. The original was made with heavy cream. I think this one is delicious, as was the original.

Serves 8

1 firm head green cabbage, about 2 ¼ pounds [1 kilo]
1 teaspoon salt
¼ cup [50 grams] sugar
½ cup [110 milliliters] cider vinegar
1 cup [225 milliliters] evaporated skimmed milk
2 tablespoons reduced fat mayonaisse
½ cup [110 grams] no-fat yogurt, drained for 1 hour
½ teaspoon fresh white pepper

Finely shred cabbage, using a food processor or hand grater, and place in a large bowl. In a small bowl, combine salt, sugar, vinegar, milk, mayonaisse, yogurt and pepper with a wire whisk. Pour milk mixture over cabbage and mix thoroughly. Refrigerate for at least 1 hour, tossing occasionally. The slaw can be made 1 day ahead.

Cucumber Salad [p]

This is a crisp, refreshing salad, easy to make ahead of time and nice to serve with many dishes. A mandoline is a handy and inexpensive gadget to use for slicing the cucumbers. My mother, Freddy Mesirow de LaViez, particularly liked this salad and I like to make it often.

Serves 8

1 ½ pounds [680 grams] English [hot house] seedless cucumbers, peeled, sliced thinly
1 ½ pounds [680 grams] sweet onions, sliced thinly [Vidalias are nice]
¾ cup [175 milliliters] white vinegar
¾ cup [175 milliliters] water
1 teaspoon salt
1 teaspoon sugar
½ teaspoon fresh white pepper

Combine all the ingredients in a glass bowl and mix well. Cover with a plate that fits inside bowl and place a weight on top of plate, [a small can of food will do]. Marinate salad in the fridge for 4 hours to overnight. Drain some of the liquid off before serving. Keeps well for a couple of days.

Cucumber Yogurt Salad [d]

I like this refreshing fat free salad. I use English cucumbers because they are practically seedless. You must drain the yogurt for several hours in a yogurt funnel or a coffee paper filter, set in a strainer or the salad will be too watery.

Serve 8

2 ¼ pounds [1 kilo] English [hot house] or Kirby cucumbers, unpeeled, sliced thinly [I use a mandoline]

salt, for sprinkling

¼ cup [4 tablespoons] snipped fresh dill

13 ounces [365 grams] no-fat plain yogurt, drained for 3 hours

salt, to taste

fresh white pepper, to taste

Sprinkle salt on cucumber slices and let drain in a colander for 30 minutes. Rinse well and pat dry with towels.

Combine cucumbers with dill and drained yogurt. Add salt cautiously, pepper to taste. Chill at least 1 hour to develop the flavor.

Greek Salad [d or p]

I include this salad and dedicate it to my friend Adrienne Hoffman, who inspires me to make Greek salad often. She is one of my best salad eaters.

Serves 8

1 medium head Iceberg lettuce, sliced about 1 pound [450 grams]

1 small head radiccio, sliced

8 ounces [225 grams] plum tomatoes, cored, cut into eights, lengthwise or 2 ounces [50 grams] Sun Dried Tomatoes [see Index] soaked for 30 minutes until soft, cut into pieces

1/2 English cucumber, peeled in stripes, halved lengthwise, sliced thinly, crosswise

1 1/2 green, red, yellow or orange bell peppers, seeds and membranes removed, sliced thinly crosswise

7 ounces [200 grams] red onions, peeled, sliced thinly crosswise, halved or Vidalias

10 pepperonicini Greek peppers, stems and seeds removed, sliced crosswise

15 Kalamata or other brine cured black olives, seeded, halved lengthwise

1 ripe avacado, peeled, halved, sliced

10 ounces [280 grams] fennel, trimmed, quartered, sliced

1/2 pound [225 grams] fresh mushrooms, sliced

a 2 ounce [55 gram] can anchovies, drained, halved

a large handful fresh basil leaves, sliced

salt, to taste

fresh black pepper, to taste

optional: 7 ounces [200 grams] Feta cheese, crumbled

1 recipe Greek Salad Dressing [see Index]

Combine all the ingredients, except cheese and dressing in a large salad bowl. Refrigerate and just before serving, add cheese, if using, and dress the salad. Toss well and serve.

Greek Salad Dressing [p]

Instead of my usual salad dressing, the Caesar Salad Dressing [see Index], I often like this dressing for Greek Salad [see Index]. It is also good on a nice mixed salad with raw vegetables.

Makes about 1 ¼ cups [300 milliliters]

handful fresh basil leaves, about 1 ounce [23 grams]
¹/₂ cup [110 milliliters] extra virgin olive oil
¹/₄ cup [55 milliliters] red wine vinegar
¹/₈ cup [28 milliliters] balsalmic vinegar
¹/₈ cup [28 milliliters] water
1 to 3 tablespoon chopped garlic, to taste
2 tablespoons Dijon mustard
¹/₂ teaspoon sugar
1 teaspoon dried oregano

Chop basil leaves. In a blender combine leaves with the rest of the ingredients. Transfer to a screw top jar. Shake well before dressing the salad.

The dressing can be prepared a week ahead of time. Keep refrigerated until used.

Green Bean Vinaigrette [p]

This is a crunchy, piquant salad that is a good "go with" for the Tomato Aspic [see Index], easy to make ahead and delicious on its own.

Serves 8

2 - 10 ounce [285 gram] packages frozen French cut green beans

a 7 ³/₄ ounce [215 gram] jar cocktail onions, drained

vinaigrette dressing:

    3 tablespoons sweet pickle relish

    2 tablespoons minced fresh parsley leaves

    ¹/₄ cup [55 milliliters] light vegetable oil [canola]

    6 tablespoons rasberry vinegar

    2 tablespoons rice vinegar

    pinch sugar

1 teaspoon salt or to taste

fresh white pepper, to taste

Bring a saucepan of salted water to a boil. Add green beans and cook for 5 minutes ONLY from time beans are added to water. Drain and add onions and toss well. Combine ingredients for vinaigrette in a jar, shaking well to mix. Add vinaigrette to beans and onions and toss to mix. Add salt and pepper, to taste. Let sit, in fridge, for 4 hours to overnight.

    Drain liquid before serving.

Middle East Vegetable Salad [p]

This typical salad of the Middle East is a light side dish, pretty to look at and yummy to eat. You must dice the vegetables by hand to keep the character of each vegetable intact. Drain the salad before serving.

Serves 8

1 ³/₄ pounds [750 grams] fresh ripe tomatoes, unpeeled
18 ounces [500 grams] English [seedless] or Kirby cucumbers, unpeeled
7 ounces [200 grams] yellow bell peppers, seeded
5 ¹/₂ ounces [150 grams] green onions, including green
4 garlic cloves
¹/₂ cup [40 grams] fresh parsley leaves
salt, to taste
fresh white pepper, to taste
2 teaspoons red wine vinegar
2 teaspoons lemon juice
lettuce leaves, to garnish

Using a very sharp knife, cut tomatoes, cucumbers and peppers into tiny dice. Slice green onions. Chop garlic and parsley in a food processor, I use a mini one.

Mix all the vegetables together in a bowl, sprinkle with salt and pepper. Add vinegar and lemon juice. Cover and refrigerate for at least 1 hour to develop the flavor, mixing occasionally. Taste and correct the seasoning.

Drain before serving on a bed of lettuce leaves. Keeps well for a day or two in the fridge.

Pepper Salad [p]

This is a different and delicious salad. Easy to make and better the next day. Great for a dinner party because it is made ahead. This is one of the dishes I make when colored peppers are at a good price.

Serves 8

1 pound [450 grams] yellow and/or orange bell peppers, seeds and membranes removed, sliced thinly lengthwise

1 pound [450 grams] red and/or white bell peppers, seeds and membranes removed, sliced thinly lengthwise

1 pound [450 grams] red onions, peeled, sliced thinly, crosswise

14 ounces [400 grams] fennel bulbs, sliced thinly, crosswise, including the large stalks and some fronds

$^1/_2$ recipe Caesar Salad Dressing [see Index], mixed with

1 $^1/_2$ tablespoons Dijon mustard

salt, to taste

fresh black pepper, to taste

Combine all the ingredients in a large salad bowl. Toss well to mix. Refrigerate for at least 6 hours to overnight, tossing occasionally.

Rasberry Vinaigrette [p]

This lovely, simple salad dressing has a nice fruity, slightly sweet flavor. I like it on a mixed green salad as it goes well with any number of main dishes.

Makes enough for 2 big salads, each serving 8, about 1 $^1/_2$ cups [350 milliliters]

$^3/_4$ cup [175 milliliters] extra virgin olive oil

$^1/_2$ cup [110 milliliters] rasberry vinegar

1/4 cup [55 milliliters] rice wine vinegar
2 tablespoons chopped garlic
1 teaspoon sugar

Place all the ingredients in a screw top jar and shake to mix. Dress salad just before serving. Keeps for weeks in the fridge.

Roasted Sweet Pepper Salad *[p]*

This is a salad I like to serve when peppers are reasonably priced. The combination of red, yellow, orange and green peppers is very beautiful and appetizing.

Serves 8

5 pounds [2.25 kilos] colored peppers, red, orange, yellow, green
olive oil cooking spray
1/2 cup [110 milliliters] cider or balsamic vinegar
3 tablespoons minced garlic
2 tablespoons minced fresh basil leaves
2 teaspoons extra virgin olive oil

Cut peppers straight across tops and across bottoms. Remove stems from tops. Cut peppers in half, remove seeds and membranes. Press pepper halves flat with palm of your hand. Place peppers and tops and bottoms on a foil lined baking sheet under a preheated broiler, about 5 inches [12 1/2 centimeters] from the heat. You might have to do this in batches. Spray peppers with olive oil spray.

Broil peppers until skin is blackened and blistered. Remove from oven as they blacken and immediately place in a paper bag, close it up and let steam until cool enough to handle, about 15 to 20 minutes.

Remove skins from peppers and slice thinly lengthwise. Place in a serving bowl.

Combine the rest of the ingredients and pour over peppers. Mix well and refrigerate for several hours to develop the flavor.

The salad can be made 2 or 3 days ahead of time.

Smoked Fish Salad [p]

For those who like smoked fish, this mild flavored salad is delicious. It can be made 2 or 3 days ahead with any kind of smoked fish. This is a favorite of mine in the summer or for an informal Brunch. I sometimes like having people for Brunch instead of Dinner.

Makes about 6 cups [1.4 liters]

1 ¹/₂ pounds [680 grams] smoked fish [any kind will do but, I do like white fish best]

3 ounces [100 grams] green onions, sliced, about 1 bunch

7 ounces [200 grams] celery, diced finely

3 to 4 tablespoons lemon juice, to taste

5 tablespoons reduced fat mayonaisse, approximately

fresh black pepper, to taste, I like lots

lettuce leaves, tomato wedges, cucumber slices, to garnish

Remove skin and bones from fish. Break fish into fairly large pieces. Add the rest of the ingredients and mix carefully with a fork. If necessary, add a bit more mayonaisse. Refrigerate, covered until ready to serve.

Serve on a bed of lettuce leaves, garnished with tomato wedges and cucumber slices.

Spinach Salad [p or d]

This is a particular favorite of mine. I prefer the salad with Blue Cheese Dressing [see Index], but it is also good if made with a pareve honey - Dijon dressing.

Serves 8

12 ounces [340 grams] baby spinach leaves, washed, dried, available in bags in the organic section of food markets

8 ounces [225 grams] fresh mushrooms, sliced

8 ounces [225 grams] onions, sliced, Vidalia or red
1/2 to 3/4 cup [60 to 70 grams] pareve bacon bits, to taste
2 hard boiled eggs, chopped finely
salt, to taste
fresh black pepper, to taste
Blue Cheese Dressing [see Index] or
pareve honey Dijon dressing

Into a large salad bowl, place spinach leaves. Add the rest of the ingredients, except dressing. This part can be prepared ahead of time and refrigerated.

Dress the salad just before serving.

Tomato - Onion Salad *[p]*

This is one of my favorite Summer salads. When tomatoes are plentiful and delicious and I have some Vidalia onions, I make this simple and flavorful salad.

Serves 8

3 1/4 pounds [1.45 kilos] [about] tomatoes, peeled
1 pound [450 grams] sweet onions, Vidalia or Maui
2 teaspoons minced garlic
1/4 cup [55 milliliters] cider vinegar
1/2 to 2 teaspoons sugar, to taste
salt, to taste
fresh black pepper, to taste, I like lots
2 teaspoons extra virgin olive oil
a large handful of fresh basil leaves, chopped

Cut tomatoes into medium dice, putting them into a bowl as they are cut. When all tomatoes are cut, pour off accumulated juices. Cut onions into medium dice and add to tomatoes. Add the rest of the ingredients. Refrigerate to develop the flavor and until ready to serve. The salad can be made one day ahead of time.

Tomato Aspic [p]

This is a very nice Tomato Aspic. It is a variation of one that my friend, Shirley Handelsman, gave me. This is not a wimpy aspic, it is thick and delicious, and full of vegetables.

Serves 8

1 package sugar free lemon gelatin
1 package sugar free lime gelatin
1 package unflavored gelatin
3 cups [700 milliliters] vegetable juice
2 cans condensed tomato soup, undiluted
3 tablespoons lemon juice
5 ounces [140 grams] celery, cut into tiny dice, 1 rib
1 bunch - 2 to 3 ounces [60 to 90 grams] green onions, sliced thinly
1 ounce [30 grams] "Sun" Dried Tomatoes [see Index], soaked in hot water, 30 minutes, drained, cut with a scissors into small pieces
1 teaspoon minced garlic
parsley sprigs, as a garnish
optional: Horseradish Sauce [see Index] as an accompaniment
optional: Green Bean Vinaigrette [see Index] as an accompaniment

Soften the 3 gelatins in $^{1}/_{2}$ cup [110 milliliters] of juice for 10 minutes. Combine the rest of the juice, tomato soup, lemon juice, celery, green onions, tomatoes and garlic in a saucepan. Bring to a boil and simmer for 5 minutes. Remove from heat and add gelatin mixture. Stir until gelatin is dissolved.

Pour aspic mixture into a cold water rinsed 7 cup [1.6 liter] ring mold. Cover with plastic wrap and chill for at least 4 hours to overnight.

Unmold aspic onto a platter, garnish with parsley, pile green beans in center, and serve with horseradish sauce on the side.

The aspic can be made several days in advance.

Tuna Salad [p]

For wonderful sandwiches or as part of an Antipasto [see Index] or as a luncheon main dish, nothing beats tuna salad. Serve with a bowl of soup, some crusty French or Italian Bread [see Index] and a nice Dessert [see Index]. I have added a special ingredient to give it a Moroccan flair, bits of Preserved Lemon [see Index].

Serves 8

4 - 6 ¼ ounce [185 gram] cans water packed tuna fish
½ Preserved Lemon [see Index], rinsed lightly, minced
2 tablespoons lemon juice from Preserved Lemon or fresh
10 ½ ounces [300 grams] sweet onions, chopped finely
7 ounces [200 grams] celery, diced finely, about ¾ cup
5 ½ ounces [150 grams] Kosher Dills [see Index], chopped
1 cup [225 grams] reduced fat mayonaisse
salt, to taste
fresh white pepper, to taste, I like lots
lettuce leaves, tomato wedges, pickle wedges, to garnish

Drain and flake tuna and place in a large mixing bowl. Add lemons and lemon juice, mix and let sit for 15 minutes. Taste and add more lemon juice if desired.

Add the rest of the ingredients and combine well. Cover and refrigerate at least 1 hour to develop the flavor.

Mound and serve on a bed of lettuce leaves, garnish with tomato and pickle wedges.

BREADS

A Few Words About Yeast Doughs

1. An oven with a pilot light or an electric oven with its electric light is a super "warm place for rising".

2. To proof yeast, mix yeast with the water and sugar called for in the recipe and let sit in a warm place for the length of time indicated or until foamy. If the yeast doesn't foam, throw it out and start again.

3. Flour measurements are approximate. If the dough is too sticky to knead, add extra flour [no need to sift], as much as 1 cup [140 grams] or so more flour may be added.

4. Do not be afraid to handle the dough, the more it is kneaded, the better the bread.

5. If the recipe states "let rise until doubled", be sure it is doubled. Time is flexible, depending on the weather and the humidity.

6. To punch down dough, make a fist and literally punch the dough while it is still in the bowl.

7. An egg white wash together with a pan of hot water in the bottom of the oven, make a crispy crust; brushing with melted margarine or egg substitute makes a soft, shiny crust.

8. Keep a razor blade in a safe place, just for slashing dough.

9. Freeze bread or cake tightly wrapped in foil. Unwrap to thaw.

Beer Bread [p]

The easiest, tastiest quick bread ever. You might never buy another loaf of bread. My friend, Marjorie Robinson, told me about this bread. It makes a great gift to take to a dinner party, along with a copy of the recipe. See Note for an interesting variation of Beer Bread.

Makes 1 loaf

a 12 ounce [340 gram] can of beer, room temperature

3 tablespoons sugar

3 cups [410 grams] self-rising flour

vegetable cooking spray

Combine beer and sugar. Add flour and mix until flour absorbs liquid. Pour batter into a greased and floured or into a sprayed non-stick 8 x 4 inch [20 x 10 centimeter] loaf pan. Let sit 15 minutes.

Bake in a preheated 375°F. [190°C.] oven for 50 minutes to 1 hour and 10 minutes, until nicely browned. The bread is good toasted, lasts for a couple days and can be frozen.

Note: To make Beer Bread with "Sun" Dried Tomatoes and Olives [p];

1 ounce [28 grams] "Sun" Dried Tomatoes [see index]

hot water, for soaking

¹/₃ cup, 2 ounces [55 grams] pimiento stuffed olives

Soak tomatoes in hot water to cover for 30 minutes. Drain, discard water and cut tomatoes into tiny pieces. Rinse olives lightly, drain and chop.

Follow directions for Beer Bread and add tomatoes and olives after mixing in flour. Continue recipe as written.

Challa *[p]*

This is a lovely challa, with a tender dough, a nicely browned crust and full of flavor. This is a relatively easy yeast bread to make. Its beautifully shaped loaf is a delight to serve and fun to mould.

Makes 2 good sized loaves

7 to 8 cups [1 to 1.14 kilos] all purpose unbleached flour
1 tablespoon salt
1 tablespoon plus 1 teaspoon sugar
2 ounces [55 grams] margarine
pinch saffron, crumbled
2 ½ cups [560 milliliters] boiling water mixed with
1 cup [65 grams] dry instant mashed potatoes flakes
2 packages dry yeast
³/₄ cup [175 milliliters] frozen egg substitute, thawed
pareve butter flavored cooking spray
¹/₄ cup [55 milliliters] frozen egg substitute, thawed
about ¹/₄ cup [30 grams] poppy seeds or sesame seeds

Place 7 cups [1 kilo] flour and salt in a large mixing bowl and set aside.

Mix 1 tablespoon sugar, margarine and saffron in 2 cups [450 milliliters] hot potato water. Stir until margarine is melted and cool to lukewarm.

Cool remaining ½ cup [110 milliliters] potato water to lukewarm. Add yeast and 1 teaspoon sugar. Proof yeast in a warm place for 15 minutes.

Make a well in center of flour and pour in yeast mixture. Mix a bit of flour with yeast mixture. Let this sponge sit in a warm place covered with a kitchen towel for 30 minutes.

Add cooled liquid mixture and egg substitute to sponge and mix until well incorporated. I use a dough hook. Knead with dough hook or turn out onto a floured surface and knead until dough is smooth and elastic, adding as much extra flour as necessary to keep dough from sticking, 8 to 10 minutes. Place dough in a clean bowl, sprayed with cooking spray, cover with a kitchen towel and let sit in a warm place to rise until doubled, 1 to 1 ½ hours.

Punch down dough, turn out onto a floured surface and knead until smooth. Return dough to bowl, resprayed, cover with a towel and let sit in a warm place to rise again until doubled, 45 minutes to 1 hour.

Punch down dough, turn out onto a floured surface and knead a bit. Divide dough into 2 equal parts. Divide each part into 3 parts. Roll each part between your hands and the surface into a cylinder about 22 inches [56 centimeters] long. Attach 3 cylinders together at one end and braid gently without stretching into a braided loaf. Pinch and turn under ends so they stay together. Repeat with second 3 cylinders to make a second loaf.

Place loaves on a sprayed and floured cookie sheet. Cover loaves with a towel and put in a warm place to rise until doubled, about 30 minutes.

Brush loaves with ¼ cup egg substitute and sprinkle liberally with seeds. Bake in a preheated 350°F. [175°C.] oven for 45 minutes to 1 hour until nicely browned. Cool on a rack. The challa can be frozen well wrapped in foil, unwrap to thaw.

Corn Bread [m or d or p]

I love anything made with cornmeal. This corn bread is simple and good and very low in fat. I use this recipe for the Corn Bread Turkey Stuffing [see Index].

Makes 1 large rectangle or 2 loaves

1 ¹/₂ cups [210 grams] all purpose unbleached flour

1 ¹/₂ cups [210 grams] yellow cornmeal

2 tablespoons baking powder

6 tablespoons sugar [80 grams]

¹/₂ cup [110 milliliters] frozen egg substitute, thawed

4 tablespoons vegetable oil or margarine, divided

1 cup [225 milliliters] skim milk or water or canned chicken broth

a 16 to 17 ounce [450 to 480 gram] can cream style corn

pareve butter flavored cooking spray

In a mixing bowl, combine all the ingredients, except 1 tablespoon oil or margarine and spray, and mix just until combined. Place 1 table-spoon oil or margarine in a sprayed 9 x 13 x 2 inch [22 ¹/₂ x 32 ¹/₂ x 5 centimeter] baking pan or ¹/₂ tablespoon each into 2 sprayed 4 x 8 inch [10 x 20 centimeter] loaf pans. Place pan or pans in a preheated 375°F. [190°C.] oven for 2 minutes. Immediately pour batter into hot pan or pans and bake for 20 to 30 minutes, depending on size of pans. Cool on a rack for 10 minutes before removing from pans or serve warm from large pan, cut into squares.

If you desire, the bread can be baked early in the day, and rewarmed in a preheated 325°F. [165°C.] oven for 10 minutes. The bread can be frozen, well wrapped in foil.

Drop Biscuits *[d or p]*

Biscuits say Southern Home Cooking to me. I like to serve them often. This is a low fat biscuit. Prepare them early in the day and bake just before serving. They can be reheated but I like them best served hot directly from the oven.

Makes 16 biscuits

2 cups [280 grams] all purpose unbleached flour
1 tablespoon baking powder
optional: ¹/₄ teaspoon baking soda, if using buttermilk
1 teaspoon salt
2 tablespoons pareve margarine, melted
1 cup [225 milliliters] no-fat buttermilk or potato water [see Note]
vegetable cooking spray

In a mixing bowl, place flour, baking powder, optional baking soda and salt. Combine liquid and margarine and add to dry ingredients, mixing just until moistened. Drop by tablespoons onto a sprayed baking sheet.

Bake in a preheated 400°F. [205°C.] oven for 12 to 14 minutes.

Serve with low or no-fat margarine, jelly, jam or Chutney [see Index], delicious.

Note: To make potato water: dissolve 5 tablespoons of dry instant mashed potatoes flakes into 1 cup [225 milliliters] boiling water.

English Muffin Bread [p]

This is an interesting and tasty bread, a successful experiment. I love to work with yeast breads so I am happy to play with something new.

Makes 2 loaves

2 $\frac{1}{2}$ cups [560 milliliters] boiling water mixed with
1 cup [60 grams] dry instant mashed potato flakes
2 packages dry yeast
2 tablespoons sugar
1 ounce [30 grams] pareve margarine
4 tablespoons white vinegar
5 to 6 cups [690 to 830 grams] all purpose unbleached flour
2 tablespoons salt
vegetable cooking spray
a bit of cornmeal

Remove $\frac{1}{2}$ cup [110 milliliters] potato water and cool to lukewarm. Mix lukewarm potato water with yeast and sugar and let proof for 10 minutes.

Combine the rest of the hot potato water with margarine and vinegar. Stir until margarine is melted and cool to lukewarm. Add yeast mixture to lukewarm liquid mixture.

Place 5 cups [690 grams] flour and salt in a large mixing bowl and add liquid. Mix with a dough hook or by hand until a dough is formed, adding as much extra flour as needed. Knead with dough hook and/or by hand until dough is smooth and elastic and no longer sticky. Form dough into a ball and place in a sprayed bowl, turning dough to cover with spray on all sides. Cover bowl with plastic wrap and a kitchen towel and let sit in a warm place until doubled, about 1 to 1 $\frac{1}{2}$ hours.

Punch down dough and turn out onto a lightly floured surface. Knead until smooth and elastic. Divide dough into 2 parts. Roll each part into a rectangle about 13 to 15 inches [32 $\frac{1}{2}$ to 37 $\frac{1}{2}$ centimeters] long. Roll up tightly, jelly roll style, starting with a long side and pinching ends against loaf as you go. Place loaves on a cornmeal sprinkled peel or cornmeal sprinkled baking sheet. Cover with plastic wrap and a towel and let rise in a warm place until doubled, about 45 minutes to 1 hour.

Lightly dust tops of loaves with flour and slash down center with a razor blade. Bake loaves in a preheated 350°F. [175°C.] oven, on a baking stone or on baking sheet, for 30 to 40 minutes until lightly browned.

Cool loaves on racks.

Bread freezes well, wrapped tightly in foil.

Garlic Bread *[d or p]*

This special treat is wonderful with any Italian dinner. It is easy to prepare ahead of time. Bake just before serving for crusty hot garlic bread.

Makes 1 large loaf

1 large loaf Italian bread

3 tablespoons extra virgin olive oil

1 $\frac{1}{2}$ tablespoons margarine, melted

2 tablespoons dried oregano

garlic granules, for sprinkling, about 2 teaspoons

optional: about $\frac{1}{2}$ cup [50 grams] grated Parmesan cheese

Cut bread in half lengthwise. Lightly score each half with a sharp knife, in a diamond pattern. Combine olive oil and margarine in a small dish. Brush each half with oil margarine mixture. Sprinkle each half with oregano, garlic and cheese, if using.

Place halves, seasoned side up, under a preheated broiler and broil until lightly toasted, about 2 minutes. Watch carefully. Let cool. Close loaf and wrap well in foil.

Just before serving, place foil wrapped loaf in a preheated 350°F. [175°C.] oven for 10 minutes.

Unwrap, slice and serve.

Irish Soda Bread [d]

This easily made quick bread is a good addition to our bread collection. It is simple, has a good flavor and texture and freezes well.

Makes 2 large or 4 small round loaves

4 cups [560 grams] whole wheat flour
3 cups [410 grams] all purpose unbleached flour
1 cup [100 grams] quick cooking oatmeal
2 tablespoons salt
2 teaspoons baking soda
1 ¹/₂ teaspoons baking powder
2 ounces [60 grams] margarine
3 cups [700 milliliters] no-fat buttermilk
³/₄ cup [175 milliliters] frozen egg substitute, thawed
3 tablespoons honey
a bit extra buttermilk
vegetable cooking spray

In a large mixing bowl, with a pastry cutter, blend dry ingredients with margarine until mixture resembles meal.

Combine buttermilk, eggs and honey. Add to flour mixture and combine well. I use a dough hook.

Turn dough out onto a lightly floured surface and knead dough until smooth. Divide dough into 2 or 4 parts and form each part into a ball. Place balls on a sprayed baking sheet. Slash an X on top of each loaf. Brush loaves with extra buttermilk.

Bake loaves in a preheated 325°F. [165°C.] oven for 1 hour to 1 hour and 10 minutes, until loaves are nicely browned.

This bread is delicious served warm. Cool on racks before freezing.

Scones *[p]*

I devised these for my daughter Becky Weisgal-Lavon, who loves scones and is always looking for non-fat foods to eat. These are truly non-fat and delicious served warm, with jam or jelly.

Makes about 18

about 2 cups [280 grams] all purpose unbleached flour
2 tablespoons sugar
4 teaspoons baking powder
$^1/_2$ teaspoon salt
1 cup [225 milliliters] skim milk

Combine dry ingredients in a mixing bowl. Add milk and mix until a dough is formed, adding more flour, if necessary, until dough is no longer sticky. Turn dough out onto a well floured surface and pat and roll dough into a rectangle $^1/_2$ inch [1 $^3/_4$ centimeters] thick. Cut scones into triangles and place on an ungreased baking sheet.

Bake scones in a preheated 300°F. [150°C.] oven for 35 minutes. Cool on a rack.

The scones can be frozen and can be rewarmed.

Sour Dough Italian Bread [p]

My love affair with delicious sour dough bread began during frequent trips to the San Francisco area. It takes some time to make this recipe and you must plan ahead but, to me, it is worth the effort. I love this bread toasted for breakfast, if there is any left over from dinner. Start the bread the day before, [assuming you have Sour Dough Starter [see Index]].

Makes 2 large loaves or 4 baguettes

Sponge

1 cup [225 milliliters] lukewarm water

2 teaspoons sugar

2 cups [280 grams] bread flour or all purpose unbleached flour

1 1/2 cups [350 milliliters] Sour Dough Starter [see Index] at
    room temperature

Bread

1 cup [225 milliliters] lukewarm water

1 teaspoon sugar

1 package dry yeast

5 to 6 cups [690 to 830 grams] bread flour or all purpose
    unbleached flour

1 tablespoon salt

1/2 teaspoon baking soda

vegetable cooking spray

a bit of cornmeal

1 egg white, mixed with

1 teaspoon water

about 1 teaspoon poppy seeds

The night before, place water and sugar in a mixing bowl. Add starter and 2 cups [280 grams] flour and mix with flat beater of a mixer until well combined. Let sit in a warm place for 12 to 24 hours, depending on your taste for sour, covered with plastic wrap and a kitchen towel.

The next day, place 1 cup [225 milliliters] water in a 2 cup measuring cup. Add 1 teaspoon sugar and yeast, mix and let sit until foamy, about 10 minutes. Add yeast mixture to sponge together with 5 cups [700 grams] flour, salt and soda. Mix until well combined, I use a dough hook. Knead by hand or with dough hook until dough is smooth and elastic, using as much extra flour as necessary. Turn out dough onto a floured surface and knead a bit. Place dough in a clean bowl, cover with plastic wrap and a kitchen towel and let sit in a warm place until doubled, 1 $1/2$ to 2 hours. I put it in an oven with the light on and the door ajar. Or put it in an oven with a pilot light. [Careful, you don't want it to be too warm.]

Punch down dough, turn out onto a floured surface and knead a bit until dough is smooth and elastic. Divide dough into 2 or 4 parts. Roll each part into a rectangle about 13 to 15 inches [32 $1/2$ to 37 $1/2$ centimeters] long. Roll up, tightly, jelly roll style, starting with a long side and pinching ends against loaf as you go. Place loaves on 2 sprayed and cornmeal sprinkled baking sheets. Cover with plastic and a towel and let sit in a warm place until doubled, about 45 minutes to 1 hour.

Slash tops of loaves diagonally, 3 or 4 times, or once down the middle, with a razor blade. Brush loaves with egg white wash. Bake in a preheated 350°F. [175°C.] oven for about 30 minutes for smaller loaves to 40 minutes for larger loaves, switching pans and racks every 10 minutes, until well browned. Cool on racks.

The bread can be frozen, well wrapped in foil. Unwrap to thaw.

3 - Stage Rye Bread #2 [p]

There is no rye flour in Israel and in order to develop this recipe, I frequently requested rye flour from the U.S. when friends came to visit. When we had the Goliath Bar-Restaurant, we had Deli sandwiches on the menu. Angel Bakery made a whole wheat bread with caraway seeds especially for us. It was an excellent substitute for the real thing. This recipe is different from my original rye bread recipe [in my first book, *Entertaining in Jerusalem*]. It is lighter and more finely textured. This is a favorite among family and friends, some say it is the best rye bread they've ever tasted. The sour dough can be made as sour as your taste dictates. Start the bread ahead of time.

Makes 4 - 1 pound [450 grams] loaves

Stage 1 - Sour

1 package dry yeast
2 cups [450 milliliters] lukewarm water
1 cup [140 grams] medium rye flour
1 cup [140 grams] bread or all purpose unbleached flour
1 teaspoon sugar

Stage 2 - Sponge

2 packages dry yeast
1 teaspoon sugar
1 cup [225 milliliters] lukewarm water
1 cup [140 grams] medium rye flour
3 cups [410 grams] bread or all purpose unbleached flour

Stage 3 - Bread Mix

1 cup [140 grams] medium rye flour
2 cups [280 grams] bread or all purpose unbleached flour, approximately
1 tablespoon sugar
1 tablespoon salt
4 tablespoons caraway seeds

vegetable cooking spray	
yellow cornmeal	
1 egg white mixed with	
1 teaspoon water [wash]	
extra caraway seeds	
a bit of kosher salt	

Whisk ingredients for sour together in a large mixing bowl. Cover with plastic wrap and let sit in a warm place for 12 to 72 hours [or longer], depending on your taste for a sour dough.

In a large mixing bowl, proof yeast with sugar in water for sponge, about 10 minutes. Using a flat beater or K beater of a mixer, add flours for sponge and sour mixture and combine well. Cover with plastic wrap and a kitchen towel and let sit in a warm place for 1 hour.

Stir down sour-sponge mixture and add ingredients for bread mix. Combine well, using dough hook. Knead dough in bowl for a few minutes. This is a slighty sticky dough. Turn out dough onto a floured surface and knead until it is no longer sticky, adding as much extra white flour as necessary. Place dough in a mixing bowl, cover with plastic wrap and a kitchen towel, and let sit in a warm place until dough has doubled in volume, about 1 hour.

Punch down dough. Turn out onto a lightly floured surface, knead for a couple of minutes and divide dough in 4 equal parts. [I use a scale.] Form each part into an oval or a round and place on 1 or 2 sprayed, corn meal sprinkled baking sheets, or place each in a sprayed loaf pan, the bottom sprinkled with cornmeal. Cover loaves with a towel and let sit in a warm place until doubled, about 30 to 40 minutes.

With a razor blade, slash each loaf down the center. Brush each loaf well with egg wash and sprinkle each loaf with a bit of caraway seeds and a bit of kosher salt.

Place a pan of boiling water in the bottom of oven. If you have a baking stone, place in oven and preheat oven to 350°F. [175°C.], at least 15 minutes. With a pizza peel, sprinkled with cornmeal, slide loaves into oven onto stone. Or place loaves on a cornmeal sprinkled baking pan. Bake loaves for 50 minutes to 1 hour, until loaves are well browned.

Remove loaves from pans or stone and cool on a rack.

The bread keeps well and can be frozen, well wrapped in foil. Unwrap to thaw.

Whole Wheat Bread [p]

What would a healthy cook book be without whole wheat bread. This bread is full of all kinds of good things, wheat germ, honey, and of course whole wheat flour. The bread freezes well and is great for sandwiches.

Makes 4 loaves, about 1 pound [430 grams] each

2 packages dry yeast

$1/2$ cup [110 milliliters] lukewarm water

1 tablespoon sugar

2 ounces [55 grams] pareve margarine, melted

$1/4$ cup [4 tablespoons] honey

$1/4$ cup [55 milliliters] frozen egg substitute, thawed

2 cups [450 milliliters] lukewarm water

1 tablespoon salt

3 tablespoons wheat germ

5 cups [700 grams] whole wheat flour

3 cups [410 grams] all purpose unbleached flour, approximately

vegetable cooking spray

1 egg white mixed with

2 teaspoons water

In a large mixing bowl, proof yeast with water and sugar in a warm place for 15 minutes. Add margarine, honey, egg, water, salt and wheat germ and mix. Using dough hook, gradually add flours and mix until well incorporated. Continue mixing with dough hook until dough is smooth and elastic. Turn out onto a lightly floured surface and knead in extra white flour if dough is still sticky.

Place dough, shaped into a ball, in a sprayed bowl, turning ball. Let sit in a warm place, covered with plastic wrap and a kitchen towel until doubled, about 1 hour to 1 hour and 15 minutes.

Punch down dough, form back into a ball, return to bowl, and let sit, covered with plastic and towel, until doubled again, about 45 minutes.

Punch down dough, turn out onto a lightly floured surface and divide dough into 4 equal parts. Place each part in a sprayed or non-stick loaf pan 4 x 8 inches [10 x 20 centimeters]. Using your knuckles push dough into pan to cover bottoms of pans. Cover pans with plastic and towel and let rise in a warm place until doubled, 30 to 40 minutes. Brush tops of loaves with egg wash.

Bake in a preheated 375°F. [190°C.] oven for 10 minutes. Turn temperature down to 350°C. [175°C.] and bake for an additional 25 to 30 minutes, until loaves are nicely browned. Remove from pans immediately and cool on racks.

The bread freezes well, wrapped in foil. Unwrap to thaw.

Sour Dough Starter [p]

After travelling to San Francisco twice a year for many years, I have become enamored of sour dough bread. After trial and error, I have finally arrived at the best sour dough starter and Sour Dough Italian Bread [see Index] with the best taste. It takes some time but to me it is worth every minute.

Makes about 2 ¹/₂ cups [560 milliliters]

1 package dry yeast

¹/₄ cup [55 grams] sugar

2 cups [450 milliliters] lukewarm water

2 cups [280 grams] bread flour or all purpose unbleached flour

1 teaspoon salt

Proof yeast and 1 tablespoon sugar in water. Let stand 10 minutes. Combine flour, the rest of the sugar and salt. Add flour mixture to yeast mixture and whisk until well mixed. Pour mixture into a 2 quart [2 liter] container, cover with cheese cloth and let stand, at room temperature for 3 days, stirring once daily.

Refrigerate covered with cheese cloth. Either use 1 ¹/₂ cups of starter every 15 to 30 days or discard 1 ¹/₂ cups. After using 1 ¹/₂ cups of starter or discarding 1 ¹/₂ cups, starter must be fed with following starter food, and it must be fed every time you use 1 ¹/₂ cups starter.

1 cup [140 grams] flour

¹/₂ cup [100 grams] sugar

1 cup [225 milliliters] lukewarm water

Whisk all the ingredients into starter and let sit at room temperature, covered with cheese cloth, for 24 hours. Refrigerate after 24 hours for 15 to 30 days again.

Keep your starter going and it will last forever.

MAIN DISHES

Brisket [m]

This delicious meal-in-a-pot is easy to make ahead of time, even the day before. Because it is cooked entirely in foil, clean up is a breeze. The aroma and taste of this dish are fantastic.

Serves 8

4 pounds [1.75 kilos] first cut lean brisket
2 pounds [900 grams] small potatoes, peeled, left whole
8 to 10 parsnips, peeled, left whole, about 1 pound [450 grams]
1 pound [450 grams] tiny carrots, peeled, left whole
1 pound [450 grams] mushrooms, washed, left whole
1 pound [450 grams] small onions, peeled, left whole
¾ cup [135 grams] dry onion soup mix [5 ounces]
1 bottle [750 milliliters] dry red wine [cheap is fine]

On a large piece of heavy duty foil [large enough to hold all the ingredients], place brisket in center. Surround meat with vegetables. Sprinkle onion soup mix over meat and vegetables. Pour wine over all. Close foil tightly so that it is airtight. Place foil packet in an open roasting pan. Bake in a preheated 450°F. [230°C.] oven for 4 hours.

Carefully open foil packet and transfer brisket to a cutting board and slice meat. Place meat slices on a large heated serving platter. Surround meat with vegetables or place vegetables in a separate bowl to serve. Skim fat from gravy, nap meat and vegetables with gravy. Serve the rest of the gravy on the side.

Or if making the day before, transfer brisket and vegetables to a casserole. Cover and chill overnight and skim fat. Transfer brisket to a cutting board, slice beef and return to casserole. Reheat brisket and vegetables in a preheated 350°F. [175°C.] oven for 30 minutes to 1 hour, until hot. The brisket can sit in a turned down oven for about ½ hour or so, if necessary.

Serve brisket with Horseradish and different Chutneys and Spiced Apple Sauce [see Index].

123

Wine Marinated Beef Stew *[m]*

This delicious meal-in-a-pot is warming, satisfying and perfect Winter fare. Don't let the word "stew" throw you off, this dish is special.

Serves 8

1 bottle dry red wine
3 tablespoons basalmic vinegar
2 bay leaves
4 garlic cloves, sliced thinly
1 teaspoon coarsely crushed black peppercorns
2 teaspoons dried basil
2 teaspoons dried thyme
2 teaspoons ground ginger
4 ¹/₂ pounds [2 kilos] thickly sliced shin beef, on the bone, trimmed of fat
salt, to taste
¹/₂ to ³/₄ cup [75 to 105 grams] all purpose unbleached flour
olive oil cooking spray
3 tablespoons extra virgin olive oil
5 ¹/₂ ounces (150 grams) leeks, sliced
10 ¹/₂ ounces (300 grams) onions, sliced
8 ounces (225 grams) carrots, chopped
2 cups [450 milliliters] beef flavored broth, from the mix, or canned
2 cups [450 milliliters] water

3 ½ pounds [1.6 kilos] tiny potatoes, left whole

1 ¾ pounds [750 grams] tiny onions, peeled, left whole

1 pound [450 grams] tiny carrots, scraped, left whole

12 ounces [350 grams] parsnips, peeled, quartered, halved

1 pound [450 grams] tiny fresh mushrooms, left whole

Mix together wine, vinegar, bay leaves, garlic, pepper, basil, thyme and ginger. Pour mixture over beef in a large container. Stir and mix to cover beef with marinade. Cover and refrigerate overnight, mixing occasionally. Next day, drain beef, reserve marinade and discard bay leaves. Cut beef off the bone and trim as much fat as possible. If necessary, cut beef into bite size. Do not discard bones.

Lightly sprinkle salt over beef pieces and dredge in flour, using all the flour. In a sprayed, non-stick large Dutch oven, heat oil until hot. Brown beef in batches, over high heat, transferring to a plate as pieces are browned. Add leeks, sliced onions and chopped carrots to pot and saute, stirring occasionally, until starting to brown. Pour broth, water, reserved marinade and bones into Dutch oven. Return meat to pot. Bring mixture to a simmer over low heat and simmer slowly, covered, stirring occasionally, until beef is barely tender, about 1 hour. Transfer mixture to an oven safe casserole, suitable for serving.

Add potatoes, onions, carrots and parsnips to casserole, mix with gravy and transfer casserole to a preheated 400°F. [205°C.] oven and bake, covered, for 1 hour. Add mushrooms and bake an additional 30 minutes.

Serve from the casserole with warm crusty Italian Bread [see Index].

Black Bean Chili *[p or d]*

I am very fond of chili, all different kinds. This version is a hearty, spicy vegetarian stew. I also am a lover of beans, so this is a very satisfying dish for me. I always "de-gas" the beans to make them easily digestable.

Makes about 12 cups [2 ³/₄ liters]

1 ¹/₂ pounds [680 grams] dried black beans [turtle], picked over for stones
water, for de-gassing
1 ¹/₂ pounds [680 grams] onions, chopped, divided
2 tablespoons minced garlic, divided
8 cups [1.8 liters] water
olive oil cooking spray
1 tablespoon extra virgin olive oil
10 ounces [300 grams] sweet green pepper, diced
a 28 ounce [800 gram] can tomatoes, chopped
8 "Sun" Dried Tomatoes [see Index], not packed in oil, cut up with a scissors
3 tablespoons chili powder
4 teaspoons ground cumin
1 tablespoon sweet paprika
2 teaspoons dried basil
2 teaspoons dried oregano

2 teaspoons dried thyme

1 teaspoon sugar

$1/2$ teaspoon ground coriander

$1/2$ teaspoon ground cayenne pepper

$1/2$ teaspoon ground bay leaf

salt, to taste

fresh black pepper, to taste

1 tablespoon cider vinegar

4 tablespoons masa harina

optional: chopped onions, grated cheese, chopped avocado, to garnish

Cover beans with 20 cups [4.5 liters] water. Bring to a boil and boil 2 minutes, cover and let sit for 1 hour. Drain and discard water.

Place de-gassed beans in an 8 quart [8 liter] kettle. Add $1/2$ of onions, $1/2$ of garlic and water. Bring to a boil and simmer, covered, until beans are almost tender, about 2 to 3 hours, depending on age of beans.

In a sprayed non-stick kettle, saute in olive oil, other half of onions, other half of garlic and green peppers, over medium heat, until vegetables are very soft, about 10 minutes. Add the rest of the ingredients, except beans, vinegar and masa. Cover and cook, over low heat, for 30 minutes.

Add beans to tomato mixture and simmer mixture for 1 to 3 hours, until beans are very tender and mixture is thick.

Add vinegar and masa harina, mix well, reheat and serve.

The chili can be made several days ahead of time and can be frozen.

If desired, serve with the garnishes, on the side.

Brazilian Black Bean Stew [m]

If you can find a variety of salamis and sausages, beef and/or turkey for this stew, the flavors will be more interesting and delicious. I once ate a similar stew in a Brazilian Restaurant in old Jaffa and adapted it to be low fat. It is one of my son Lawrence Weisgal's favorite dishes. I like to make this the day before because it intensifies the flavor and the ribs are easier to trim of any extra fat when they are cold.

Serves 8

1 pound [450 grams] dry black beans, picked over for stones
water for de-gassing
water, for cooking
8 or 10 beef back ribs, about 5 to 6 pounds [2 ¹/₂ kilos]
salt, for sprinkling
fresh black pepper, for sprinkling
1 ¹/₃ pounds [600 grams] assorted beef and/or turkey salamis and sausages, sweet and spicy
olive oil cooking spray
1 tablespoon extra virgin olive oil
1 ¹/₃ pounds [600 grams] onions, sliced thinly
14 ounces [400 grams] onions, chopped
4 large garlic cloves, chopped
salt, to taste
fresh black pepper, to taste

Place beans and 12 cups [2.7 liters] water in an 8 quart [8 liter] kettle and bring to a boil. Boil for 2 minutes, cover and let sit for 1 hour. Drain and discard water.

In same kettle, barely cover beans with fresh cold water and bring to a boil. Cover and simmer over low heat, until beans are soft and tender, adding more water as necessary, about 2 to 4 hours, depending on age of beans. Keep warm over very low heat.

While beans are cooking, trim ribs of as much fat as possible. Season well with salt and pepper. Place ribs on a rack in an open, foil lined roasting pan and bake in a preheated 400°F. [205°C.] oven until well browned, about 1 hour.

If you are cooking these the day before, cool and chill. Remove and cut away as much fat as possible.

If not cooking ahead, remove ribs from oven, discard fat in pan and cut away as much fat as possible from ribs.

Return ribs to rack and rewarm or keep warm in a slow 200°F. [90°C.] oven.

Cut salamis and sausages into bite size pieces. Place in a large saucepan and cover with cold water. Bring to a boil, cover and simmer for 15 minutes. Drain, discard liquid and set aside.

In a sprayed non-stick pan, saute, in oil, onion slices, over medium high heat, until golden brown, stirring frequently. Remove onion slices with a slotted spoon to paper towels to drain. Set aside.

Respray same pan, and saute chopped onion and garlic until golden and soft. Scoop up about 1 1/2 cups [350 milliliters] of cooked beans with some liquid and add to onion garlic mixture. Place mixture in a food processor and mash to a paste. [Or use a potato masher.] Return mixture to the rest of the beans, add salt and pepper to taste and bring to a simmer. Simmer, covered for 30 minutes. Add cut up salamis and sausages to bean mixture with onion slices. Simmer an additional 30 minutes.

Serve stew with ribs on the side, 1 rib to a person. The ribs are very large and meaty and one rib is usually enough.

Brisket, ala Sophie [m]

This is a delicious brisket. It is easy to make ahead of time and is a whole meal-in-a-pot. While it is cooking, the aroma in the house is mouth watering. Sophie Macht was the originator of this recipe for which she was justly well known. I have adapted and adopted it to be my own. Make this the day before you want to serve it. By special request, I am repeating this recipe from my first book.

Serves 8 to 10

4 pounds [1.75 kilos] first cut lean brisket
salt, to taste
fresh black pepper, to taste
3 tablespoons whole pickling spice
2 bay leaves
10 ½ ounces [300 grams] onions, diced finely
2 ribs celery, diced finely
3 to 4 teaspoons minced garlic
1 ¼ cups [300 milliliters] Beef Stock [see Index] or canned
1 ¼ cups [300 milliliters] dry red wine
3 pounds [1.35 kilos] leeks, weight before cleaning, white and   pale green parts only, washed well, halved
8 to 10 parsnips, peeled, left whole, about 1 pound [450 grams]
8 to 10 carrots, peeled, left whole, about 1 pound [450 grams]
12 ½ ounces [350 grams] celery root, peeled, cut into 8 to 10 wedges
1 ½ pounds [680 grams] potatoes, peeled, quartered
sweet paprika, for sprinkling
1 pound [450 grams] shallots, peeled, left whole
1 pound [450 grams] mushrooms, washed, left whole

The day before, season brisket with salt and pepper. Brown meat well under a preheated broiler on both sides, about 8 to 10 minutes for each side. Set aside on a plate.

In a large roasting pan with a lid, place pickling spices, bay leaves, onions, celery and garlic. Add broth and wine to pan. Place brisket on top of spices, together with any juices that have accumulated from brisket. Surround meat with leeks, parsnips, carrots, celery root and potatoes. Sprinkle paprika over meat and vegetables. Cover and bake in a preheated 375°F. [190°C.] oven for 3 hours. Add shallots and mushrooms to pan and let cool. Refrigerate overnight in pot.

The next day, remove meat from pot and any fat that may have accumulated. Slice meat thinly. Return meat to pot, re-cover and bake an additional hour in a preheated 375°F. [190°C.] oven.

The brisket can sit in a turned down oven for about ¹/₂ hour or so, if necessary.

Transfer sliced brisket to a platter, nap with defatted pan juices and surround with vegetables or place vegetables in a separate serving bowl.

Serve brisket with Horseradish and different Chutneys and Spiced Apple Sauce [see Index].

Flank Steak [m]

This easily prepared and succulent steak is the only kind of steak I serve when entertaining. I marinate it most of the day and broil it just before serving.

Serves 8

2 to 3 flank steaks, total weight about 4 ¹/₂ pounds [2 kilos]

about ¹/₂ cup [120 grams] prepared mustard [your choice]

4 teaspoons finely chopped garlic

salt, to taste

fresh black pepper, to taste

With a very sharp knife, lightly score steaks on both sides in a diamond pattern. Combine mustard and garlic. Thinly spread mustard mixture over both sides of meat. Place steaks on a rack in a foil lined pan to marinate for 6 hours at room temperature or overnight in fridge. Just before serving, lightly sprinkle with salt and pepper to taste. Place steaks on a rack in a foil lined pan.

Broil meat about 2 inches [5 centimeters] from heat for 3 to 4 minutes on each side for rare meat. Slice diagonally across the grain into thin slices to serve.

The steaks are delicious prepared on an outdoor or indoor grill.

Cabbage Rolls - Sweet and Sour *[m]*

This is a lightened version of my Russian Grandmother, Elizabeth Brown Mesirow's stuffed cabbage. My Moroccan house helper in Israel, Sima Suissa, made it exactly the same way as my grandmother. When we were studying Hebrew in Israel, our teacher asked each of us to make a national or family dish. It was so interesting how many dishes from so many different countries are almost the same.

Makes about 22 medium small rolls

1 ³/₄ to 2 ¹/₄ pounds [800 grams to 1 kilo] Napa cabbage
boiling water
³/₄ cup [150 grams] raw Basmati rice, rinsed
1 pound [450 grams] ground turkey
³/₄ pound [340 grams] lean ground beef
9 ¹/₂ ounces [275 grams] onions, chopped finely
³/₄ cup [175 milliliters] cold water
3 large garlic cloves, chopped finely
2 teaspoons salt, or to taste
¹/₂ teaspoon fresh black pepper
¹/₂ teaspoon sweet Hungarian paprika
4 ¹/₂ cups [1 liter] tomato juice
a 15 ounce [420 gram] can tomato sauce
2 ¹/₂ tablespoons brown sugar
1 tablespoon Worcestershire sauce
1 teaspoon salt, or to taste

fresh black pepper, to taste

6 tablespoons lemon juice

Tabasco sauce, to taste

Cut off bottom of Napa cabbage, separate leaves and wash well in cold water. Place leaves in an 8 quart [8 liter] kettle and cover leaves with boiling water. Let sit for about 20 minutes, until leaves soften. Don't wash kettle.

Soak rice in 1 cup [225 milliliters] boiling water for 10 minutes. Drain. Combine and mix well, rice, meat, onions, cold water, garlic, salt, pepper and paprika.

Cut largest leaves of cabbage in $^1/_2$ and start stuffing and rolling cabbage leaves, using about $^1/_4$ cup measure. Place meat mixture on one end. Fold over cabbage leaf to enclose meat. Fold in sides and roll up, making a cabbage envelope. Turn seam side down onto a plate. Continue rolling and stuffing the same way until all meat is used.

In same kettle, place whatever cabbage is left over on bottom. Carefully lay cabbage rolls on top. Discard any juices left on plate.

Combine and mix well, tomato juice, tomato sauce, sugar, Worcestershire, salt, pepper, lemon juice and Tabasco. Pour mixture over cabbage rolls, making sure rolls are covered with liquid, adding a bit more tomato juice, if necessary.

Slowly bring rolls to a boil. Simmer covered, for 2 hours. The recipe can be completed up to this point ahead and kept in fridge for a few days or frozen before continuing. Thaw and/or rewarm to a simmer before continuing.

Uncover and bake in a preheated 350°F. [175°C.] oven for 45 minutes. The rolls can be kept warm in oven, turned down to low or over a low flame on top of stove, covered, for a short time.

Choucroute Garni [m]

This is another whole meal-in-a-pot that I am very partial to. It is easy to make ahead of time, even the day before and is most satisfying winter fare. The first time I made this, my guests were very leery of this dish until they tasted it and then I received raves. Choucroute garni is sauerkraut with smoked meats.

Serves 8 generously

3 ½ pounds [1.55 kilos] assorted spicy turkey sausages
olive oil cooking spray
2 teaspoons extra virgin olive oil
2 ½ pounds [1 kilo] onions, sliced thinly
2 tablespoons chopped garlic
18 ounces [500 grams] carrots, sliced thinly
4 pounds [900 grams] fresh bag sauerkraut, drained, rinsed well, drained again, not canned
2 cups [450 milliliters] Chicken Broth [see Index] or canned
1 bottle Reisling wine
a cheesecloth bag containing 40 juniper berries and
3 bay leaves
4 ½ pounds [2 kilos] smoked turkey wing drummettes or turkey legs
2 ¼ pounds [1 kilo] Yukon Gold potatoes [8 to 10], peeled
fresh black pepper, to taste
¼ teaspoon ground cloves

Cut sausages in half lengthwise and cut crosswise into large bite size pieces. Fry sausages in a well sprayed large wide Dutch oven, with oil added, until well browned. Remove sausages with a slotted spoon to paper towels to drain and set aside.

In same pot, saute onions, garlic and carrots until well wilted, about 10 to 15 minutes, stirring occasionally. Add sauerkraut, cover, and cook for 10 minutes, stirring and mixing occasionally. Add broth, wine, cheesecloth bag, turkey and potatoes. Bring to a boil, cover and simmer over low heat for 45 minutes.

Remove potatoes to a bowl and set aside. Fish out turkey. Remove skin and cut meat off the bone and cut into bite size. Return turkey meat to pot. Discard bones. This part of recipe can be completed ahead of time, even the day before.

Reheat choucroute until hot. Add sausages and mix. Simmer for 30 minutes, covered. Add potatoes and heat until potatoes are warmed through, about 20 to 30 minutes.

Transfer potatoes to a serving bowl. Transfer sauerkraut mixture to a casserole suitable for serving. Serve with assorted mustards and with Horseradish [see Index].

The choucroute can wait in a low oven or over very low heat for 30 minutes or so, if necessary.

Rack of Lamb [m]

This is one of my most special and elegant main dishes. All preparations can be done ahead of time, but it must be roasted at the last minute. I wait until my guests are seated at the table and pop the racks into the oven. By the time soup and salad are served and finished, the racks of lamb are ready to serve, beautiful and delicious.

Serves 8 generously

salt, to taste
fresh black pepper, to taste
1 tablespoon extra virgin olive oil
4 racks of lamb, bones frenched, trimmed of most fat, rest of fat scored
8 tablespoons Roasted Garlic pulp [see Index]

Lightly sprinkle salt and pepper all over racks of lamb. Heat oil in a large non-stick fry pan until very hot, but not smoking. Quickly brown racks one at a time on meaty parts. Cool slightly. Spread a coating of garlic puree, 2 tablespoons for each rack, over meaty parts of racks. Set aside until 30 minutes before serving.

Roast racks, meaty [fat] side up, in a foil lined open roasting pan in a preheated 450°F. [230°C.] oven for 25 minutes for well rare meat. Add 5 minutes for medium rare.

Cincinnati Chili *[m]*

On my first trip to Cincinnati, to visit friends, the Shenks, I became intrigued with my first taste of the famous "Cincinnati Chili". It was different from any other chili that I had tasted and I now favor this version. It has a slightly spicy sweet taste that is hard to describe. Try it and serve with the tradional accompaniments to make this up to "5 ways". Each garnish is a "way" and each extra "way" adds up to "5-Way Cincinnati Chili".

Makes about 20 to 24 cups [4 $\frac{1}{2}$ to 5 $\frac{1}{2}$ liters]

olive oil cooking spray
1 teaspoon extra virgin olive oil
1 $\frac{1}{2}$ pounds [680 grams] onions, chopped
12 ounces [340 grams] celery, chopped
2 $\frac{1}{2}$ tablespoons minced garlic
4 pounds [1.75 kilos] ground turkey
8 cups [1.8 liters] defatted Beef Stock [see Index] or canned
a 28 to 32 ounce [800 to 900 gram] can chopped tomatoes
a 12 ounce [340 gram] can tomato paste
6 to 8 tablespoons chili powder, to taste
4 tablespoons lemon juice
1 to 2 tablespoons sugar, to taste
4 bay leaves
4 teaspoons ground cinnamon
2 to 3 teaspoons salt, to taste
2 teaspoons fresh black pepper
1 teaspoon ground cloves
1 teaspoon ground cumin
1 teaspoon ground allspice
optional; spaghetti, kidney beans, chopped raw onions, cooked rice, oyster crackers, as traditional accompaniments, if desired, to make Cincinnati Chili "5 Ways"

Heat a sprayed 8 quart [8 liter] non-stick kettle, and add olive oil. Saute onions, celery and garlic, over medium heat until vegetables are very soft, about 15 minutes.

Add turkey and saute, breaking up lumps, until meat loses its color, about 15 minutes, stirring frequently.

Add beef stock and the rest of the ingredients, except accompaniments. Simmer chili, uncovered, for 1 1/2 to 2 hours, stirring occasionally. Taste and correct the seasoning. The chili should be slightly soupy. Pick out and discard bay leaves.

Serve the chili with the accompaniments, if desired.

The chili can be made several days ahead of time and can be frozen.

Muffaletta [m]

This sandwich is a New Orleans original. This is my Kosher version, which is quite delicious. Make just one and cut into eighths for an hors' d'oeuvre, or make two and cut each into fourths for an informal main course.

Makes 1 muffaletta sandwich [double for 2]

---

about a 10 ounce [290 gram] round loaf sour dough Italian bread

2 tablespoons extra virgin olive oil, divided

1 cup [225 milliliters] Olive Salad [see Index], divided

4 ounces [110 grams] lean corned beef, sliced thinly

4 ounces [110 grams] smoked turkey, sliced thinly

4 ounces [110 grams] salami, sliced thinly

Cut bread in half horizontally. Remove almost all of the crumb [reserve for another use]. Brush each half with 1 tablespoon olive oil. Place 1/2 cup [110 milliliters] olive salad evenly over each half of bread. Put half of corned beef evenly over bottom half of bread on top of olive salad. Put half of turkey over top of corned beef. Put half of salami over top of turkey. Repeat layers of corned beef, turkey and salami. Cover meats with top half of bread, containing olive salad.

Wrap loaf in plastic wrap and wrap whole thing in aluminum foil. Place a wooden board on top of sandwich and place a heavy weight on top of board. Refrigerate for several hours before serving. The sandwich can be made and kept wrapped for up to 3 days.

Cut into eighths or fourths and serve. Delicious!

Cous Cous with Short Rib Stew [m]

This is a great whole meal in a pot dish. I use short ribs which become sweet and succulent after the long roasting and braising. Sima Suissa, who worked for me in Jerusalem taught me the rudiments of cous cous. Traditionally at least 7 different kinds of vegetables must be included, beside the meat, which could be chicken, if that is your desire. This dish is easier made the day before so that the congealed fat can be removed.

Serves 8

2 cups [360 grams] dried chick peas

water for de-gassing

water for cooking

5 to 6 pounds [2 $\frac{1}{2}$ kilos] short ribs, well trimmed of fat

salt, for sprinkling

fresh black pepper, for sprinkling

garlic granules, for sprinkling

12 cups [2.7 liters] water

8 thin carrots, about 1 pound [450 grams], peeled, left whole

8 thin or split parsnips, about 1 pound [450 grams] peeled, left whole

11 $\frac{1}{2}$ ounces [325 grams] onions, quartered lengthwise
   through root

3 $\frac{1}{2}$ ounces [100 grams] celery tops, with leaves, sliced

a 28 ounce [800 gram] can whole peeled tomatoes, cored,
   squeezed through the fingers

1 tablespoon chopped garlic

1 bay leaf

1 teaspoon ground turmeric

$\frac{1}{2}$ teaspoon ground ginger

pinch saffron, crumbled in fingers

salt, to taste

fresh black pepper, to taste

1 pound [450 grams] fresh pumpkin or winter squash, seeds
   removed and discarded, cut into large [8] chunks, peeled

8 ounces [230 grams] zucchini, trimmed, cut into 8 or 9 large chunks

a 16 to 17 ounce [460 gram] box cous cous, cooked according to
   box directions, using some of the broth from stew plus water,
   see Note

Place chick peas and 20 cups [4.5 liters] water into a large pot. Bring to a boil, boil for 2 minutes, turn off heat, cover and let sit for 1 hour. Drain and discard water.

Place soaked chick peas back into same pot. Add water to cover by about 2 inches [5 centimeters]. Bring to a boil, cover and simmer until chick peas are just tender, about 2 to 3 hours.

Sprinkle ribs with salt, pepper and garlic granules and place on a rack in a foil lined baking pan. Roast in a preheated 475°F. [245°C.] oven, turning once for about 45 minutes, until ribs are well browned. Discard fat which has melted off.

Transfer ribs to an 8 quart [8 liter] kettle with 12 cups [2.7 liters] water. Bring to a boil, skimming the froth as it rises. Add chick peas, carrots, parsnips, onions, celery, tomatoes, garlic, bay leaf, turmeric, ginger and saffron. Return to a boil and simmer for 1 1/2 hours. Let cool.

Remove meat from stew, discard bones and fat, and cut meat into bite sized pieces. Return meat to stew and chill until fat congeals.

Skim fat from stew, bring to a boil and add pumpkin and zucchini and simmer an additional 30 minutes until pumpkin and zucchini are barely tender.

Serve over cous cous. The stew can be kept warm for about an hour, if necessary.

Note: If cous cous is too grainy and not fluffy, add more liquid than what is called for on the box. The cous cous will absorb the extra liquid and become very fluffy and light.

Corned Beef [m]

This is corned beef starting from scratch. Buy a whole, lean brisket and begin the process. It takes about a week or so to corn the beef and 1 day to cook and eat this delicious meat.

Serves 8 for dinner with leftovers

6 ¹/₄ to 6 ¹/₂ pounds [3 kilos] whole, lean brisket
6 to 8 cloves garlic
5 tablespoons kosher salt [coarse]
4 teaspoons saltpeter
3 crushed bay leaves
2 teaspoons black peppercorns
2 teaspoons whole allspice
5 whole cloves
1 teaspoon mustard seeds
water
6 ounces [170 grams] celery, sliced in hunks
6 ounces [170 grams] [small] onion, peeled, left whole
6 ounces [170 grams] carrots, cut into hunks
1 teaspoon salt
1 teaspoon black peppercorns
water
optional: about a 5 pound [2.25 kilo] head of cabbage

Cut garlic cloves into slivers, pierce meat all over and insert garlic slivers. Place meat in a container, large enough to hold it and enough water to submerge it.

Combine salt, saltpeter, bay leaves, pepper, allspice, cloves and mustard seeds. Sprinkle mixture over meat and add water to cover. Put a plate on top of meat and a weight on top of plate, to keep meat submerged. Refrigerate meat for about 1 week or so, turning it every day.

You can freeze meat at this point, thaw before continuing recipe, or you can cook it now.

Scrape off and discard spices, you can leave garlic in meat if desired. Place meat in a pot, cover with water and bring to a boil. Drain and discard water and start again. Place meat in a pot, cover with water and bring to a boil, skimming the froth as it rises. Add celery, onion, carrots, salt and pepper. Cover, and simmer for 2 to 2 ½ hours until tender. During last 15 minutes, if desired, add cabbage, cut into 8 wedges.

Remove meat to a cutting board, slice and serve. Serve cabbage on the side. Or let corned beef cool and refrigerate. Slice cold the next day.

Roasted Rib of Beef [m]

This simple dish is to me the height of elegance. It makes a showy centerpiece for a special dinner. I like to serve roast beef with York-shire Pudding [see Index]. Put the roast beef in the oven as your guests walk in the door. It will be ready to eat after cocktails, hors' d'oeuvres, soup and salad.

Serves 8

about a 6 pound [2.75 kilo] standing rib roast, 3 or 4 ribs

Roasted Garlic pulp [see Index]

about 1 ½ to 2 tablespoons seasoned salt, for sprinkling

Trim beef of almost all fat, but leave a thin layer. Lightly score fat layer in a diamond pattern. Spread garlic pulp all over roast beef. Sprinkle a good coating of seasoned salt all over beef.

Roast on a rack in a foil lined baking pan, fat side up, in a pre-heated 425°F. [220°C.] oven for 1 hour and 15 minutes for rare meat.

Meat Loaf [m]

We love meat loaf, hot with gravy or cold in sandwiches. I like to serve this with boiled potatoes and Sauerkraut [see Index]. I always make enough to have leftovers. If you serve 8, you will have enough for sandwiches the next day.

Makes 2 loaves, each serving 8

2 pounds [900 grams] ground turkey
3 ³/₄ pounds [1.7 kilos] extra lean ground beef
2 pounds [900 grams] lean ground veal
18 ounces [500 grams] onions, diced finely
1 cup [225 milliliters] frozen egg substitute, thawed
3 slices stale bread [Challa is good, see Index]
1 tablespoon salt or to taste
1 teaspoon fresh black pepper
1 to 1 ¹/₂ tablespoons minced garlic, to taste
4 cups [900 milliliters] cold defatted Beef Stock [see Index] or canned, divided

In a large mixing bowl, combine meats, onions, egg substitute, crumbled bread, salt, pepper, garlic and 1 ¹/₂ cups [350 milliliters] of stock. [I use my hands.] Divide mixture into 2 parts and form each part into an oval. Place ovals in a heavy roasting pan with a lid. Pour the rest of the stock over meat loaves.

Bake covered in a preheated 375°F. [190°C.] oven for 1 ¹/₂ hours. Uncover and bake an additional 30 minutes, until tops are nicely browned.

Slice and serve with defatted pan juices on the side, in a sauceboat.

The meat loaf can be made ahead and reheated, covered, in a preheated 300°F. [150°C.] oven for 30 to 40 minutes.

The second meat loaf freezes well, tightly wrapped in foil.

Meat Loaf ala Aran Kay [m]

This is my daughter Aran's meat loaf. She is a very inventive cook and it is fun to exchange ideas with her, albeit by long distance telephone. We always cook together when I visit her in California. This recipe makes 2 loaves, one to use now and one to freeze for another dinner.

Makes 2 loaves, each serving 8

olive oil cooking spray
3 tablespoons extra virgin olive oil, divided
1 ¼ pounds [580 grams] onions, chopped coarsely
4 teaspoons chopped garlic
3 ¾ pounds [1.7 kilos] extra lean ground beef
2 pounds [900 grams] ground veal
2 pounds [900 grams] ground turkey
1 cup [80 grams] quick or ground old fashioned oatmeal
1 bottle 14 ounce [400 gram] ketchup
1 to 1 ½ tablespoons salt, to taste
fresh black pepper, to taste
3 cups [700 milliliters] water

In a sprayed large fry pan, add 2 tablespoons of oil and heat until hot. Add onions and garlic and saute until onions are well browned, stirring frequently, about 20 minutes. Set aside.

Combine beef, veal and turkey. Add oatmeal, ketchup, salt, pepper and onion mixture, mixing until well combined. Divide mixture into 2 parts and form a loaf of each part. Place loaves in a baking pan and rub the 1 tablespoon oil over tops of loaves. Pour water into bottom of baking pan.

Bake loaves in a preheated 400°F. [205°C.] oven for 1 hour and 15 minutes. If loaves brown too quickly, lay a piece of foil over tops of loaves. Wrap well in foil to freeze.

Moussaka [m]

A delicious Greek dish that is a whole meal-in-a-pot. I like to serve it with the Greek Salad [see Index]. It sounds involved but it is quickly put together and can be prepared ahead of time and baked just before serving.

Serves 8

2 pounds [900 grams] eggplant, unpeeled, cut lengthwise into
    $^1/_2$ inch [1 centimeter] slices

salt, for sprinkling

2 pounds [900 grams] ground turkey

10 $^1/_2$ ounces [300 grams] onions, chopped

olive oil cooking spray

6 teaspoons extra virgin olive oil, divided

4 $^1/_4$ cups [950 milliliters] defatted Chicken Broth [see Index] or
    canned, divided

3 $^1/_2$ ounces [100 grams] tomato paste

salt, to taste

$^1/_2$ teaspoon fresh black pepper

1 $^1/_2$ tablespoons chopped garlic

2 pounds [900 grams] potatoes, peeled, sliced thinly, rinsed in
    cold water

12 $^1/_2$ ounces [350 grams] fresh mushrooms, sliced

$^1/_2$ cup [110 milliliters] frozen egg substitute, thawed

3 tablespoons lemon juice

1 $^1/_2$ tablespoons Dijon mustard

$^1/_2$ cup [75 grams] all purpose unbleached flour

salt, to taste

fresh white pepper, to taste

pinch ground allspice

Sprinkle salt lightly on both sides of eggplant slices and let sit in a colander to drain for 30 minutes. Rinse well and drain. Place eggplant slices into a pot of boiling water and simmer for 5 minutes. Drain, lay on paper towels and set aside.

In a sprayed non-stick Dutch oven, add 2 teaspoons of olive oil and saute meat and onions until meat loses it color and onions have softened, stirring frequently. Add $3/4$ cup [175 milliliters] of broth, tomato paste, salt, black pepper and garlic. Simmer mixture, uncovered, stirring occasionally, until meat is tender, about 30 minutes. Set aside.

In a separate pan, sprayed, toss potatoes in 2 teaspoons of olive oil until lightly coated with oil. Sprinkle lightly with salt and cook over low heat, covered, until potatoes are barely tender, about 15 minutes, turning occasionally. Set aside.

In a separate pan, sprayed, saute mushrooms in last 2 teaspoons of oil, stirring occasionally, until mushrooms are tender, about 15 minutes. Sprinkle lightly with salt and pepper. Set aside.

Whisk egg substitute, lemon juice and mustard together. Whisk flour into the rest of the cold broth until smooth. In a saucepan, combine broth mixture with egg mixture. Place mixture over medium heat and heat whisking constantly, until sauce comes to a boil and has thickened. Add salt and pepper to taste and add allspice. Set aside.

In a sprayed baking pan, 9 x 13 x 2 $1/2$ inches [22 $1/2$ x 32 $1/2$ x 6 $1/4$ centimeters], suitable for serving, layer as follows:

a thin layer of sauce on bottom
a layer of $1/2$ of meat
a layer of $1/2$ of potatoes
a layer of $1/2$ of eggplant slices
a layer of $1/2$ of mushrooms
evenly spread a layer of $1/2$ of sauce over all

Repeat layers of meat, potatoes, eggplant and mushrooms with other $1/2$ of each. Spread the rest of the sauce over all. This part can be prepared ahead of time and can be frozen.

Bake the moussaka in a preheated 375°F. [190°C.] oven for 1 hour.
Serve from the pan, cut into squares.

Osso Bucco [m]

This is one of Italy's finest dishes, hearty, satisfying and warming. By special request, I frequently make Osso Bucco for my friend Philip Macht. I like to serve this dish with an interestingly shaped pasta noodle or Nuckerl or Spaetzle [see Index]. Try this delicious stew, you'll love it.

Serves 8

6 ½ pounds [3 kilos] 8 large veal shank pieces about 2 inches [5 centimeters] thick, well trimmed of fat	
salt, for sprinkling	
fresh white pepper, for sprinkling	
olive oil cooking spray	
1 green pepper, cored, seeded, membranes removed, cut into thick strips lengthwise	
5 ½ ounces [150 grams] carrots, peeled, chopped	
7 ounces [200 grams] onions, chopped	
1 rib celery, with leaves, chopped	
3 large garlic cloves, chopped, about 1 tablespoon	
8 ounces [225 grams] fresh mushrooms, sliced	

1 cup [225 milliliters] dry red wine

2 cups [450 milliliters] defatted Beef Stock [see Index] or canned

3 ½ ounces [100 grams] tomato paste

4 strips lemon peel, without the white

½ cup [40 grams] chopped fresh parsley leaves

salt, to taste

fresh white pepper, to taste

Lightly sprinkle salt and pepper on veal shanks. Place them on a rack in a foil lined baking sheet and roast in a preheated 450°F. [230°C.] oven for 45 minutes, turning after 20 minutes, until veal is lightly browned. Transfer veal to paper towels to drain.

In a large, well sprayed, non-stick kettle, saute, over medium low heat, green pepper, carrots, onions, celery, garlic and mushrooms until well softened.

Combine wine, stock and tomato paste in a bowl.

Add veal to kettle, mixing with vegetables and add wine mixture. Combine well, cover and bring to a simmer. Simmer for 1 hour. Add lemon peel, parsley, salt and pepper. Simmer for an additional 30 minutes to 1 hour, until veal is very tender.

Transfer the osso bucco to a casserole dish and serve.

The dish can be prepared ahead of time and refrigerated or frozen. Bring to room temperature before reheating to serve.

Paella [m]

This is one of Spain's greatest dishes for entertaining. A whole meal-in-a-pot, it is easily prepared ahead of time. I like to serve this with Tapenade, Gaspacho and Sangria [see Index].

Serves 8

2 tablespoons extra virgin olive oil
2 tablespoons lemon juice
6 garlic cloves, minced
$1/2$ teaspoon dried thyme
$1/2$ teaspoon fresh white pepper
1 tablespoon chopped fresh parsley or fresh coriander leaves
salt, to taste
1 $1/2$ pounds [680 grams] skinless, boneless chicken breasts, trimmed of fat
1 $1/2$ pounds [680 grams] skinless, boneless chicken thighs, trimmed of fat
1 pound [450 grams] assorted sausages, hot, spicy and sweet
olive oil cooking spray
1 $1/2$ pounds [680 grams] onions, chopped coarsely
12 ounces [340 grams] fresh mushrooms, sliced
2 cups [350 grams] long grain rice, raw
$3/4$ teaspoon saffron threads, crumbled
3 tablespoons capers, drained
$3/4$ cup [175 milliliters] dry white wine
5 cups [1.2 liters] hot Chicken Broth [see Index] or canned

a 28 ounce [800 gram] can tomatoes, chopped coarsely

2-14 ounce [400 gram] cans artichoke hearts, drained, halved or
   frozen

10 $\frac{1}{2}$ ounces [300 grams] shelled peas, fresh or frozen

7 ounces [200 grams] black olives, seeded, halved, about 18

a 3 ounce [90 gram] jar pimiento, sliced

Combine oil, lemon juice, garlic, thyme, pepper, parsley and salt. Spread over chicken pieces and coat well. Set aside to marinate for at least 30 minutes.

In a saucepan, blanch sausages, pricked in several places, for 10 minutes. Drain on paper towels and slice into bite sized pieces. Set aside.

In a sprayed non-stick fry pan or Dutch oven, saute chicken pieces, still coated with marinade, on high heat, until browned, about 5 minutes on each side. Set aside.

In same pan, resprayed, saute onions and mushrooms until lightly browned. Transfer onions and mushrooms to a 6 quart [5 $\frac{1}{2}$ liter] casserole pot or Paella pan, suitable for serving. Add rice to casserole and mix well with onion mushroom mixture. Combine saffron, capers, wine and broth and add this mixture to casserole and mix well. Add tomatoes to casserole and mix. Add chicken pieces, sausages and artichokes to casserole and mix well. This part of recipe can be prepared ahead of time. Set aside until 1 hour before serving time.

Cover casserole tightly and bring slowly to a simmer. Simmer for 20 minutes. Add peas, olives and pimiento and mix well. Cover and simmer an additional 5 to 10 minutes until liquid is absorbed.

The Paella can be kept warm in a slow 250°F. [120°C.] oven for $\frac{1}{2}$ hour, covered.

Serve from the casserole.

Short Rib Daube *[m]*

A daube is a marinated and slowly braised meat stew. It is a classic French dish which, I am sure, has as many variations as households. This fragrant and delicious dish is easy to make, but should be started 2 days ahead of time. I use short ribs because they invite long slow cooking and become very sweet and tender.

Serves 8

4 ²/₃ pounds [2.1 kilos] short ribs, trimmed of fat, on the bone	
salt, for sprinkling	
fresh black pepper, for sprinkling	
Marinade	
	5 cups [1.2 liters] dry red wine
	2 teaspoons dried thyme, crumbled
	2 teaspoons dried rosemary, crumbled
	2 bay leaves
	2 tablespoons chopped garlic
	salt, to taste
	coarsely ground black pepper, to taste
olive oil cooking spray	
1 ¹/₂ pounds [680 grams] onions, halved, sliced thinly	

7 ounces [200 grams] celery, chopped

8 ounces [225 grams] carrots, chopped

2 tablespoons chopped garlic

3 tablespoons all purpose unbleached flour

5 cups [1.2 liters] beef broth, from the mix or canned

a 14 ¹/₂ ounce [415 gram] can diced tomatoes

salt, to taste

fresh black pepper, to taste

Sprinkle ribs with salt and pepper. Roast ribs on a rack in a foil lined open roasting pan in a preheated 300°F. [150°C.] oven for 1 ¹/₄ hours. Let cool slightly. Discard foil and fat.

Combine ingredients for marinade. Place ribs in a pot just large enough to hold them in one layer. Pour marinade over ribs and marinate for 24 hours. Strain marinade into a bowl. Discard spices.

Saute, in a sprayed large non-stick Dutch oven, onions until browning. Add celery, carrots and garlic. Saute until vegetables are well softened. Add flour and stir to mix well. Add ribs, marinade, beef broth and tomatoes. Bring to a boil and transfer pot to a preheated 325°F. [165°C] oven for 3 hours, until meat is tender. Chill until fat congeals. Skim fat and discard. Transfer meat to a cutting board. Cut meat into bite size pieces. Discard bones, fat and gristle. Taste gravy for seasoning. Bring daube to a simmer and simmer for an additional hour.

Serve with noodles, rice, pasta or dumplings.

Ribs in Barbeque Sauce [m]

I have friends who are rib aficionados. They are constantly after me to have a rib dinner. There are 3 different recipes for ribs. Take your pick or have all 3. These meaty ribs have a little bite to them, they are wonderful. Start them the day before.

Serves 8

10 pounds [4 kilos] beef back ribs, well trimmed of fat

salt, for sprinkling

fresh black pepper, for sprinkling

garlic granules, for sprinkling

a 15 ounce [420 gram] can tomato sauce

1 cup [225 milliliters] cider vinegar

6 ounces [175 grams] prepared Horseradish [see Index] [³/₄ cup] or store bought

6 tablespoons lemon juice

6 tablespoons lime juice

¹/₂ cup [110 milliliters] bottled chili sauce

4 tablespoons brown sugar

2 tablespoons Worcestershire sauce
2 tablespoons Dijon mustard
1 to 2 tablespoons minced garlic, to taste
2 teaspoons Tabasco sauce

Sprinkle ribs on both sides with salt, pepper and garlic granules. Place ribs on a rack in 1 or 2 foil lined baking pans, in 1 layer. Bake in a preheated 400°F. [205°C.] oven for 40 minutes, turning ribs after 20 minutes.

Cool ribs. Discard fat in pans, discard foil and wash pans. Although most of the fat will melt away during this initial baking, after ribs are cool, scrape away as much visible fat as possible.

Combine tomato sauce with the rest of the ingredients. Dip each rib in sauce until well covered. Return ribs to baking pans, relined with foil, cover and refrigerate overnight, dipping ribs in sauce at least 2 more times.

Bake ribs, in baking pans in a preheated 300°F. [150°C.] oven for 1 to 1 ½ hours until hot and crispy. Serve ribs with any left-over sauce, heated to boiling point, on the side.

The ribs can sit in oven, turned down to 250°F. [120°C.] for ½ hour or so, if necessary.

The ribs can be frozen after baking. Thaw before reheating in a preheated 300°F. [150°C.] oven for ½ hour.

Ribs in Spicy Sauce [m]

When I lived in Minneapolis during my college days, I went to a "Rib Joint" for ethnic food. They had nicely spiced ribs, which I never forgot. These are as close as I could remember. If you like spicy, this is the sauce for you; not biting, but delicious with just the right amount of heat. These are my personal favorites.

Serves 8

10 pounds [4 kilos] beef back ribs, well trimmed of fat
salt, for sprinkling
fresh black pepper, for sprinkling
garlic granules, for sprinkling
24 ounces [680 grams] bottled chili sauce
a 15 ounce [420 gram] can tomato sauce
5 ½ ounces [150 grams] apple jelly [2/3 cup]
4 tablespoons cider vinegar
2 tablespoons dry mustard
2 tablespoons Worcestershire sauce
1 tablespoon Tabasco sauce
1 to 2 tablespoons minced garlic, to taste
½ to 1 teaspoon ground cayenne pepper, to taste

Sprinkle ribs on both sides with salt, pepper and garlic granules. Place ribs on a rack in 1 or 2 foil lined baking pans, in 1 layer. Bake in a preheated 400°F. [205°C.] oven for 40 minutes, turning ribs after 20 minutes.

Cool ribs. Discard fat in pans, discard foil and wash the pans. Although most of the fat will melt away during this initial baking, after ribs are cool, scrape away as much visible fat as possible.

Combine chili sauce with the rest of the ingredients. Dip each rib in sauce until well covered. Return ribs to baking pans, relined with foil, cover and refrigerate overnight, dipping ribs in sauce at least 2 more times.

Bake ribs, in baking pans, in a preheated 300°F. [150°C.] oven for 1 to 1 ½ hour until hot and crispy. Serve ribs with any left-over sauce, heated to boiling point, on the side.

The ribs can sit in oven, turned down to 250°F. [120°C.] for ½ hour or so, if necessary.

The ribs can be frozen after baking. Thaw before reheating in a preheated 300°F. [150°C.] oven for $^1/_2$ hour.

Roast Beef Hash *[m]*

This is a wonderful way to use left-over roast beef. It is similar to a meat loaf but flat and slightly crispy.

Serves 8

olive oil cooking spray
1 tablespoon extra virgin olive oil
18 ounces [500 grams] onions, chopped
1 $^1/_2$ tablespoons chopped garlic
13 ounces [370 grams] fresh mushrooms, sliced
1 $^1/_2$ tablespoons all purpose unbleached flour
1 $^1/_2$ cups [350 milliliters] Beef Stock [see Index] or canned
1 $^1/_3$ pounds [600 grams] potatoes, unpeeled
1 $^1/_2$ pounds [680 grams] left-over cooked roast beef, chopped coarsely
1 $^1/_2$ teaspoons Worcestershire sauce
2 teaspoons salt, to taste
fresh black pepper, to taste

In a sprayed Dutch oven with oil added, saute onions until softened. Add garlic and mushrooms and saute until browning. Add flour, mix well and add beef stock, stirring. Cook until thickened, about 3 to 5 minutes. Remove from heat and cool.

Parboil potatoes for about 30 minutes, just until barely tender. Cool slightly, peel and dice tiny. Cool.

Combine onion mixture with roast beef. Add potatoes and toss to mix well. Add Worcestershire, salt and pepper and mix.

Turn roast beef hash mixture into a sprayed 13 x 10 x 2 inch [32 $^1/_2$ x25 x 5 centimeter] baking pan, suitable for serving. This part can be prepared ahead until about 1 hour before serving or frozen, well wrapped for later serving.

Bake in a preheated 400°F. [205°C.] oven for 45 minutes.

Cut into squares and serve from baking pan.

Ribs In Soy - Beer Sauce [m]

These ribs have an interesting flavor, kind of mild but definitely asser-tive and delicious. They are the favorite, of the 3 rib recipes, of some of my friends. Start them the day before.

Serves 8

10 pounds [4 kilos] beef back ribs, well trimmed of fat
salt, for sprinkling
fresh black pepper, for sprinkling
garlic granules, for sprinkling
1 cup [225 milliliters] light soy sauce
1 cup [225 milliliters] dark beer
1 cup [225 milliliters] Dijon mustard
$^1/_3$ cup [75 milliliters] honey
10 ounces [280 grams] onions, chopped finely
2 tablespoons Worcestershire sauce
1 $^1/_2$ tablespoons minced garlic
2 teaspoons Tabasco sauce

Sprinkle ribs on both sides with salt, pepper and garlic granules. Place ribs on racks in 1 or 2 foil lined baking pans. Bake in a preheated 400° F. [205°C.] oven for 40 minutes, turning ribs after 20 minutes.

Cool ribs, discard fat in pans, discard foil and wash pans. Although most of the fat will melt away during this initial baking, after ribs are cool, scrape away as much visible fat as possible.

Combine soy sauce and the rest of the ingredients. Dip each rib in soy beer sauce until well covered. Return ribs to baking pans, relined with foil, cover and refrigerate overnight, dipping ribs in sauce at least 2 more times.

Bake ribs, in baking pans, in a preheated 300°F. [150°C.] oven for 1 to 1 $^1/_2$ hours until hot and crispy. Serve with any left-over sauce, heated to boiling point, on the side.

The ribs can sit in oven, turned down to 250°F. [120°C.] for $^1/_2$ hour or so, if necessary.

The ribs can be frozen after baking. Thaw before reheating in a preheated 300°F. [150°C.] oven for $^1/_2$ hour.

Poached Salmon [p]

This simple and delicious main dish was devised by my friend Marjorie Moch. I serve it often in the summer for dinner because it is served cold. It is also suitable as a light luncheon main dish. I like to serve it with my light Tartar Sauce [see Index] on the side.

Serves 8

8 salmon steaks, cut 1 ¼ inches [3 centimeters] thick, about 5 pounds [2.25 kilos] total

salt, for sprinkling

fresh white pepper, for sprinkling

6 ½ ounces [185 grams] onions, sliced

1 lemon, unpeeled, sliced thinly, seeded

8 bay leaves

2 cups [450 milliliters] cider vinegar

2 cups [450 milliliters] water

2 teaspoons chopped garlic

2 teaspoons sugar

Sprinkle fish lightly on both sides with salt and pepper. Lay fish steaks in 2 large fry pans in one layer, 4 to each pan. Layer onion slices and lemon slices over fish. Place bay leaves in pans. Combine vinegar, water, garlic and sugar. Mix until sugar is dissolved. Divide mixture in two and pour over fish in pans.

Bring vinegar broth to a boil and simmer, covered for 7 to 10 minutes. Let fish cool as poached, covered. Chill in poaching liquid overnight in fridge, covered. Discard bay leaves.

Drain and serve with onion and lemon slices and tartar sauce.

Fish Stew - Kosher Bouillabaisse *[p]*

This is a dish for very special friends. It is a superb fish stew. It looks complicated but it isn't. Most of it can be prepared ahead of time. Serve with Aioli [see Index], a garlicky mayonaisse that is traditional with bouillabaisse, and with a crusty French or Italian Bread [see Index].

Serves 8

Stock

5 ounces [140 grams] onions, chopped, 1 medium
2 ounces [55 grams] carrots, peeled, chopped, 1 medium
fish heads and bones or 2 fish bouillion cubes
$^1/_2$ teaspoon crushed black peppercorns
1 bay leaf
$^1/_2$ teaspoon dried thyme
2 tablespoons chopped fresh parsley leaves
3 cups [700 milliliters] water
$^1/_2$ cup [110 milliliters] dry white wine

Stew

pareve butter flavored cooking spray
1 $^1/_2$ teaspoons margarine or extra virgin olive oil
3 large garlic cloves, chopped
7 ounces [200 grams] leeks, white and light green parts only, sliced, weight after cleaning

5 ½ ounces [150 grams] onions, chopped	
2 ounces [55 grams] carrots, peeled, chopped	
1 ½ pounds [680 grams] tomatoes, peeled, diced, fresh or canned	
7 ounces [200 grams] potatoes, peeled, diced finely, about 2 medium	
3 strips orange peel, without white pith	
¼ teaspoon ground bay leaf	
2 to 3 sprigs Spanish saffron, crumbled in fingers	
salt, to taste	
fresh white pepper, to taste	
splash dry white wine	
fish stock [see above]	
3 ½ pounds [1.6 kilos] assorted non oily fish filets, cubed	
[red snapper, striped bass, haddock, halibut, reserve heads and bones for stock]	

Make the stock: combine all the ingredients except wine, in a 5 to 6 quart [5 ½ liter] Dutch oven. Bring to a boil and simmer for 5 minutes. Add wine and simmer an additional 15 minutes ONLY. Strain stock, discard solids, and set aside broth. This part as well as the preparation of the rest of the ingredients can be prepared ahead of time.

In same pot, sprayed, add margarine or oil and saute garlic, leeks and onions until well wilted. Add carrots, tomatoes, potatoes, orange peel, parsley and bay leaf. Bring to a boil and simmer, covered, for 10 minutes. Add stock and the rest of the ingredients and simmer, covered, an additional 15 minutes.

Serve with a spoon of Aioli [see Index] in each bowl.

Stuffed Peppers [m]

A pleasant and homey main course, this is a dish that everyone seems to remember from childhood. I use colored peppers because they are more digestable than the green ones and are very pretty on the table.

Serves 8

4 "Sun" Dried Tomatoes [see Index], not packed in oil
8 sweet bell peppers, red, yellow, green, purple [no orange]
5 ounces [140 grams] raw rice
5 ounces [140 milliliters] hot defatted Beef Stock [see Index] or canned
1 ³/₄ pounds [800 grams] ground turkey
10 ounces [280 grams] onions, chopped finely
4 large garlic cloves, chopped finely
2 teaspoons Worcestershire sauce
2 egg whites
salt, to taste
fresh black pepper, to taste

Sauce

a 12 ounce [340 gram] can tomato paste
3 cups [800 milliliters] liquid, water plus soaking liquid from dried tomatoes

2 tablespoons brown sugar

3 tablespoons lemon juice

2 teaspoons Worcestershire sauce

1 teaspoon chili powder

1 teaspoon dried thyme

salt, to taste

fresh black pepper, to taste

Soak dried tomatoes in hot water, to cover, for 30 minutes. Reserve liquid for sauce. Cut up tomatoes finely. Set aside.

Cut straight across tops of peppers, reserving tops. Remove seeds and white membranes. Place peppers in a large kettle of boiling water. Return water to a boil. Remove peppers and let drain upside down until cool. Blanch tops in boiling water for 30 seconds. Drain and chop tops.

Soak rice in hot broth for 15 minutes. Combine rice mixture with meat, onions, garlic, Worcestershire, egg whites, chopped pepper tops, tomatoes, salt and pepper. Place peppers in a deep baking dish or pan large enough to hold them in one layer. Divide meat mixture among peppers.

With a wire whisk, combine ingredients for sauce. Spoon sauce over peppers and cover pan with foil. This part can be prepared ahead. Refrigerate or freeze until ready to complete recipe. Thaw before baking.

Bake peppers, covered with foil, in a preheated 350°F. [175°C.] oven for 1 1/2 hours, basting occasionally. Remove foil and bake an additional 30 minutes, basting occasionally.

Texas Style Chili [m]

After writing my first cookbook, I went on a trip around the U.S. to help publicize the book. When I was in Houston, Texas, I was interviewed by the Food Editor of the Houston Chronicle. As she was glancing through the book, she eagerly examined the recipe for Texas Chili. She turned to me with satisfaction when she saw that the list of ingredients included Masa Harina, a must in any recipe for "Texas" chili. This is my low fat Texas Chili.

Makes about 14 cups [3 liters]

3 ½ pounds [1.6 kilos] turkey thighs
olive oil cooking spray
1 tablespoon extra virgin olive oil
6 large garlic cloves, chopped
18 ounces [500 grams] onions, chopped
2 ½ pounds [1.2 kilos] ground turkey
a 4 ounce [110 gram] can chopped green chilis
6 to 8 tablespoons chili powder, to taste
1 tablespoon dried oregano
1 teaspoon ground cumin
salt, to taste
fresh black pepper, to taste
¾ cup [95 grams] masa harina
6 to 8 cups [1.4 to 1.8 liters] defatted Beef Stock [see Index] or canned
3 ½ tablespoons cider vinegar
¼ to ½ teaspoon hot red pepper flakes, to taste

Remove skin, fat and bone from thighs and cut into small dice [this takes a while].

In a sprayed non-stick kettle, in oil, saute onions, garlic and turkey dice until browning, stirring frequently [meat will actually turn a dark tan]. Add ground turkey and continue sauteing until turkey loses its color, stirring very frequently, and breaking up lumps.

Add green chilis, 6 tablespoons chili powder, oregano, cumin, salt and pepper. Cook, stirring, for 2 minutes. Sprinkle masa over mixture and stir until well combined. Add 6 cups [1.4 milliliters] stock, vinegar and pepper flakes, stir until combined. Bring to a boil, turn heat to very low, cover and simmer 2 hours, stirring occasionally, adding more stock as needed to prevent burning. Taste and correct the seasoning after 1 hour, adding more chili powder if desired.

The chili can be made 3 days ahead and can be frozen.

Serve with beans on the side, if desired.

Fresh or Pickled Tongue [m]

I don't serve tongue very often, but I have some friends, who request it all the time. For them, I dedicate this recipe. When I lived in Israel, my dog would stand up at the kitchen window, sniffing the delicious aroma of cooking tongue. She was eagerly waiting for the scraps, which were always her treat.

Serves 8 tongue lovers

1 fresh or pickled beef tongue, about 3 pounds [1.35 kilos]
10 $^1/_2$ ounces [300 grams] onions, sliced
1 large carrot, unpeeled, sliced
2 celery ribs, with leaves, cut into large hunks
2 large garlic cloves, halved
3 bay leaves
10 lightly crushed black peppercorns
2 tablespoons salt
water

Place all the ingredients in an 8 quart [8 liter] kettle. Add enough water to barely cover tongue. Bring to a boil and simmer, covered, for about 3 $^1/_2$ hours, until tongue is tender.

Transfer tongue to a cutting board and let it cool slightly. Remove skin, bones and gristle. [These, together with strained out vegetables are wonderful for the dog.]

Strain broth and return to kettle. Return tongue to broth to sit until ready to serve. Reheat tongue in broth, if desired.

When ready to serve, slice tongue thinly and place on a serving platter to serve with various mustards and Horseradish [see Index].

Reserve broth to use in making soups. It adds a lot of flavor to Lentil/Split Pea Soup or Vegetable Soups [see Index].

Turkey Chili *[m]*

This is a good regular chili, spicy and full of flavor, a successful transition to low fat cooking. I like spicy so guide yourself accordingly. One winter night while testing recipes for this book, I made all three chilis in the book and invited lots of people from my building to a "Casual Chili Party". It was a successful tasting and everyone enjoyed being part of the experiment.

Makes about 20 cups [4 ½ liters]

olive oil cooking spray
3 ¾ pounds [1 ¾ kilos] ground turkey
2 pounds [900 grams] onions, chopped finely
8 large garlic cloves, minced
9 ounces [250 grams] spicy, hot turkey sausage, casing removed, chopped
3 ⅓ pounds [1 ½ kilos] tomatoes, canned or fresh, peeled, chopped coarsely
an 18 ounce [510 gram] can tomato paste
2 to 3 tablespoons canned pickled jalapeno peppers, chopped
3 to 6 tablespoons chili powder, to taste

2 teaspoons dried thyme
2 teaspoons dried oregano
2 teaspoons dried basil
2 teaspoons sugar
$\frac{1}{2}$ teaspoon hot paprika
$\frac{1}{2}$ teaspoon red pepper flakes
$\frac{1}{4}$ teaspoon ground bay leaf
$\frac{1}{4}$ teaspoon ground cumin
3 heaping tablespoons beef soup powder or bouillion cubes
salt, to taste
fresh black pepper, to taste
optional: 2 cans red kidney beans, rinsed, drained

In a well sprayed 8 quart [8 liter] kettle, saute, over medium high heat, turkey, onions, garlic and sausage, stirring frequently, until meat loses its color, and breaking up lumps. Add the rest of the ingredients, except beans, and bring to a boil, stirring occasionally. Simmer, covered, for 1 $\frac{1}{2}$ hours, stirring occasionally.

Taste, correct seasoning, and add beans, if using. Simmer, covered, an additional hour, stirring occasionally.

Skim fat and serve. Or refrigerate overnight and remove fat. Reheat to serve.

The chili can be made several days ahead of time and can be frozen.

Veal Shanks with Beans, Carrots and Parsnips [m]

This wholesome, hearty stew is a meal-in-a-pot; great for entertaining. This is another dish that can be prepared ahead of time and frozen if desired. Veal shanks are wonderful and marry well with many other ingredients.

Serves 8

8 large veal shank pieces, about 2 inches [5 centimeters] thick, well trimmed of fat, about 6 ²/₃ pounds [3 kilos]
salt, for sprinkling
fresh white pepper, for sprinkling
garlic granules, for sprinkling
olive oil cooking spray
2 teaspoons extra virgin olive oil
1 ¹/₂ cups [350 milliliters] dry white wine
1 cup [225 milliliters] water
3 cups [700 milliliters] defatted Chicken Broth [see Index] or canned
1 ¹/₂ tablespoons dried thyme
pinch ground cloves

a 14 $\frac{1}{2}$ ounce [410 gram] can diced tomatoes
a 12 ounce [340 gram] can tomato paste
20 ounces [550 grams] onions, chopped coarsely
4 large garlic cloves, chopped
8 carrots, 1 bunch, about 1 pound [450 grams], peeled, trimmed, left whole, save and freeze tops for soup
8 parsnips, about 1 pound [450 grams] peeled, trimmed, left whole
4 -20 ounce [570 gram] cans cannelinni beans, drained, rinsed

Sprinkle veal with salt, pepper and garlic granules. Heat a well sprayed non-stick large Dutch oven with oil added, until hot. Brown veal in batches, on both sides, about 10 minutes for each batch. Transfer veal to a plate as it is browned. Add wine to Dutch oven and bring to a boil, scrapping up all brown bits. Transfer to an 8 quart [8 liter] kettle and add veal to kettle along with any juices that have accumulated. Put Dutch oven aside. Add water, broth, thyme, tomatoes and tomato paste to kettle. Bring to a boil and simmer for about 2 hours, barely covered, until veal is almost tender, stirring occasionally.

In Dutch oven, resprayed, saute onions and garlic until browning. Add this mixture to veal mixture along with carrots and parsnips. Simmer an additional 30 to 45 minutes, until carrots and parsnips are tender. Add salt and pepper to taste. Add beans and simmer an additional 15 minutes.

The stew can be made 3 or 4 days ahead and can be frozen.

Veal Goulash with Nuckerl [m]

I am partial to veal in almost any form. This is a particularly tasty dish and I like to make it often. Most people enjoy the veal and love the Nuckerl [see Index], an Hungarian dumpling that I learned to make from my mother in law, Aranka Weisgal.

Serves 8

4 ¹/₂ pounds [2 kilos] boneless lean veal
1 ¹/₂ tablespoons salt, or to taste
1 teaspoon fresh white pepper
olive oil cooking spray
2 tablespoons extra virgin olive oil
20 ounces [580 grams] onions, sliced thinly
3 garlic cloves, chopped
¹/₂ cup [75 grams] all purpose unbleached flour
4 to 5 cups [900 to 1.2 liters] water
2 tablespoons whole caraway seeds
1 tablespoon sweet Hungarian paprika
1 recipe cooked Nuckerl [see Index]

Trim all fat from veal and cut veal into bite size cubes. Sprinkle with salt and pepper.

In a sprayed Dutch oven, in olive oil, brown onions and garlic. Add veal cubes, in batches, and brown, over high heat, stirring frequently. As veal is browned, transfer with a slotted spoon, to an 8 quart [8 liter] kettle. Sprinkle veal and onions with flour and mix well. Add water to Dutch oven and bring to a boil, scraping up all browned bits left in pot. Transfer water to kettle and add caraway and paprika.

Bring mixture to a boil, cover, and simmer stew for 1 ¹/₂ to 2 hours, until veal is very tender, stirring occasionally, and adding more water if necessary.

The stew can be prepared ahead up to this point. Refrigerate until ready to reheat or freeze. Thaw before reheating.

Reheat stew until hot, add nuckerl, stir to mix nuckerl with gravy and heat until nuckerl are heated through, about 25 to 30 minutes, stirring frequently. Note: do not freeze nuckerl, they do not freeze well.

PASTA

Roast Beef Enchiladas [m]

There is life after roast beef sandwiches for left-over roast beef. This is one of the ways in which I use leftover roast beef. [Also try Roast Beef Hash [see Index]]

Makes 16 enchiladas, serving 8

olive oil cooking spray
1 teaspoon extra virgin olive oil
11 ounces [315 grams] onions, chopped
1 tablespoon chopped garlic
1 to 1 ¹/₂ tablespoons chili powder, to taste
1 teaspoon salt, to taste
fresh black pepper, to taste
1 pound [450 grams] leftover roast beef, chopped [see Note]
an 8 ounce [225 gram] can tomato sauce
16 eight inch [20 centimeter] flour tortillas
1 recipe prepared Hot Sauce for Enchiladas [see Index] or bought prepared sauce

In a sprayed Dutch oven with oil added, saute onions until well softened. Add garlic and saute. Add chili powder, salt and pepper and mix. Add roast beef and tomato sauce and cook, stirring occasionally, about 5 to 10 minutes. Transfer to a bowl and let cool.

Place about ¹/₃ cup [75 milliliters] filling on each tortilla and roll up tightly. Lay seam side down in 1 or 2 sprayed baking pans. Pour enchilada sauce over rolled tortillas, covering well.

This part can be prepared ahead and covered with film, until about 30 minutes before serving or frozen, well wrapped in foil, for later serving. Thaw before baking.

Bake in a preheated 350°F. [175°C.] oven for 15 to 20 minutes until hot and bubbly. Serve, allowing 2 per person.

Note: If desired, ground beef, lightly sauteed, can be substituted for leftover roast beef.

Bell Pepper Sauce for Pasta [d]

When colored sweet peppers are at a special price, I make this sauce and have a dinner party or freeze it for a future dinner. This is an unusual pasta sauce; it has no tomatoes, no meat and almost no fat. Great for serving vegetarian guests and the flavor is terrific.

Serves 8

1/4 cup [55 milliliters] extra virgin olive oil
olive oil cooking spray
9 sweet bell peppers, red, yellow, orange, green, about 4 pounds [1.9 kilos], seeded, sliced thinly lengthwise
9 1/2 ounces [275 grams] red onions, sliced thinly
9 1/2 ounces [275 grams] sweet onions, sliced thinly, Vidalia or Spanish
12 ounces [340 grams] fresh mushrooms, sliced
3 tablespoons chopped garlic
1 cup [225 milliliters] dry white wine
1 1/2 cups [350 milliliters] pareve chicken flavored soup, from the mix
3/4 cup [175 milliliters] Dijon mustard
2 bunches green onions, chopped
5 ounces [135 grams] grated Parmesan cheese, 1 1/3 cups
salt, to taste
fresh white pepper, to taste
1 1/2 pounds [680 grams] fettucini or spaghetti, cooked al dente

Heat oil in a sprayed large Dutch oven. Saute peppers until tender, about 15 to 20 minutes, stirring occasionally. Remove peppers with a slotted spoon to a bowl. Add onions, mushrooms and garlic to Dutch oven and saute until tender, about 15 minutes, stirring occasionally.

Combine soup with mustard and white wine and add to onion mixture in Dutch oven. Bring to a boil and simmer until sauce thickens, about 8 minutes. Add peppers to sauce.

This part of the recipe can be done ahead of time. Refrigerate, covered, for 1 or 2 days or freeze for longer storage. Thaw and bring to a simmer before continuing with recipe.

Add green onions and Parmesan, mix well, taste, and add salt and pepper, if needed.

Pour sauce over pasta in a large serving bowl and serve.

Marinara Sauce *[p]*

A simple, all purpose tomato sauce that is outstanding by itself or as a basic ingredient in other pasta sauces. I can't say enough about the excellent flavor of this sauce.

Enough for 1 $1/2$ pounds [680 grams] pasta, serving 8

2 - 28 to 32 ounce [800 to 900 gram] cans Italian peeled tomatoes
2 tablespoons chopped garlic
5 anchovy filets, cut up
$1/4$ cup [55 milliliters] extra virgin olive oil
salt, to taste
fresh black pepper, to taste

Empty tomatoes into a bowl. Cut out core end and break up tomatoes by squeezing through your fingers. Set aside.

Simmer garlic and anchovies gently in oil over very low heat, mashing anchovies with the back of a spoon, until garlic is golden, about 5 minutes. Add tomatoes with their juices. Bring to a boil over high heat and boil vigorously until juices are cooked down and sauce has thickened, stirring frequently, about 25 to 30 minutes. Add salt and pepper to taste.

Lasagne [d]

This simple lasagne is delicious, easy to put together ahead of time and can be frozen. I like to have one of these in my freezer for unexpected guests. It always makes a hit. This lasagne is my son Samuel Weisgal's favorite.

Serves 8 generously

1 recipe Mushroom Tomato Sauce [see Index]
8 lasagne noodles, about 7 ounces [200 grams]
8 ounces [225 grams] low fat cottage cheese, drained 1 hour
2 cups [200 grams] grated Parmesan cheese
6 ounces [175 grams] part-skim milk Mozzarella cheese,
shredded or sliced

Make mushroom tomato sauce and set aside.

In an 8 quart [8 liter] kettle of boiling salted water, cook lasagne noodles until al dente, about 8 minutes. Drain, rinse with cold water and lay on towels to dry.

In a large baking pan, about 12 ½ x 10 ½ x 3 inches [32 x 27 x 7 ½ centimeters] suitable for serving, layer as follows:

1. a thin layer of sauce
2. layer of 4 lasagne noodles [slightly overlapping]
3. layer of cottage [use all]
4. layer of sauce [use one half]
5. layer of Parmesan [use one half]
6. layer of 4 noodles [slightly overlapping]
7. layer of Mozzarella [use all]
8. layer of sauce [use second half]
9. layer of Parmesan [use second half]

This part of recipe can be prepared ahead and set aside until about 1 hour before serving or can be frozen. Thaw before baking.

Bake in a preheated 350°F. [175°C.] oven for 1 hour.

Cut into squares to serve.

Eggplant Parmesan [d]

This is a tasty rendition of the classic Italian vegetarian dish. I make it often for my vegetarian friends.

Serves 8

1 recipe Mushroom Tomato Sauce [see Index]

1 ³/₄ to 2 ¹/₄ pounds [800 to 1 kilo] eggplant

salt, for sprinkling

5 ¹/₂ ounces [150 grams] part-skim milk Mozzarella cheese, shredded

2 cups [200 grams] grated Parmesan cheese [7 ounces]

16 ounces [450 grams] low fat cottage cheese, drained for 30 minutes

olive oil cooking spray

Prepare Mushroom Tomato Sauce and set aside.

Thinly slice eggplant lengthwise into ¹/₂ inch [1 centimeter] slices. Lightly sprinkle salt on both sides of each slice and let eggplant drain in a colander for 30 minutes. Rinse and drain. Place eggplant in a pot of boiling water and simmer for 10 minutes. Drain and lay on kitchen towels to cool.

In a sprayed au gratin pan or large baking pan, about 13 x 9 x 2 inch [33 x 23 x 5 centimeters] suitable for serving, layer as follows:

1. a thin layer of sauce
2. layer of eggplant slices [use one third]
3. layer of Mozzarella [use all]
4. layer of sauce [use one third]
5. layer of Parmesan [use one half]
6. layer of eggplant slices [use one third]
7. layer of cottage [use all]
8. layer of sauce [use one third]
9. layer of eggplant slices [use last third]
10. layer of sauce [use last third]
11. layer of Parmesan [use second half]

This part can be prepared ahead of time. Set aside until about 1 hour before serving or freeze, well wrapped, for later serving.

Bake in a preheated 375°F. [190°C.] oven for 45 minutes to 1 hour, until bubbly. Let sit, covered with foil, for 15 minutes, before cutting into squares to serve from pan.

173

Meat Ball Sauce for Pasta [m]

My grandson, Benjamin Lavon, is a lover of spaghetti with meat balls. I devised this recipe especially for him. This is a great dish to serve for almost any large or small group of people. It seems that everyone likes pasta.

Makes about 90 - 1 ½ inch [3 3/4 centimeter] meat balls, and
     enough sauce for 1 ½ pounds [680 grams] pasta

2 ¼ pounds [1 kilo] very lean ground beef
2 ½ pounds [1.2 kilos] ground turkey
¾ cup [175 milliliters] frozen egg substitute, thawed
½ cup [85 grams] dried onion soup mix
½ to 1 tablespoon garlic granules, to taste
salt, to taste
fresh black pepper, to taste
1 recipe Marinara Sauce [see Index]
a 12 ounce [340 gram] can tomato paste
1 teaspoon sugar, to taste

Combine two meats with egg substitute, soup mix, garlic, salt and pepper in a bowl. Make tiny meat balls with moistened hands. In a kettle, combine Marinara Sauce with tomato paste and sugar. Bring to a simmer and add meat balls. Simmer, covered, for 1 hour, carefully stirring occaionally to keep meat balls from sticking. Simmer, uncovered, for an additional hour until sauce is thickened, adding more sugar, if necessary.

Serve over your favorite pasta.

The sauce can be frozen.

174

Noodle Kugel [Pudding] [d]

This is a delicious way to serve noodles. I dedicate this recipe to friend, Eileen Eiselsberg, who loves a Noodle Kugel. I like to serve the kugel at our break fast dinner after Yom Kippur, as we always have a dairy meal.

Serves 8 easily [maybe more]

14 ounces [400 grams] no yolks wide noodles
2 ounces [55 grams] margarine
1/2 cup [110 milliliters] frozen egg substitute, thawed
7 ounces [200 grams] low fat cottage cheese, drained for 1 hour
7 ounces [200 grams] no-fat sour cream substitute
1/4 cup [60 grams] no-fat plain yogurt, drained for 1 hour
1/3 cup [70 grams] sugar
1 teaspoon ground cinnamon
1 1/2 teaspoons vanilla
1 tablespoon grated orange peel, about 1/2 an orange
14 ounces [400 grams] apples, peeled, cored, sliced thinly
4 1/2 ounces [125 grams] white raisins
4 egg whites
butter flavored cooking spray
2 tablespoons sugar mixed with
1 heaping teaspoon ground cinnamon

Cook noodles in boiling water until al dente, about 10 minutes. Drain well, return to pot and add margarine. Mix until margarine is melted. Set aside.

In a mixing bowl, combine egg substitute, cottage, sour cream, yogurt, sugar, cinnamon, vanilla, orange peel, apples and raisins. Add mixture to noodles and mix thoroughly.

Quickly beat egg whites until stiff. Fold whites into noodle mixture, combining gently but thoroughly. Pour noodle mixture into a sprayed 13 x 9 x 2 inch [33 x 23 x 5 centimeter] 3 quart [3 liter] baking dish, suitable for serving. Sprinkle cinnamon sugar mixture evenly over top.

Bake in a preheated 400°F. [205°C.] oven for 45 minutes. Serve the pudding from the baking dish, either hot or at room temperature.

The kugel can be baked a day ahead of time and reheated in a 350° F. [175°C.] oven for 15 minutes.

Baked Rigatoni [d]

I have a special friend who loves baked rigatoni. I dedicate this to
Adrienne Hoffman and often make this especially for her. Using eggplant, roasted in the oven, makes this a very "meaty" dish. I am partial
to any leftovers of this dish, reheated.

Serves 8 easily

1 recipe Mushroom Tomato Sauce [see Index]

salt, for sprinkling

12 ounces [340 grams] eggplant, unpeeled, cut into 1 ¹/₂ inch
    [3 ³/₄ centimeter] cubes

olive oil cooking spray

12 ounces [340 grams] dry rigatoni

12 ounces [340 grams] low fat cottage cheese, drained for 1 hour

12 ounces [340 grams] part-skim milk Mozzarella cheese, shredded

²/₃ cup [70 grams] grated Parmesan cheese

Make mushroom tomato sauce.

Lightly sprinkle salt on eggplant cubes and let drain in a colander
for 30 minutes. Rinse, drain well and pat dry. Lay in 1 layer on a sprayed
foil lined baking sheet and spray eggplant cubes. Roast in a preheated
400°F. [205°C.] oven until just beginning to brown, about 20 to 25
minutes. Add eggplant cubes to sauce and mix to combine.

Cook rigatoni until al dente. Drain, rinse with cold water, drain
and set aside.

In a 3 x 10 ¹/₂ x 12 ¹/₂ inch [7 ¹/₂ x 27 x 32 centimeter baking pan,
sprayed well, layer as follows:

1. a layer of 3 ladles of sauce [6 ounce ladle]
2. layer of ¹/₂ of rigatoni
3. layer of cottage cheese, use all
4. layer of 3 ladles sauce
5. layer of rest of rigatoni
6. layer of Mozzarella cheese, use all
7. layer of rest of sauce
8. layer of Parmesan cheese, use all

Bake rigatoni in a preheated 375°F. [190°C.] oven for about 40 minutes, until lightly browned and bubbly.

The rigatoni can sit in oven, turned down to 250°F. [120°C.] for half an hour or so, if necessary.

The rigatoni can be frozen either unbaked or baked. No need to thaw to cook but add another 20 minutes to cooking time.

Pasta Salad [d]

This is more than a salad, it is a light main dish for a summer evening. It is aromatic and full of flavor with lots of different tastes in each bite.

Serves 8

1 pound [450 grams] bows [pasta]
5 ¹/₂ ounces [150 grams] Pesto [see Index]
2 ounces [60 grams] "Sun" Dried Tomatoes [see Index]
hot water for soaking
8 ounces [225 grams] frozen peas, thawed
7 ounces [200 grams] smoked salmon [I buy ends and pieces]
4 ounces [110 grams] shelled pine nuts, lightly toasted
vinaigrette sauce:
4 ounces [110 grams] extra virgin olive oil, ¹/₂ cup
2 ounces [55 grams] basalmic vinegar, ¹/₄ cup
2 ounces [55 grams] red wine vinegar, ¹/₄ cup
2 tablespoons chopped garlic
1 tablespoon Dijon mustard
salt, to taste
fresh black pepper, to taste

Cook bows in boiling water until al dente, about 9 minutes. Drain, place in a large serving bowl and while still warm, mix with pesto until well combined. Cool.

Soak tomatoes in hot water to cover for 45 minutes. When very soft, cut into medium sized pieces with a scissors. Add to bowl with pasta. Add peas, salmon and nuts. Lightly moisten with vinaigrette sauce to taste. [You will probably have some leftover, refrigerate until needed for another time.] Add salt and pepper to taste.   177

Sausage Sauce For Pasta or Pizza [m]

This delicious sauce is wonderful with rigatoni or other tubular pasta. It is hearty and filling. It can also be spread as a meat topping for pizza.

Makes enough for 1 ½ pounds [680 grams] pasta

18 ounces [500 grams] assorted turkey and beef sausages and salamis, spicy and sweet
water
olive oil cooking spray
1 tablespoon extra virgin olive oil
1 ½ pounds [680 grams] ground turkey or lean ground beef
9 ½ ounces [275 grams] onions, chopped
2 ½ ounces [75 grams] celery, chopped, 1 large rib
3 ½ ounces [100 grams] green peppers, chopped
3 to 5 garlic cloves, chopped
4 ounces [110 grams] fresh mushrooms, sliced
an 8 ounce [225 gram] can tomato paste
a 14 to 16 ounce [425 gram] can diced tomatoes
2 tablespoons dry beef soup powder

$^1/_2$ teaspoon salt, or to taste

fresh black pepper, to taste

2 teaspoons dried basil

2 teaspoons dried oregano

$^1/_2$ teaspoon dried thyme

$^1/_8$ teaspoon ground bay leaf

sugar, to taste

2 tablespoons chopped fresh parsley leaves

In a saucepan, place sausages and salamis, pricked with a fork. Add water to cover and bring to a boil. Simmer for 10 minutes. Drain, cut meats into bite size and set aside.

In a sprayed 5 quart [5 liter] kettle, add oil and heat. Saute turkey or beef, breaking up lumps, until meat loses its color. Add onions, celery, peppers and garlic and saute until vegetables soften, about 10 minutes. Add mushrooms and saute an additional 5 minutes. Add sausages and salamis and the rest of the ingredients, except parsley, and bring to a boil. Cover and simmer for 1 $^1/_2$ hours, stirring frequently. Taste, correct seasoning and simmer for an additional hour. Add parsley and stir to mix.

The sauce can be made several days ahead of time and can be frozen.

Spinach Lasagne, Alma [d]

When we lived in Jerusalem, we had many friends among the foreign
correspondents that were stationed there. Alma Claiborne was one of
the wives who became part of the Israeli scene, learning Hebrew and
generally joining in. She and her husband, Bill, became good friends
of our family. Alma invented this recipe and I've added to it. I hope she
likes the changes that I've made. It is delicious, thank you, Alma.

Serves 8

1 ¹/₂ pounds [680 grams] frozen cut spinach leaves, thawed
2 pounds [900 grams] low fat cottage cheese, drained for 1 hour
2 teaspoons salt
pinch ground nutmeg
pinch dried marjoram
olive oil cooking spray
5 ¹/₂ ounces [150 grams] onions, chopped finely
4 garlic cloves, chopped finely
2 ounces [50 grams] margarine
¹/₃ cup [55 grams] all purpose unbleached flour
2 cups [450 milliliters] hot skim milk
2 teaspoons salt
¹/₂ teaspoon fresh white pepper
1 teaspoon dried sweet basil
1 teaspoon dried oregano
pinch ground cayenne pepper
¹/₂ cup [110 milliliters] frozen egg substitute, thawed
10 ¹/₂ ounces [300 grams] part-skim milk Mozzarella cheese, shredded
²/₃ cup [70 grams] grated Parmesan cheese
8 dry lasagne noodles, uncooked

Combine drained and squeezed spinach with cottage cheese, salt, nutmeg and marjoram in a mixing bowl.

Saute in a sprayed non-stick fry pan, onions and garlic until well softened. Add onion mixture to spinach mixture and combine well. Set aside.

In a saucepan melt margarine, add flour and whisk until combined. While whisking constantly, add hot milk all at once. Cook, stirring until sauce is thick and smooth. Add salt, pepper, basil, oregano and cayenne. Let sauce simmer for 10 minutes over low heat, stirring frequently. Remove from heat. Add a bit of hot sauce to eggs to warm eggs, beating well. Add warmed eggs to the rest of the sauce, reheat sauce until thick, stirring.

In a sprayed baking pan about 3 x 10 x 12 inches [7 $\frac{1}{2}$ x 25 x 30 centimeters] layer as follows:

1. a thin layer of sauce
2. layer of 4 uncooked lasagne noodles [slightly overlapping]
3. layer of spinach mixture [use all]
4. layer of sauce [use one half]
5. layer of Mozzarella [use all]
6. layer of 4 uncooked lasagne noodles [slightly overlapping]
7. layer of sauce [use the rest]
8. layer of Parmesan [use all]

Place baking pan on a foil lined baking sheet and bake in a preheated 350°F. [175°C.] oven for 1 hour to 1 hour and 10 minutes, until puffed and bubbly. Remove from oven, cover with foil and let sit for 10 minutes before cutting into squares to serve.

The lasagne can be frozen before cooking, well covered with foil. If frozen, thaw and follow baking directions. It can also be frozen after cooking. Thaw and reheat in a preheated 300°F. [150°C.] oven for 30 minutes.

Mushroom Tomato Sauce [p]

This is a thick meaty sauce without any meat. It is my standby for vegetarian and dairy dishes. I like it with spaghetti and different lasagnas [see Index] and many pasta dishes.

Makes 8 cups [1.8 liters]

olive oil cooking spray
1 ¹/₂ teaspoons extra virgin olive oil
12 ounces [340 grams] onions, chopped finely
5 ounces [135 grams] green peppers, diced finely
3 large garlic cloves, chopped
12 ounces [340 grams] fresh mushrooms, sliced
a 12 ounce [340 gram] can tomato paste
2 - 14 ¹/₂ ounce [415 gram] cans diced tomatoes
1 tablespoon Worcestershire sauce
2 to 4 teaspoons sugar, to taste
1 ¹/₄ teaspoons dried oregano
³/₄ teaspoon salt
1 teaspoon dried basil or 1 tablespoon fresh basil leaves, sliced
fresh white pepper, to taste
3 sprigs fresh parsley leaves, minced
1 cup [225 milliliters] water
¹/₂ cup [110 milliliters] dry red wine

In a sprayed 5 quart [5 liter] kettle, heat oil until hot. Saute onions, peppers and garlic until well softened, stirring occasionally, about 15 minutes. Add mushrooms and saute over high heat for 10 minutes, stirring frequently. Add the rest of the ingredients, bring to a boil and simmer, covered, stirring occasionally, for 2 hours. Add more water if necessary. The sauce can be frozen.

Spinach Gnocchi [d]

These lovely dumplings can be served as a light supper entree or as a side dish at a dinner. I like to serve them with a sprinkling of Parmesan cheese, but served with a tomato or cheese sauce can make the dish more substantial as an entree. The gnocchi have a pronounced spinach flavor.

Serves 8 generously

20 ounces [580 grams] frozen chopped spinach, cooked, drained well, squeezed of water
salt, to taste
fresh black pepper, to taste
1 tablespoon margarine
1 $^1/_2$ pounds [680 grams] low fat cottage cheese, drained 1 hour
$^1/_2$ teaspoon ground nutmeg
2 cups [280 grams] all purpose unbleached flour
$^1/_2$ cup [110 milliliters] frozen egg substitute, thawed
grated Parmesan cheese, to garnish
optional: pasta sauce or cheese sauce, to garnish

Add salt, pepper and margarine to well drained and squeezed spinach.

Beat cottage in a food processor until smooth. Add spinach mixture, pulse to mix. When well mixed, add nutmeg, flour and eggs. Continue pulsing until mixture is well combined.

Dip a tablespoon in water and scoop up some spinach mixture and let it drop into a large pot of boiling salted water. When gnocchi have risen to top, let cook for a minute or two and then remove with a slotted spoon to a colander to drain. Continue making gnocchi in the same manner until all dough is used. Set aside, covered, until just before ready to serve.

Reheat gnocchi in boiling water to cover for just a minute or two, drain, sprinkle with Parmesan cheese or nap with sauce and serve.

Vegetable Lasagne [d]

I like this "change of pace" lasagne. It is full of vegetables, low in calories and very tasty. The lasagne noodles are not cooked ahead to prevent the lasagne from being soggy. The whole dish can be assembled and frozen or just refrigerated for a day or two before baking.

Serves 8 generously

5 ounces [135 grams] broccoli

5 ounces [135 grams] carrots

3 ¹/₂ ounces [100 grams] zuchinni

3 ¹/₂ ounces [100 grams] yellow squash

7 ¹/₂ ounces [210 grams] cauliflower

7 ounces [200 grams] asparagus

3 ¹/₂ ounces [100 grams] spinach leaves

6 baby corns about 2 ¹/₂ ounces [75 grams]

3 ¹/₂ ounces [100 grams] fresh mushrooms

olive oil cooking spray

¹/₂ recipe Marinara Sauce [see Index]

8 dry lasagne noodles, uncooked

12 ounces [340 grams] no-fat cottage cheese, drained for 1 hour

12 ounces [340 grams] part-skim milk Mozzarella cheese, shredded

2 ounces [55 grams] grated Parmesan cheese, ¹/₂ cup

salt, to taste

fresh black pepper, to taste

2 teaspoons dried basil

2 teaspoons dried oregano

2 teaspoons granulated garlic

1 teaspoon sugar

Bring a large pot of water to a boil to blanch vegetables prepared in following manner and for following times. Separate broccoli into florets and stems. Peel and slice stems thinly. Blanch florets and stems for 3 minutes, remove with a slotted spoon and set aside in a large bowl. Peel carrots and slice thinly or shred. Blanch for 3 minutes, remove with slotted spoon and set aside in bowl. Trim and halve lengthwise zuchinni and yellow squash and slice thinly. Blanch for 1 minute, remove with slotted spoon and set aside in bowl. Separate cauliflower florets and slice thinly. Blanch for 3 minutes, remove with slotted spoon and set aside in bowl. Break off tough ends of asparagus [reserve for soup, see Index], and slice on the diagonal 3/4 inch [2 centimeters] thick. Blanch for 2 minutes, remove with slotted spoon and set aside in bowl. Wash and trim spinach. Blanch for 1 minute, drain and set aside in the bowl. Add to bowl, baby corn, sliced on the diagonal thinly and mushrooms, sliced thinly. Gently combine vegetables. Add salt and pepper to taste. Combine basil, oregano, garlic and sugar in a small dish. Set aside

In a sprayed lasagne or baking dish 10 x 12 x 3 inches [25 x 30 x 7 1/2 centimeters] layer as follows:
1. a thin layer of sauce
2. layer of 4 uncooked lasagne noodles, overlapping slightly
3. layer of 1/2 of vegetables
4. layer of 1/2 of sauce
5. layer of cottage, use all
6. sprinkle all over with 1/2 of herb mixture
7. layer of 4 uncooked lasagne noodles, overlapping slightly
8. layer of rest of vegetables
9. layer of Mozzarella, use all
10. layer of rest of sauce
11. sprinkle rest of herb mixture over all
12. layer of Parmesan, use all

Up to this point, recipe can be made ahead of time. Refrigerate for a day or two or freeze. Thaw before baking.

Cover lasagne with foil and place on a foil lined baking sheet. Bake in a preheated 425°F. [220°C.] oven for 1 hour.

Let sit, covered for 15 minutes before cutting into squares to serve.

POULTRY

Chicken Musakhan [m]

This is a very special Middle Eastern Arab dish, delicious and easy to prepare ahead of time. I like using Cornish hens, they are exactly the right size for serving. Everyone gets to eat some of the white and dark meat of the chicken. This is a very different dish. The sumac is available in stores that carry Middle Eastern foods and some specialty stores.

Serves 8

4 Cornish hens, about 1 ¹/₂ pounds [680 grams] each

salt, for sprinkling

fresh white pepper, for sprinkling

sweet paprika, for sprinkling

ground ginger, for sprinkling

olive oil cooking spray

3 ³/₄ pounds [1.7 kilos] onions, chopped coarsely

1 ¹/₂ tablespoons extra virgin olive oil

6 tablespoons ground sumac

4 mini pitas, about 4 inches [10 centimeters], split horizontally

Cut hens on each side of backbone and remove backbone, [reserve for soup]. Cut hens in half, splitting down center of breast. I use a scissors. Remove small rib bones with the scissors [very easy to do]. Trim excess skin and any fat. Lightly sprinkle hens with salt, pepper, paprika and ginger.

Roast hens on a rack in a foil lined open roasting pan, skin side up, in a preheated 375°F. [190°C.] oven for 35 minutes. Set aside to cool. Discard pan juices.

In a large sprayed non-stick fry pan or Dutch oven, saute onions in olive oil until well softened, about 15 minutes. Add sumac and combine well. Remove from heat and set aside to cool.

Spray 2 large baking pans, suitable for serving. Lay 4 split pitas

186

halves in each pan in one layer, inside up. Divide ½ of onion mixture evenly among pita halves. Lay ½ hen on each pita on on top of onions, skin side down. Divide the rest of the onion mixture evenly over hens. This part can be prepared ahead of time and refrigerated until ready to continue, even the day before.

Bake hens in a preheated 375°F. [190°C.] oven for 1 hour.

Serve each person ½ hen together with the pita it rests on.

Garlic Chicken [m]

For all garlic lovers, and I am one of the biggest, I dedicate this dish. It is fragrant and mouth wateringly good. Enjoy!

Serves 8

4 Cornish hens, about 1 ½ pounds [680 grams] each
salt, for sprinkling
fresh white pepper, for sprinkling
sweet Hungarian paprika, for sprinkling
1 cup [225 milliliters] dry white wine
1 cup [55 grams] chopped parsley leaves, 2 ounces
⅓ cup [60 grams] finely chopped garlic, 2 ounces
pinch saffron
¼ teaspoon ground bay leaf

Cut hens on each side of backbone and remove it [reserve for soup]. Cut hens in half, splitting down center of breast. I use a scissors. Trim excess skin and any fat. Remove small rib bones with the scissors, very easy to do. Sprinkle hens with salt, pepper and paprika.

Roast hens, skin side up, on a rack in a foil lined roasting pan in a preheated 375°F. [190°C.] oven for 30 minutes. Transfer hens to 1 or 2 baking dishes suitable for serving. Leave oven on. Discard pan juices.

Combine wine, parsley, garlic, saffron and bay leaf. Pour mixture over hens covering well. Return hens to oven in baking dish to roast for 45 minutes, until well browned, turning and basting every 15 minutes.

Chicken Cacciatore [m]

I use Cornish hens in this dish instead of chicken. The hens, actually baby chickens, make serving especially easy. The sauce makes linguini or fettucini a natural accompaniment. With a light soup, a salad and a vegetable side dish, you have a substantial and satisfying meal.

Serves 8

4 Cornish hens, about 1 ½ pounds [680 grams] each
fresh white pepper, for sprinkling
sweet paprika, for sprinkling
dried sweet basil, for sprinkling, about 2 tablespoons
dried oregano, for sprinkling, about 2 tablespoons
olive oil cooking spray
1 tablespoon extra virgin olive oil
18 ounces [500 grams] onions, sliced crosswise in thick slices
13 ½ ounces [380 grams] green peppers, seeded, sliced lengthwise in thin slices
4 large garlic cloves, sliced thinly
8 ounces [225 grams] fresh mushrooms, sliced
2 - 28 ounce [800 gram] cans tomatoes, chopped
a 6 ounce [170 gram] can tomato paste
2 teaspoons salt, or to taste
1 tablespoon dried oregano
1 tablespoon dried sweet basil
½ teaspoon fresh black pepper
½ cup [110 milliliters] dry red wine
2 tablespoons chopped fresh parsley leaves

Cut hens on either side of backbone and remove it [reserve for soup]. Cut hens in half cutting down middle of breast. I use a scissors. Trim excess skin and any fat. Cut out little rib bones, using the scissors [very easy to do]. Lightly sprinkle hens with pepper, paprika, basil and oregano.

Roast hens on a rack in a foil lined open roasting pan, skin side up in a preheated 375°F. [190°C.] oven for 30 minutes. Remove from oven and let cool. Discard pan juices.

In a sprayed Dutch oven, heat olive oil until hot. Saute onions, peppers, garlic and mushrooms until well softened. Add tomatoes, tomato paste, salt, oregano, basil and pepper. Bring mixture to a boil and simmer for 15 minutes. Add wine and parsley and a bit of water if it seems dry. This part can be prepared in advance. Store chickens and sauce, separately, in the fridge. If desired, chickens and sauce can be frozen separately.

Place hens in a large casserole dish, suitable for serving, and add sauce, mixing enough to blend hens with sauce. Bring mixture, covered, slowly to a boil and bake in a preheated 350°F. [175°C.] oven for about 1 hour to 1 hour and 15 minutes. The cacciatore can sit in a turned down oven for 20 to 30 minutes, if needed.

Serve with linguini or spinach fettucini.

Lemon Pepper Chicken with Mushrooms [m]

Sometimes the simplest and easiest dishes taste the best, this is delicious.

Serves 8

1 pound [450 grams] fresh mushrooms, sliced

olive oil cooking spray

4 Cornish hens, about 1 ½ pounds [680 grams] each

lemon pepper, for sprinkling, about 2 tablespoons

Layer mushrooms over bottom of a well sprayed 13 x 10 x 2 ½ inch [32 ½ x 25 x 6 ¼ centimeter] baking dish, suitable for serving.

Cut hens on each side of backbone and remove, [reserve for soup]. Cut hens in half, splitting down center of breast. I use a scissors. Trim excess skin and any fat. Remove small rib bones with the scissors, very easy to do. Sprinkle hens on each side with lemon pepper. Lay hens, skin side up, on mushrooms. Let marinate 6 hours to overnight.

Roast hens in a preheated 400°F. [205°C.] oven for 1 hour, until nicely browned. Serve each guest ½ hen together with some mushrooms.

Chicken with Tomatoes and Carrots [m]

A simple tasty dish with an Italian flair, easily made ahead of time. I like to serve this over pasta. Round out the meal with an Antipasto [see Index], Italian Bread [see Index] and fruit for dessert. My friend Esther Merzel suggested this dish.

Serves 8

4 Cornish hens, about 1 ½ pounds [680 grams] each
fresh white pepper, for sprinkling
hot paprika, for sprinkling
dried sweet basil, for sprinkling, about 3 to 5 tablespoons
a bit of ground allspice, for sprinkling, about 2 teaspoons
a 28 ounce [800 gram] can crushed tomatoes
an 8 ounce [225 gram] can tomato sauce
1 pound [450 grams] onions, chopped finely
6 to 8 garlic cloves, chopped finely, to taste
1 tablespoon honey
¾ cup [175 milliliters] cream sherry
1 ¾ pounds [800 grams] large carrots, halved lengthwise, halved crosswise
1 to 1 ½ pounds [450 to 680 grams] pasta [I like spaghetti]

Cut hens on each side of backbone and remove it [reserve for soup]. Cut hens in half, splitting down center of breast. I use a scissors. Trim excess skin and any fat. Remove small ribs with the scissors [very easy to do]. Lightly sprinkle hens with pepper, paprika, basil, and allspice.

Roast hens on a rack in a foil lined open roasting pan, skin side up, in a preheated 375°F. [190°C.] oven for 20 minutes. Pour off juices into a container, skim off fat and reserve gravy.

Combine tomatoes, tomato sauce, onions, garlic, honey, sherry and reserved gravy in a bowl.

In a baking pan, suitable for serving, and large enough to fit hens in a single layer [they can overlap slightly], lay carrot pieces. Place hens over carrots, skin side up. Pour tomato mixture over hens and carrots. This part can be completed ahead of time. Refrigerate until time to complete recipe.

Bake hens in a preheated 375°F. [190°C.] oven for 1 to 1 ½ hours.

Serve each person ½ hen with some carrots and serve with pasta.

Roast Goose [m]

This is a good choice for Holiday fare. It is meaty and filling. If you follow the recipe, there is almost no fat. I like the Potato - Chestnut Stuffing [see Index], baked separately, to go with the goose.

Serves 8 to 10

11 ½ pounds [5.25 kilos] goose, thawed, if frozen

a bit of lemon juice

salt, for sprinkling

fresh white pepper, for sprinkling

ground ginger, for sprinkling

sweet paprika, for sprinkling

1 orange, halved, seeded

½ onion, peeled, scored

Remove as much fat as possible from goose cavity and from neck area. Prick goose SKIN all over on fatty parts.Bring a large kettle of water, with lemon juice added, to a boil. Plunge goose into boiling water for 1 minute. Remove goose and drain. Sprinkle goose, inside and outside with salt, pepper, lots of ginger and paprika. Place orange and onion inside goose.

Roast goose on a rack in a foil lined baking pan, in a preheated 450°F. [230°C.] oven for 20 minutes.

Remove goose from oven, lower oven temperature to 275°F. [135° C.], pour off any fat that has accumulated, and prick goose SKIN all over. Replace goose in oven.

Roast goose for 4 ½ hours, pricking regularly and removing fat regularly. Discard orange and onion.

Carve goose as you would a turkey and serve with stuffing on the side.

Chicken Fricassee [with Dumplings] [m]

This hearty "stick to the ribs" chicken dish is a great winter time treat. I make this with Cornish hens but chicken parts are equally suitable. Any of the various Dumplings [see Index] are a suitable "go with".

Serves 8

4 Cornish game hens, about 1 ½ pounds [680 grams] each or 6 pounds [2.7 kilos] chicken parts, breasts, thighs, legs
salt, for sprinkling
fresh white pepper, for sprinkling
all purpose unbleached flour, for dredging, about ¼ cup [35 grams]
olive oil cooking spray
2 tablespoons extra virgin olive oil
9 ounces [250 grams] onions, chopped
4 ½ ounces [130 grams] carrots, chopped
2 celery ribs, 4 ounces [115 grams], chopped
6 cups [1.4 liters] defatted Chicken Broth [see Index] or canned
½ teaspoon ground bay leaf
1 teaspoon ground ginger
pinch ground cloves
salt, to taste

fresh white pepper, to taste

1 tablespoon chopped fresh parsley leaves

1 recipe Dumplings [see Index]

Cut hens on each side of backbone and remove it [reserve for soup]. Cut hens in half, splitting down center of breast. I use a scissors. Trim excess skin and fat. Remove small rib bones, with the scissors, very easy to do. Cut each half hen in half. Sprinkle hen quarters or chicken parts with salt and pepper and dredge in flour, shaking off excess.

In a sprayed non-stick fry pan, add 1 tablespoon oil and saute hen or chicken pieces over medium high heat, in batches, on both sides until browned, adding other tablespoon of oil as needed. Remove from pan as browned to paper towels to drain. Transfer pieces to an 8 quart [8 liter] kettle.

In same fry pan, resprayed, if necessary, saute onions, carrots and celery until softened, about 5 minutes. Transfer vegetables to kettle. Add broth, bay leaf, ginger and cloves to kettle and bring to a simmer. Simmer for 1 hour. Remove hens or chicken pieces to a plate, cover and keep warm. Taste gravy, add salt and pepper as needed.

Make dumplings and add to simmering gravy. Steam for 20 minutes without peeking, until dumplings are done. Remove dumplings with a slotted spoon to a bowl. Add parsley to gravy and mix. Return hens or chicken pieces to kettle and any juices that may have accumulated. Mix carefully with gravy. Heat until hot.

Serve with dumplings on the side, napped with gravy.

Chicken Sesame [m]

Sesame seeds are sweet, crunchy, nutty and delicious. The seeds marry particularly well with chicken. I think this is one of the tastiest chicken dishes that I make. It has a kind of Middle Eastern feeling.

Serves 8

4 Cornish game hens, about 1 ½ pounds [680 grams] each

salt, for sprinkling

fresh white pepper, for sprinkling

all purpose unbleached flour, for dredging, about ¼ cup [35 grams]

olive oil cooking spray

2 tablespoons extra virgin olive oil

about ⅓ cup [55 grams] sesame seeds

3 tablespoon chopped fresh parsley leaves

Cut hens on each side of backbone and remove it [reserve for soup]. Cut hens in half, splitting down center of breast. I use a scissors. Trim excess skin and any fat. Remove small rib bones, with the scissors, very easy to do. Cut each half hen in half. Sprinkle hen quarters with salt and pepper and dredge in flour, shaking off excess.

In a sprayed non-stick fry pan, add 1 tablespoon oil and saute hen quarters, over medium high heat, in batches, on both sides until browned, adding other tablespoon of oil as needed. Remove from pan as browned to paper towels to drain. Transfer quarters to a baking dish, suitable for serving.

Toast sesame seeds in a 250°F. [120°C.] oven for about 10 minutes, watch carefully they burn very quickly.

Sprinkle seeds on both sides of hen quarters, covering hens well. The recipe can be prepared up to this point ahead of time.

Transfer baking pan to a preheated 350°F. [175°C.] oven for 30 minutes, sprinkle with chopped parsley and serve.

Duck [m]

This is a crispy duck. I like to serve this with Sweet and Sour Red Cabbage [see Index] and Spiced Apple Sauce [see Index]. Start the duck the day before.

Serves 8

3 - 4 ¹/₂ to 5 pound [2 to 2 ¹/₂ kilo] ducklings
lemon juice
lite soy sauce, for rubbing
fresh white pepper, for sprinkling
ground ginger, for sprinkling
sweet paprika, for sprinkling

The day before, remove as much fat as possible from duck cavity and neck area. Rub ducks all over with your fingers and knuckles to loosen skin. Cut off wing tips and reserve for gravy. Reserve giblets, neck and liver for Giblet Gravy [see Index]. Make giblet gravy.

Wash ducks inside and out. Prick SKIN of ducks well on fat parts. Bring a large kettle of water, with a little lemon juice added, to a boil. Plunge ducks, one at a time, into boiling water for about 1 minute. Remove ducks and drain.

Rub ducks all over with soy sauce. Sprinkle some soy sauce inside ducks. Sprinkle ducks with pepper, a generous amount of ginger and paprika inside and out.

Place ducks, breast side up, on a rack in a foil lined roasting pan, or place ducks on vertical roasters. Roast in a preheated 475°F. [245°C.] oven for 20 minutes. Remove from oven, turn oven heat to 275°F. [135° C.]. Remove fat from bottom of roasting pan or vertical roasters, prick duck skin on fatty parts again and put back into oven.

Roast ducks for 4 hours, pricking occasionally and draining fat and juices into a container, periodically. Skim fat from these drippings and discard. Reserve juices for gravy. Add juices to gravy.

Remove ducks from oven and let cool. Cover well and refrigerate until well chilled. I do this overnight.

Cut ducks into serving pieces. Remove as much visible fat as possible. Place ducks on a rack in a foil-lined roasting pan. Place in a preheated 275°F. [135°C.] oven for 1 hour, until hot and serve.

The ducks can be held in a slow 200°F.[90°C.] oven for ¹/₂ hour, if necessary.

Chicken Paprikash *[m]*

I learned this dish from our Hungarian cousin Klari Kaufman. Use very good Hungarian paprika and the chicken will taste of its Hungarian roots. My son in law, Zev Lavon, says it reminds him of his mother, Ilana Lavon. I usually make this with legs and thighs but breasts can be substituted.

Serves 8 generously

7 to 8 pounds [3 ½ kilos] chicken legs and thighs, skin removed
salt, for sprinkling
fresh white pepper, for sprinkling
olive oil cooking spray
1 tablespoon extra virgin olive oil
1 ³⁄₄ pounds [800 grams] onions, sliced
1 tablespoon ground caraway
4 tablespoons sweet Hungarian paprika
1 cup [225 milliliters] no-fat non-dairy creamer
2 tablespoons white vinegar
1 recipe cooked Nuckerl or Spaetzle [see Index]

Lightly sprinkle salt and pepper on chicken pieces and set aside.

In a sprayed large Dutch oven, in olive oil, saute onions until golden. Add caraway and paprika, stir well and brown slightly, about 2 minutes. Add chicken pieces, mix well to coat with onion mixture.

Cover tightly and simmer over low heat, until chicken is tender, about 1 to 1 ½ hours. Transfer chicken pieces to a heated platter and keep it warm.

Or set aside for up to 2 days or freeze for longer storage. Freeze chicken and sauce separately.

Combine creamer and vinegar and add to gravy. Heat until hot, mixing until well combined. Return chicken to pot, together with any juices that may have accumulated. Heat over low heat until hot, stirring occasionally,

Serve with Nuckerl or Spaetzle [see Index], napped with some of the gravy.

Roast Chicken [m]

I use game hens [really baby chickens] which are perfect and convenient to serve. I find that 1/2 hen per person is an adequate portion. This is a tasty, satisfying and simple dish. I like to serve roasted chicken with interesting side dishes and homemade bread.

Serves 8

4 Cornish hens, about 1 ½ pounds [680 grams] each

salt, for sprinkling

fresh white pepper, for sprinkling

ground ginger, for sprinkling

sweet paprika, for sprinkling

Cut hens on each side of backbone and remove it [reserve for soup]. Cut hens in half, splitting down center of breast. I use a scissors. Trim excess skin and any fat. Remove small ribs with the scissors, very easy to do. Sprinkle hens on both sides with salt, pepper, lots of ginger and paprika. Place hens on a rack in a foil lined baking pan.

Roast hens in a preheated 400°F. [205°C.] oven for 30 to 40 minutes, until hens are brown and crispy.

Spicy Barbeque Chicken [m]

Cornish hens are used in this dish instead of chicken. The hens, actually baby chickens, make serving especially easy. I cook these in the oven as I live in an apartment but the chickens are delicious done outside on a barbeque. You can start these the day before or early in the day. They are just slightly spicy.

Serves 8

4 Cornish hens, about 1 ½ pounds [680 grams] each

Spicy Dry Rub [see Index]

a 28 ounce [800 gram] can crushed tomatoes

3 ½ ounces [100 grams] onions, chopped finely

1 heaping tablespoon chopped garlic

⅛ teaspoon ground cayenne pepper

½ teaspoon Tabasco sauce

½ teaspoon dried tarragon

1 teaspoon hot paprika

1 teaspoon sweet paprika

1 teaspoon fresh black pepper

2 teaspoons dry mustard

2 teaspoons chili powder

1 tablespoon sugar

1 tablespoon soy sauce

2 tablespoons salt

3 tablespoons Worcestershire sauce

4 tablespoons red wine vinegar

Cut hens on either side of backbone and remove it [reserve for soup]. Cut hens in half splitting down middle of breast. I use a scissors. Trim excess skin and any fat. Cut out little rib bones, using the scissors, very easy to do. Cut each half in half. Lightly sprinkle hens all over with spicy dry rub.

Roast quarters on a rack in a foil lined baking pan in a preheated 400°F. [205°C.] oven for 20 minutes, turning after 10 minutes. Set aside.

Combine the rest of the ingredients, for the sauce, in a saucepan. Bring to a boil, cover, and simmer for 10 minutes, stirring occasionally.

Dip each hen quarter into sauce and lay in an open roasting pan in one layer. Pour the rest of the sauce over hens. Let marinate in fridge for 4 hours to overnight, turning 2 times. Drain excess sauce before cooking.

Roast hens on a rack in a foil lined open roasting pan, in a preheated 400°F. [205°C.] oven for 45 minutes total, turning every 15 minutes. Or roast on a barbeque grill for same length of time.

Transfer hens to a platter and serve.

Turkey Gumbo *[m]*

Gumbo is a famous, flavorful and spicy New Orleans stew. Served over rice it is almost a whole meal-in-a-pot. This gumbo makes fantastic use of leftover turkey and its gravy. The two necessary components of gumbo, okra and filé powder, are included in this recipe. I am especially fond of this gumbo.

Serves 8

olive oil cooking spray
14 ounces [400 grams] onions, chopped
7 ounces [200 grams] green peppers, diced small
9 ounces [250 grams] celery, chopped, 2 large ribs
7 ounces [200 grams] cabbage, chopped
6 garlic cloves, chopped
¹/₂ cup [40 grams] chopped parsley leaves
a 28 ounce [800 gram] can tomatoes, cut up, with juice
6 cups [900 milliliters] turkey or Chicken Broth [see Index] or canned
leftover turkey giblet gravy, if available [I always have leftover gravy] 4 cups [900 milliliters] if possible or extra broth as necessary
1 smoked turkey leg, about 9 ounces [250 grams]
5 ¹/₂ ounces [150 grams] smoked turkey wing tips, about 3
1 pound [450 grams] spicy turkey sausages, blanched 15 minutes, sliced into bite size,

salt, to taste

fresh black pepper, to taste

$1/4$ teaspoon dried red pepper flakes or to taste

1 teaspoon dried thyme

1 teaspoon dried basil

1 teaspoon dried oregano

$1/2$ teaspoon ground bayleaf

4 to 5 cups [900 to 1.2 liters] diced leftover turkey, dark and
white meat

20 ounces [580 grams] okra, sliced, fresh or frozen

2 tablespoons filé powder

In a sprayed 8 quart [8 liter] kettle saute onions, peppers, celery, cabbage, garlic and parsley over low heat, stirring occasionally, until vegetables are well softened, about 25 minutes. Add tomatoes, broth, gravy, turkey leg and wing tips and bring to a boil. Add sausages, salt, pepper, red pepper, thyme, basil, oregano and bay leaf. Turn to a simmer and simmer for 30 minutes, covered, stirring occasionally.

Remove smoked turkey pieces, discard skin and bones, cut meat into dice, return to kettle along with diced turkey and okra. Simmer until okra is tender, about 15 minutes.

The gumbo can be completed up to this point 2 days ahead of time or frozen.

Return to a simmer before adding filé powder just before serving. Filé thickens the stew and can become stringy if cooked for any length of time after being added to gumbo.

Serve over steamed Rice [see Index].

Roast Turkey [m]

I am famous for this recipe, which I have updated for living at sea level in the U.S. The secret of this turkey is not to overcook. This is an American fetish. I promise you that the turkey will be done, organisms will be killed and if you follow the time exactly, you will get raves. This is always Holiday fare for our family. I always cook a larger turkey than I need just for the leftovers. You must use a fresh killed turkey for best results.

Allow 3/4 pound [340 grams] per person

The day before, clean and season turkey. Sprinkle inside and outside all over with salt, fresh white pepper, lots of ground ginger and a light sprinkling of sweet paprika. Cover loosely and refrigerate overnight. Reserve neck, giblets and liver for gravy. Make Giblet Gravy [see Index].

The next day just before putting turkey in the oven, if you desire, stuff turkey with cold stuffing of your choice [see Index] [see Note] and wrap turkey well with heavy duty foil, well sprayed with cooking spray, covering wing tips, leg ends and any other protruding parts with extra padded foil, so as not to puncture outer foil covering. Roast according to following chart.

Preheat oven to 450°F. [230° C.]
Ready to cook weight [after cleaning] unstuffed:
5.5 to 9 pounds [2.5 to 4 kilos] - 2 hours to 2 ½ hours
9 to 13 pounds [4.5 to 6 kilos] - 2 ½ hours to 2 ¾ hours
13 to 17 pounds [6 to 7.7 kilos] - 2 ¾ hours to 3 hours
17 to 21 pounds [7.7 to 9.5 kilos] - 3 hours to 3 ¼ hours
22 to 25.5 pounds [10 to 11.5 kilos] 3 ¼ hours to 3 ½ hours

Half an hour before turkey is done, open and fold back foil so that turkey can brown. Remove from oven, re-cover with foil and let turkey sit for 15 minutes before slicing.

Decide on your serving time and count backwards to determine time to preheat oven [allow 15 minutes]. Don't forget the 15 minutes sitting time before slicing. Re-covering turkey with foil after removing it from the oven keeps it warm and allows juices to be absorbed by turkey. ENJOY!

Note: Refrigerate prepared stuffing as bacteria can grow in warm stuffing. I prefer to bake the stuffing separate from the turkey. Follow directions for stuffing recipe of your choice [see Index].

VEGETABLES AND SIDE DISHES

Artichokes *[p]*

Artichokes, served hot, are an unusual and special vegetable. Served cold and halved, they make an interesting first or salad course. Artichokes are very cheap in Israel so we had them often.

Allow one artichoke per person

Buy artichokes that are tightly closed without any brown bruising. Have ready a large bowl of water, to which juice of $1/2$ lemon has been added. Cut off stem close to bottom. Break off lower leaves, about 2 rows. With a scissors, cut straight across top of each remaining leaves, cutting off the thorny tip, going round and round artichoke. With a sharp knife, cut off top of artichoke about 1 or 2 rows down. As each artichoke is prepared, wash well and drop into acidulated water bath.

Half fill a large kettle with salted water. Add juice of half a lemon and drop in squeezed lemon. Bring water to a boil and add artichokes. Simmer for about 45 minutes until tender. Test with a skewer inserted into center.

Drain artichokes upside down and serve hot with melted margarine or cold, cut in half, with choke removed and served with a mustard vinaigrette.

Bean Medley *[p]*

I often prepare these beans when making Chili [see Index]. They are also a nice side dish with other meals. "De-gassing" the beans makes them more digestible for most people. I am amazed by the number of people who love beans.

Makes about 10 cups [2.25 liters]

¹/₂ pound [225 grams] dry red kidney beans, about 1 ¹/₂ cups heavy, picked over for stones
¹/₂ pound [225 grams] dry black beans [turtle beans], picked over for stones
¹/₂ pound [225 grams] dry small white pea or navy beans, picked over for stones
water, for de-gassing
1 onion, halved lengthwise through root, stuck with
4 whole cloves
2 or 3 whole bay leaves
2 large garlic cloves, sliced thinly
8 cups [1.8 liters] water
a 28 ounce [800 gram] can whole tomatoes, chopped
olive oil cooking spray
1 tablespoon extra virgin olive oil
18 ounces [500 grams] onions, peeled, chopped

4 or 5 large garlic cloves, chopped
1 teaspoon dried thyme
1 teaspoon dried basil
1 teaspoon dried oregano
1 teaspoon dried cumin
pinch ground allspice
2 $1/2$ teaspoons sugar
1 tablespoon chili powder
salt, to taste
fresh black pepper, to taste

Cover beans with 20 cups [5.8 liters] water, bring to a boil and boil for 2 minutes. Cover and let sit for 1 hour. Drain and discard water. This degasses the beans.

Place beans in an 8 quart [8 liter] kettle. Add halved onion, with cloves, bay leaves, sliced garlic and 8 cups [1.8 liters] water. Bring to a boil and simmer, covered, until beans are almost tender, about 1 $1/2$ hours, stirring occasionally. Drain beans and discard onion and bay leaves. Return beans to kettle and add tomatoes.

In a sprayed non-stick fry pan, in olive oil, saute chopped onions and garlic, until browned, stirring frequently, about 15 minutes. Add onion mixture to beans along with the rest of the ingredients, except salt and pepper. Simmer until beans are soft, about 1 hour. Add salt and pepper, to taste. The beans can be made several days ahead and can be frozen.

Broccoli and Spinach Bake [d]

This side dish is an interesting vegetable combination. The acidic taste of spinach is contrasted by the sweetness of the broccoli. I prepare this ahead of time, even the day before, and bake it just before serving. My friend Selma Pustin suggested this recipe.

Serves 8

1 $^1/_3$ pounds [600 grams] broccoli florets [reserve stalks for
    another use or buy just florets]

2 - 10 ounce [280 gram] packages frozen chopped spinach

1 tablespoon [15 grams] margarine

butter flavored cooking spray

2 tablespoons all purpose unbleached flour

1 $^1/_2$ cups [350 milliliters] hot skim milk

$^1/_2$ cup [55 grams] grated Parmesan cheese

$^1/_8$ teaspoon ground nutmeg

pinch ground cayenne pepper

salt, to taste

fresh white pepper, to taste

Cook broccoli in boiling salted water until very soft. Drain, chop coarsely and set aside.

Cook spinach according to package directions. Drain and squeeze by handfuls, all liquid from cooked spinach. Set aside.

Melt margarine in a sprayed saucepan. Add flour and whisk until well combined. Add hot milk all at once whisking constantly and cook sauce until it thickens. Add cheese, nutmeg, cayenne, salt and pepper. Remove from heat and add to spinach mixing with a fork, until well combined. Add spinach mixture to broccoli and combine.

Pour broccoli spinach mixture into a 2 $^1/_2$ quart [2 $^1/_2$ liter] casserole dish suitable for serving. This part can be prepared ahead. If prepared a day or two in advance refrigerate until about 1 hour before serving.

Bake in a preheated 325°F. [165°C.] oven for 20 to 30 minutes until hot and bubbly. The casserole can wait in a turned down oven for 30 minutes or so.

Broccoli [p]

Broccoli is a lovely vegetable to serve to a group. It is colorful, marries well with many main dishes and appeals to lots of people. I often prepare it in the morning and reheat on a steamer rack just before serving. You can serve it with a sauce but I prefer it plain or with a bit of reduced calorie margarine.

Serves 8

2 ¹/₂ pounds [1.1 kilos] broccoli
water to cover
¹/₂ lemon
salt, to taste

Separate broccoli into manageble florets and stalks. Trim all leaves and peel stalks. Cut stalks diagonally into bite size.

Bring a large kettle filled with enough water to cover broccoli, to a boil. Squeeze lemon into water and drop in squeezed lemon. Add salt to taste. Add broccoli and cook until crisp tender [even a little less as it will continue to cook a bit].

Serve.

If you are preparing broccoli early in the day, drain it and cool it in a large colander under cold running water. Place a steamer basket in a casserole dish and fill with broccoli. Just before serving, add a bit of water to casserole and reheat broccoli, covered, until steaming.

If you add broccoli to rolling boiling water, it will remain a bright green. If you add broccoli to cold water and then bring it to a boil, it will lose its bright green color.

Corn Cakes [p]

This terrific side dish can be made ahead and rewarmed just before serving. The cakes can be frozen for a month or so. Thaw and warm as an appetizer or a side dish at dinner. I think they are very unique.

Makes about 28 regular size, 60 small size

1 $^3/_4$ pounds [800 grams] canned corn, drained, reserve liquid
about $^3/_4$ cup [105 grams] all purpose unbleached flour
2 egg whites
2 teaspoons sugar
$^3/_4$ cup [175 milliliters] corn liquid [plus water, if necessary]
salt, to taste
fresh white pepper, to taste
vegetable cooking spray

Lightly crush corn with a potato masher or in a food processor. Mix corn with the rest of the ingredients, except spray, to make a thick pancake mixture. Measure 4 tablespoons [$^1/_4$ cup measure] for each cake and saute in a well sprayed non-stick fry pan, in batches, over medium heat, until cakes are browned on each side, respraying pan as necessary. Drain cakes on paper towels. Keep warm in a 250°F. [120°C.] oven until all cakes are done. [Or make them half size to serve to a large party or as an hors' d'oeurve.] Serve.

The cakes can be prepared a day or 2 ahead and reheated in oven or microwave or they can be frozen. Thaw before reheating.

Carrot Cakes [p]

These little cakes are an interesting and unusual way to serve carrots as a vegetable side dish. Made half size, they are also suitable as an hors'd'oeuvre.

Makes about 28 regular size, 60 small size

2 cups [280 grams] all purpose unbleached flour
4 teaspoons baking powder
4 tablespoons snipped fresh chives
2 tablespoons chopped fresh parsley leaves
1 teaspoon dried thyme
1 tablespoon ground ginger
2 teaspoons salt
fresh white pepper, to taste
2 teaspoons Worcestershire sauce
1 tablespoon brown sugar
¹/₈ teaspoon ground nutmeg
2 ¹/₂ cups [560 milliliters] water
¹/₂ cup [110 milliliters] frozen egg substitute, thawed
2 ¹/₄ pounds [1 kilo] carrots, peeled, shredded
vegetable cooking spray

Combine flour, baking powder, chives, parsley, thyme, ginger, salt, pepper, Worcestershire, sugar, nutmeg, water and egg substitute. Gradually add carrots and mix well. Let sit covered for ¹/₂ hour.

Measure 4 tablespoons [¹/₄ cup] for each cake and saute in a well sprayed non-stick fry pan, in batches, over medium heat, until cakes are brown on each side, re-spraying pan as necessary. Drain cakes on paper towels. Keep warm in a 250°F. [120°C.] oven until all cakes are done. [Or make them half size to serve at a large party or as an hors' d'oeuvre.] Serve.

The cakes can be prepared a day or 2 ahead and reheated in oven or microwave or they can be frozen. Thaw before reheating.

Farfel [m or p]

Farfel is a simple side dish, nice to serve instead of rice or noodles or potatoes. It is quickly and easily made and is very low fat.

Serves 8

vegetable cooking spray

12 ounces [340 grams] onions, diced finely

1 tablespoon margarine or extra virgin olive oil

12 ounces [340 grams] farfel [short cut rice or pea shaped macaroni]

1 teaspoon salt

4 cups [900 milliliters] hot defatted Chicken Broth [see Index] or pareve chicken flavored soup, from the mix

In a sprayed Dutch oven, saute onions in margarine or oil until well browned. Add the rest of the ingredients and mix well. Cover and simmer over low heat for 25 minutes, stirring occasionally. Serve.

Peas and Mushrooms [p]

I use Portobello mushrooms in this simple but flavorful side dish. It is quickly and easily made. Prepare it early in the day and reheat in the microwave just before serving.

Serves 8

11 ½ ounces [325 grams] Portobello mushrooms

olive oil cooking spray

¾ cup [175 milliliters] water

1 pound [450 grams] frozen petite green peas

1 teaspoon dried thyme, crumbled in your fingers

salt, to taste

fresh black pepper, to taste

Wash mushrooms well. Cut off stems and reserve for another use. Halve caps and slice each half thinly. In a well sprayed non-stick fry pan, saute mushroom caps for 5 minutes. Add water and simmer caps, uncovered, for 10 minutes. Add peas, thyme, salt and pepper. Stir well and remove from heat.

Drain and serve.

Or drain and set aside in a microwave safe bowl, covered with film, until just before serving. Reheat in a microwave on high for 2 to 3 minutes, until hot.

Polenta [d or p]

Polenta is a particular favorite of mine to serve at Italian dinners. This is a simple dish, easy to prepare ahead of time and with an optional variation for a dairy or meat meal.

Serves 8

1 ¹/₂ cups [210 grams] yellow corn meal
1 ¹/₂ cups [350 milliliters] cold water
2 teaspoons salt
4 cups [900 milliliters] boiling water
pareve butter flavored cooking spray
optional: 1 cup [100 grams] grated Parmesan cheese
optional: bottled or homemade salsa as a garnish

Mix corn meal with cold water and salt. Slowly pour corn meal mixture into rapidly boiling water and whisk constantly. Turn down heat and cook over low heat, stirring frequently, until very thick and smooth, about 15 minutes.

Pour mixture into 2 sprayed non-stick loaf pans, 4 x 8 inches [10 x 20 centimeters]. Chill until firm and cold.

Unmold loaves onto a cutting board and slice each loaf into 8 slices. Place slices in one layer in a foil lined shallow baking pan. Spray each slice with cooking spray. If using, sprinkle half of cheese evenly over slices.

Broil slices about 4 inches [10 centimeters] from heat until lightly browned, about 3 to 5 minutes. Turn slices carefully. Spray each slice with cooking spray. Sprinkle second half of cheese, if using, evenly over slices. Broil second side until lightly browned. The polenta can be kept warm in a slow oven until ready to serve, if necessary.

Serve with warmed salsa, if desired.

Polenta Polo Grill [d]

This delicious polenta is a variation of one that I ate at the hugely successful Polo Grill, run by my friends, the Kaplans, here in Baltimore. Chef Marmelstein gave me his recipe and I adapted it for this book.

Serves 8

3 cups [700 milliliters] evaporated skim milk

1 cup [175 grams] semolina flour [available in Italian markets]

2 ounces [55 grams] Gorgonzola cheese, crumbled

salt, to taste

fresh black pepper, to taste

all purpose unbleached flour, for dusting

butter flavored cooking spray

2 teaspoons margarine, divided

In a saucepan, bring milk to a boil. Slowly whisk in semolina. Cook over very low heat, stirring frequently, until very thick and smooth, about 15 minutes. Add cheese and mix until cheese is melted. Add salt and pepper, to taste.

Pour mixture into an 8 x 8 inch [20 x 20 centimeter] baking pan. Chill until firm and cold. Cut into quarters. Cut each quarter, on the diagonal, in half, making 8 triangles.

Lightly dust triangles with flour and saute, in batches, in a sprayed non-stick fry pan, with margarine added, 1 teaspoon at a time, until lightly browned on each side.

Keep warm in a slow oven or rewarm in a microwave and serve warm.

Potato Kugel [p]

I make this ahead of time and reheat it for dinner. It is crusty on the outside and moist in the middle. Almost everyone likes this delicious pudding.

Serves 8

about 3 ¹/₃ pounds [1.5 kilos] potatoes, peeled
1 pound [450 grams] onions, minced
1 whole egg
1 cup [225 milliliters] frozen egg substitute, thawed
1 tablespoon salt
³/₄ teaspoon fresh white pepper
¹/₂ to ³/₄ cup [75 to 105 grams] all purpose unbleached flour
olive oil cooking spray
1 tablespoon margarine, ¹/₂ ounce [15 grams]

Shred potatoes and place immediately into a bowl of cold water. This is an important step as it keeps potatoes white. Drain well and squeeze by handfuls to remove as much moisture as possible.

In a large bowl, place potatoes, onions, egg, egg substitute, salt and pepper. Mix with a large fork. Add flour as necessary to absorb excess moisture.

In a well sprayed 9 x 11 x 2 inch [22 ¹/₂ x 27 ¹/₂ x 5 centimeter] baking pan, suitable for serving, add margarine. Place pan in a preheated 375°F. [190°C.] oven for 3 minutes. Remove pan from oven and add potato mixture to sizzling pan, tamping down and smoothing top. Bake uncovered for 1 hour.

Just before serving, reheat pudding in a preheated 375°F. [190° C.] oven for 15 minutes.

Cut into squares and serve from baking pan.

Sweet and Sour Red Cabbage [p]

This delicious vegetable side dish can be eaten hot or cold. I pariularly like to serve it with Roast Duck [see Index].

Serves 8

2 ¹/₂ pounds [1.15 kilos] red cabbage
salt, for sprinkling
vegetable cooking spray
8 ounces [225 grams] red onions, sliced thinly
12 ounces [340 grams] tart apples, peeled, cored, sliced
³/₄ cup [175 milliliters] dry red wine
³/₄ cup [175 milliliters] pareve beef flavored or chicken flavored soup, from the mix or vegetable broth
1 ¹/₂ tablespoons brown sugar
¹/₂ cup [110 milliliters] basalmic vinegar
salt, to taste
fresh white pepper, to taste
1 ¹/₂ tablespoons whole caraway seeds

Remove outer leaves of cabbage head. Quarter, core and shred cabbage. Lightly sprinkle salt on cabbage and place in a colander to wilt for 30 minutes. Rinse and drain well.

Spray a Dutch oven and heat over medium high heat. Add onions and saute until well wilted. Add cabbage, cover and steam, over medium low heat for 10 minutes. Add the rest of the ingredients and stir to mix. Cover and simmer mixture for 1 ¹/₂ hours, stirring occaionally. Uncover, taste and add more sugar or vinegar, if needed. Simmer an additional 10 minutes, uncovered.

Serve hot or cold.

The cabbage can be made ahead and reheated, and can be frozen.

Red Beans and Rice [p]

For some this is almost the perfect food nutritionally. I like to serve this dish as a side with Chili [see Index] as an alternative to Bean Medley [see Index] which I also serve with Chili. Red beans and rice have a wonderful and varied flavor, suitable as a side dish with many main courses.

Serves 8 or more

12 ½ ounces [350 grams] small dry red beans
15 cups [3.37 liters] water, for degassing
water, for cooking
9 ounces [250 grams] onions, quartered, stuck with
4 whole cloves
20 ounces [580 grams] fresh tomatoes, peeled or canned
4 to 8 garlic cloves, sliced, to taste
2 bay leaves
4 sprigs fresh parsley, chopped
salt, to taste
fresh black pepper, to taste
2 tablespoons [55 grams] vegetable oil
18 ounces [500 grams] onions, chopped

1 tablespoon chopped garlic

1 ¹/₂ cups [270 grams] raw rice

pareve beef flavored soup, from the mix, as needed, about 2 ¹/₂ to 4 cups [1 liter]

Place beans in a large kettle, add 15 cups [3.37 liters] water and bring to a boil. Boil for 2 minutes, cover and let sit for 1 hour. Drain. This degasses the beans.

Place beans in a 4 quart [4 liter] pot and add enough water to cover beans by about 2 inches [5 centimeters]. Add quartered onions, with cloves, tomatoes, sliced garlic, bay leaves and parsley. Bring to a boil and simmer, covered, stirring occasionally, until beans are tender, 2 to 4 hours, depending on age of beans. Add water as necessary to keep beans covered.

Drain beans over a bowl and reserve liquid. Discard onions, with cloves, and bay leaves. Add salt and pepper to taste. Set aside.

In same pot, in oil, saute chopped onions and garlic until well softened. Add rice and saute for 3 minutes. Measure reserved bean liquid and add enough soup to measure 4 ¹/₂ cups [1 liter]. Add liquid to rice mixture, bring to a boil and boil, covered for 7 minutes.

Transfer rice mixture to a 3 ¹/₂ quart [3 ¹/₂ liter] casserole. Add beans and combine well. This part can be prepared ahead of time [even 2 days] until about 1 hour before serving.

Bake in a preheated 350°F. [175°C.] oven for 20 to 30 minutes, until all liquid is absorbed.

Serve from the casserole.

Ratatouille [p]

This is a good ratatouille, made with oven roasted vegetables and almost no oil. It is an excellent side dish to go with any kind of meat or chicken or fish. I also like it for lunch or as a light snack.

Makes about 3 ½ quarts [3 liters]

2 ¼ to 2 ½ pounds [1 kilo] eggplant, unpeeled, cut into ½ inch [1 ¾ centimeter] slices, crosswise
salt, for sprinkling
1 whole head garlic
olive oil cooking spray
2 ¼ pounds [1 kilo] onions, cut crosswise into ½ inch [1 ¾ centimeter] slices
1 ½ pounds [680 grams] green bell peppers, halved, cored, seeded, membranes discarded, cut into wide strips, lengthwise
1 ½ pounds [680 grams] zucchini squash, unpeeled, halved lengthwise
2 ¼ pounds [1 kilo] tomatoes, cored, halved, seeded
4 ½ ounces [125 grams] celery, sliced thickly
3 ounces [90 grams] leeks, white part only, sliced thickly
1 tablespoon salt, or, to taste
handful fresh basil leaves, sliced, or 1 tablespoon dried basil
handful fresh parsley leaves, chopped coarsely
1 teaspoon fresh black pepper

Sprinkle eggplant slices with salt and let drain in a colander for 30 minutes. Rinse, drain and set aside.

Remove papery skin from garlic head without exposing cloves. Cut off top of garlic head, lightly spray and wrap head in a piece of aluminum foil. Bake in a preheated 450°F. [230°C.] oven for 30 minutes, until it is very soft. Do not turn off oven. Squeeze out garlic pulp from cloves and set aside.

Spray 2 or 3 shallow baking pans. Lay eggplant, onions, green peppers, zucchini and tomato slices in pans in one layer. Place pans in lower and middle part of oven and roast vegetables for about 20 minutes until lightly browned, switching pans and racks after 10 minutes. Let cool slightly and remove tomato skins and pepper skins, if possible. [This is not too important, although I prefer the skins off.]

Cut all vegetables into large dice and place in an 8 quart [8 liter] kettle together with garlic pulp and the rest of the ingredients. Simmer stew for 1 hour, stirring occasionally.

Cool and store in jars in the fridge. The ratatouille keeps well for at least 2 weeks.

Rice [m or p]

You can use any kind of long grain rice to make steamed rice, but I prefer Basmati or any of the other aromatic rices. These rices can stand on their own and are delicious. Rice is a staple in the Middle East.

Makes about 6 cups [280 grams]

2 cups [360 grams] long grain aromatic rice, rinsed

olive oil cooking spray

1 teaspoon extra virgin olive oil

3 cups [700 milliliters] water or chicken, vegetable or beef broth

salt, to taste

Spray a saucepan, add oil and heat pan. Add rice and saute stirring until rice becomes a little translucent, about 3 minutes. Add liquid, cover and bring to a boil. Turn heat to the lowest possible heat and steam for 20 minutes without peeking. Turn off heat and let sit covered for an additional 10 minutes.

Cooked rice can be frozen. Thaw before reheating in oven or microwave.

Roasted Corn [p]

This is not only the easist way to prepare corn for a crowd, but it is the most delicious, also the easiest to husk. I often fix the corn early in the day and rewarm it in the microwave for a quick and simple vegetable.

Peel back husk without removing it, to expose silk. Carefully remove as much silk as possible and refold husk back around corn. Half fill a sink with water and soak corn for about 10 to 15 minutes while oven is preheating to 450°F. [230°C.].

Shake off water and roast corn directly on a rack for 10 to 12 minutes depending on how fresh corn is. Remove corn from oven and place on racks to cool just until it can be handled easily. Husk corn and place on plates and serve or cover with plastic wrap.

Just before serving, rewarm corn on high in microwave until hot.

Serve with reduced calorie margarine and salt and pepper, if desired.

Roasted Garlic Potatoes [p]

This is a simple potato side dish for garlic lovers. Crunchy on the outside, tender on the inside and very easy to prepare.

Serves 8

1 ¹/₂ pounds [680 grams] tiny red potatoes
2 ¹/₂ tablespoons finely chopped garlic
salt, to taste
fresh black pepper, to taste
about 1 tablespoon sweet Hungarian paprika
olive oil cooking spray

Wash unpeeled potatoes well and slice into ¹/₂ inch [1 ³/₄ centimeter] slices. Place in a mixing bowl together with garlic. Sprinkle with salt, pepper and paprika and mix carefully with a large fork. Spray a 13 x 10 inch [32 ¹/₂ x 25 centimeter] baking pan and add potato mixture spreading evenly. Spray potatoes and mix.

Bake in a preheated 450°F. [230°C.] oven for 25 to 30 minutes, turning and mixing once or twice, until potatoes are nicely browned.

Sauerkraut [p]

This is a regular side dish that I serve with Meat Loaf [see Index] and Roast Turkey [see Index]. Sauerkraut is a traditional Thanksgiving vegetable in Maryland. I also like it cold or hot on sandwiches.

Serves 8

2 pounds [900 grams] fresh sauerkraut
1 ¹/₂ tablespoons caraway seeds
10 juniper berries, tied in a piece of cheese cloth
1 cup [225 milliliters] dry white wine
water, as needed
optional: salt, to taste

Rinse and drain sauerkraut. Combine all the ingredients, except salt, in a saucepan. Bring to a boil, cover and simmer for 3 or 4 hours, adding water as necessary, stirring occasionally. Discard cheese cloth with juniper berries. Add salt to taste.

The sauerkraut can be prepared a week or so in advance.

Succotash [p]

I love the smell of succotash cooking. It just makes my mouth water. It can be made all year round with frozen vegetables but it is very special in the summer with corn freshly cut off the cob. I also love to eat the leftovers cold the next day.

Serves 8 hungry people

2-10 ounce [280 gram] packages frozen baby lima beans
1 ½ cups [350 milliliters] water
1 ½ pounds [680 grams] fresh white [Silver Queen] corn, cut from the cob, about 6 to 7 ears, or frozen white corn
salt, to taste
fresh black pepper, to taste, I like lots
optional: no-fat or reduced fat margarine

Place lima beans and water in a medium saucepan and bring to a boil. Simmer, covered until beans are tender, about 30 minutes. Add corn, salt and pepper and simmer until corn is tender, about 5 minutes.

Turn into a serving bowl and add margarine to taste, if desired.

Southern Stewed Green Beans [m]

These beans are cooked slowly for a long time. I love the smoky flavor of these "over cooked" beans. The pot "likker" asks for a piece of Rye Bread or Biscuit [see Index] to sop up the juices.

Serves 8

4 cups [900 milliliters] water
2 pounds [900 grams] frozen whole green beans or fresh, trimmed
3 to 5 ounces [90 to 140 grams] smoked turkey wing tip or piece of wing
salt, to taste
fresh black pepper, to taste
garlic granules, to taste

In a saucepan, bring water to a boil. Add beans and turkey. Bring back to a boil, turn heat down and simmer for 1 hour. Add salt, pepper and garlic to taste and simmer an additional 30 minutes.

Spinach - Rice Bake [d]

My friend Louise Cavagnaro [Cavi] gave me this very nice recipe. It combines 2 vegetables that I like in an interesting dish. It is easy to prepare ahead and bake just before serving or baked ahead and re-heated just before serving.

Serves 8

a 10 ounce [280 gram] package frozen, chopped spinach
1 cup [225 grams] frozen egg substitute, thawed
²/₃ cup [150 milliliters] skim milk
2 tablespoons margarine, melted, cooled
1 large shallot, minced
3 tablespoons finely chopped parsley leaves
1 teaspoon Worcestershire sauce
1 teaspoon seasoned salt
¹/₂ teaspoon dried thyme
¹/₂ teaspoon ground nutmeg
3 cups [420 grams] cooked brown rice, [1 cup raw]
³/₄ cup [75 grams] grated Parmesan cheese
olive oil cooking spray

Cook spinach according to package directions. Drain well. [No need to squeeze.]

Combine egg substitute, milk, margarine, shallot, parsley, Worcestershire, salt, thyme and nutmeg. Add spinach, rice and cheese and mix with a fork to combine well. Pour into a sprayed 8 inch [20 centimeter] square baking pan and spread evenly.

Bake in a preheated 325°F. [165°C.] oven for 50 minutes. Spray the top and bake an additional 10 minutes.

Cut into squares to serve.

Stewed Tomatoes [p]

I like to make this when summer tomatoes are at their peak. In the winter, I use a good brand of canned diced tomatoes. I devised this recipe especially for my friend Lois Macht, who loves stewed tomatoes.

Serves 8

3 ³/₄ pounds [1.7 kilos] tomatoes, peeled, cut into dice
12 ounces [340 grams] green peppers, diced finely
12 ounces [340 grams] onions, chopped
¹/₃ cup [21 grams] fresh basil leaves, packed tightly, sliced
2 teaspoons minced garlic
salt, to taste
fresh black pepper, to taste
1 to 2 teaspoons sugar, to taste

Combine all the ingredients in a saucepan. Bring to a simmer and simmer, uncovered, until tomatoes are tender and dish is very thick, about 1 ¹/₂ to 2 hours.

Stewed tomatoes can be made as much as a week ahead of time.

Baked Stuffed Potatoes *[p]*

This tasty side dish was invented by Barry Bogarad, chef, friend and son of my very good friend, Joan Bogarad.

Serves 8

4 russet potatoes, about 2 ¹/₃ pounds [1 kilo] total
about 1 ¹/₂ cups [350 milliliters] vegetable broth, divided
pareve butter flavored cooking spray
7 ounces [200 grams] onions, chopped
1 tablespoon chopped garlic
5 ¹/₂ ounces [150 grams] mushrooms, chopped coarsely
a 10 ounce [280 gram] package chopped spinach, thawed,
**   squeezed**
pinch ground nutmeg
salt, to taste
fresh black pepper, to taste

Bake potatoes until fork tender. Set aside.

In a sprayed non-stick fry pan, saute onions until well browning and starting to caramelized. Add garlic and mushrooms and saute until mushrooms are tender. Add spinach, nutmeg and about ³/₄ cup [175 milliliters] vegetable broth and continue cooking until spinach is tender. Set aside.

Cut potatoes in half lengthwise. Scoop out potato flesh, leaving a thin shell of potato inside skin. Chop potatoes in a food processor with enough vegetable broth added until potatoes are creamy and fluffy. Add salt and pepper to taste.

Combine spinach mixture and potato mixture until well mixed. Divide and pile mixture into potato shells. Place stuffed potatoes in a baking pan large enough to hold potatoes in one layer. This part can be prepared ahead, even a day ahead. Cover and refrigerate. Bring to room temperature before baking.

Bake potatoes in a preheated 350°F. [175°C.] oven until potatoes are heated through, about 30 minutes.

Vegetable Latkes *[p]*

This wonderful side dish can be served hot or cold. Latkes are also good as a first course or appetizer. Make them half size to serve a large party. Save the blanching water for soup.

Makes 20 to 24 latkes

water, for blanching
a 10 ounce [280 gram] package frozen chopped spinach
4 ounces [115 grams] parsnips, peeled, shredded
6 ounces [175 grams] carrots, peeled, shredded
1 pound [450 grams] corn, fresh, frozen or canned
5 ounces [135 grams] onions, chopped
9 ounces [250 grams] zucchini, shredded
1 tablespoon chopped garlic
²/₃ cup [150 milliliters] blanching water
¹/₂ cup [110 milliliters] frozen egg substitute, thawed
³/₄ cup [105 grams] all purpose unbleached flour
2 teaspoons baking powder
1 tablespoon Worcestershire sauce
salt, to taste
fresh black pepper, to taste
olive oil cooking spray
1 tablespoon extra virgin olive oil, divided

Bring a medium saucepan half filled with water to a boil. Blanch vegetables, one at a time, for 2 minutes each. Remove vegetables with a slotted spoon. Drain well. Squeeze spinach and zucchini by handfuls until almost dry. Reserve water for another use. Reserve ²/₃ cup (150 milliliters) for recipe.

Combine vegetables with the rest of the ingredients and mix well. Using a ¹/₄ cup measure for each latke, saute, in batches, in a sprayed non-stick fry pan with oil added as needed. Respray for each batch.

Transfer latkes, as they are browned to a baking sheet to rewarm before serving or freeze, well wrapped for later serving.

Rewarm in a microwave or in oven, just before serving.

The latkes can be made half size to serve at a large party or as an appetizer.

Wild Rice *[m or p]*

This is a simple but elegant dish. It is very tasty and has a slight crunch. Wild rice is a suitable side dish with any number of entrees and I like to serve it often.

Serves 8

vegetable cooking spray
5 ¹/₂ ounces [150 grams] onions, chopped
1 ¹/₂ cups [270 grams] wild rice, rinsed
2 ¹/₂ cups [560 milliliters] Chicken Broth [see Index] or canned
or pareve chicken flavored soup, from the mix or
vegetable broth

In a well sprayed non-stick saucepan, saute onions until well softened. Add rice and broth. Bring to a boil, cover and simmer for 35 minutes. Remove from heat and let sit, covered, for 15 minutes and serve.

The rice can be prepared ahead of time and reheated in the microwave. The rice can be frozen.

Yorkshire Pudding [p]

This is a favorite of my family. I always serve this with Roasted Rib of Beef, Rack of Lamb and Flank Steak [see Index]. Yorkshire pudding is similar to popovers. It puffs up high around the edges and stays soft in the middle. It makes a lovely presentation at the table. Serve it with any gravy on the side.

Serves 8

2 cups [280 grams] all purpose unbleached flour
1 teaspoon salt
2 cups [450 milliliters] water
2 eggs
½ cup [110 milliliters] frozen egg substitute, thawed
2 tablespoons margarine
vegetable cooking spray

Place flour and salt in a mixing bowl. Whisk in water, whisking until smooth. Add eggs and egg substitute and continue beating until large bubbles form. Cover and let sit at room temperature for at least 1 hour. This part of recipe can be completed early in the day, if desired.

Place margarine in a sprayed au gratin or large baking pan, suitable for serving. Preheat oven to 375°F. [190°C.] Place pan in oven for 3 minutes, until margarine is melted and sizzling. Re-beat pudding mixture and pour into sizzling pan. Immediately place in oven and bake for 30 to 40 minutes, until well puffed and golden.

Zucchini Cakes [m or p]

I sometimes serve these little cakes as an appetizer and sometimes as a side dish at dinner. They are unusual, tasty and easy to make. As squash is readily availabe all year round, they are a convenient vegetable to serve. They are practically non-fat.

Makes 26 to 28 cakes

1 ³/₄ pounds [800 grams] zucchini squash	
salt, for sprinkling	
3 egg whites	
¹/₄ cup [55 milliliters] canned chicken broth or pareve chicken flavored soup, from the mix	
5 ¹/₂ ounces [150 grams] onions, chopped finely, 1 medium	
2 teaspoons sugar	
³/₄ cup [105 grams] all purpose unbleached flour	
salt, to taste	
fresh white pepper, to taste	
pareve butter flavored cooking spray	

Shred unpeeled, washed and trimmed squash. [I use the 2 x 2 shredding disk on my food processor.] Sprinkle with salt and let wilt in a colander for 30 minutes. Rinse and drain well, squeeze out all moisture by handfuls. Mix squash with the rest of the ingredients, except spray.

Measure 4 tablespoons [¹/₄ cup] for each cake and fry them in a well sprayed non-stick fry pan, in batches, over medium high heat, until cakes are brown on each side, respraying pan as necessary. Drain on paper towels. Keep warm in a 250°F. [120°C.] oven until all cakes are done. (Or make them half size to serve at a large party.) Serve.

The cakes can be prepared a day or 2 ahead and reheated in oven or microwave or they can be frozen. Thaw before reheating.

DESSERT

Mandel Brot, Frances [p] [Biscotti]

This delious cookie is great with coffee or just as a snack. Easy and quick to make. Thank you Frances Rubenstein for this recipe. I've enjoyed making, serving and eating these cookies.

Makes about 70

3/4 cup [150 grams] sugar

1/3 cup [75 milliliters] light vegtable oil [safflower]

3/4 cup [175 milliliters] frozen egg substitute, thawed

2 teaspoons baking powder

2 1/2 to 3 cups [350 to 410 grams] all purpose unbleached flour

8 ounces [225 grams] shelled walnuts, chopped

2 teaspoons vanilla

vegetable cooking spray

1 1/2 tablespoons cinnnamon mixed with

4 tablespoons sugar

Combine all the ingredients, except spray and cinnamon sugar mixture, in a mixing bowl. Turn out dough onto a well floured surface. Knead until dough is well combined and no longer sticky, adding as much extra flour as needed.

Divide dough into 3 parts. Roll each part into a log about 12 inches [30 centimeters] long. Place logs well apart on a non-stick or lightly sprayed baking sheet. Flatten logs slightly.

Bake in a preheated 350°F. [175°C.] oven for 25 to 30 minutes until lightly colored. Remove from oven and let cool on baking sheet on a rack for 10 minutes. Leave oven on.

Cut logs diagonally, into slices about 3/4 inch [2 centimeters] thick. Place slices, cut side down, back on baking sheet and sprinkle each cookie with cinnamon sugar mixture. Return baking sheet to oven to bake for 7 minutes. Turn slices over and sprinkle each with cinnamon sugar mixture. Bake for an additional 7 minutes. Transfer slices to racks to cool. Store in an airtight container for 2 weeks.

231

Applesauce Cake [p]

This is a light, moist and spicy cake, easy to make and very low in fat. If you would like, raisins and/or nuts can be added, but I like it just as is. This recipe makes 2 loaves, 1 to eat now, 1 to freeze for another time. I have gotten raves for this cake. I make it in a food processor but it also can be done with a mixer.

Makes 2 loaves, each serving 8 [or more]

1 ¹/₂ cups [435 grams] canned natural applesauce
2 teaspoons ground cinnamon
¹/₂ teaspoon ground nutmeg
¹/₂ teaspoon ground allspice
or 1 ¹/₂ cups [435 grams] Spiced Apple Sauce [see Index]
2 ounces [55 grams] pareve margarine
1 ¹/₂ cups [300 grams] brown sugar, packed firmly
³/₄ cup [175 milliliters] frozen egg substitute, thawed
2 ¹/₂ cups [300 grams] all purpose unbleached flour
1 tablespoon baking powder
1 teaspoon baking soda
¹/₂ teaspoon salt
vegetable cooking spray
powdered sugar, for dusting

In a mixing bowl, combine well, applesauce with cinnamon, nutmeg and allspice. Set aside. Or use homemade spiced apple sauce.

In a food processor or a mixer, cream margarine with sugar until fluffy. Add egg substitute slowly, beating constantly. Add dry ingredients, mixed together, alternately with applesauce mixture, pulsing or beating until batter is combined. Pour batter into 2 sprayed, non-stick 4 x 8 inch [10 x 20 centimeter] loaf pans.

Bake in a preheated 325°F. [165°C.] oven until cake springs back when lightly touched, about 45 minutes.

Cool cakes on a rack in pans for 5 minutes. Turn out and finish cooling on the rack.

Dust tops of cakes with sifted powdered sugar. Slice and arrange overlapping slices on a plate and serve.

Apple Crisp [p]

A delicious, easily prepared "Apple Pie" with no crust. It goes well with any kind of dinner. When I have apples that are no longer crispy, I make this dessert or Spiced Apple Sauce [see Index.]

Serves 8

2 ²/₃ pounds [1.2 kilos] apples, peeled, cored, sliced

2 tablespoons lemon juice

1 tablespoon ground cinnamon

1 teaspoon ground nutmeg

¹/₂ teaspoon ground allspice

¹/₂ teaspoon ground cloves

4 ounces [110 grams] shelled pecans, chopped

¹/₂ cup [50 grams] oatmeal, ground up in a processor

¹/₂ cup [70 grams] all purpose unbleached flour

¹/₂ cup [100 grams] brown sugar

¹/₄ cup [55 milliliters] light vegetable oil [safflower]

vegetable cooking spray

In a mixing bowl, combine apples, lemon juice, cinnamon, nutmeg, allspice and cloves. Mix well with a fork to coat apples with spices.

In another mixing bowl, combine pecans, oatmeal, flour, sugar and oil, mixing well, until crumbly.

In a well sprayed 10 inch [25 centimeter] deep dish pie plate, place apple mixture, spreading evenly. Evenly spread pecan mixture over top of apples.

Bake in a preheated 375°F. [190°C.] oven for 1 hour.

Serve from pie dish.

The crisp can be baked 1 day ahead of time and reheated for 15 minutes, if desired, or it can be served cold.

[It is also good served with low or no-fat whipped topping, if desired.]

Apple Struedel [p]

It is not very difficult to work with fillo leaves. Keep your leaves covered with a damp towel to prevent them drying out and you won't have a problem. I like the versatility of these leaves. I make Dried Fruit Struedel [see Index] at the same time as I make these and freeze the portion that I don't use for another time.

Makes 4 struedels, each cut into 7 or 8 portions

2 ¹/₄ pounds [1 kilo] tart apples, peeled, cored, chopped coarsely
8 ounces [225 grams] shelled walnuts, chopped coarsely, 2 cups
1 ¹/₂ cups [150 grams] dried cranberries
juice of 1 lemon
grated rind of 1 lemon
1 tablespoon ground cinnamon
¹/₈ teaspoon ground nutmeg
12 sheets fillo dough leaves
1 ¹/₂ to 2 ounces [40 to 60 grams] margarine, melted
pareve butter flavored cooking spray
about 3 tablespoons dried fine bread crumbs

Combine apples, walnuts, cranberries, lemon juice, lemon rind, cinnamon and nutmeg in a mixing bowl.

Lay 1 fillo leaf on a flat surface, keeping other leaves covered with a damp kitchen towel. Spray lightly and brush lightly with margarine. Repeat 2 more times making a pile of 3 fillo leaves. Sprinkle top fillo leaf with ³/₄ tablespoon bread crumbs. Leaving a wide border, spread about 1 ¹/₂ cups [350 milliliters] of filling along long side of leaves. Carefully fold border over filling and roll up dough with filling, jelly roll style, as tightly as possible, folding in ends as you go. Place seam down on an ungreased baking sheet.

Repeat above 3 more times, making 4 struedels. Score tops of struedel rolls with a serrated knife into 7 or 8 portions.

Bake struedels in a preheated 375°F. [190°C.] oven for 20 to 25 minutes, until nicely browned.

Immediately cut rolls into portions and serve; or cut into portions, cool on a rack, wrap carefully and freeze; or cut into portions and put aside until later, to reheat and recrisp in a 300°F. [150°C.] oven for 20 minutes before serving.

Baked Apples [p]

Baked apples are a nostalgia dish for me. When my brother, Bob de LaViez, and I were children, it was a special treat for us when my mother would make baked apples. I hope you like my version of this old fashioned dish.

Serves 8

8 small Golden Delicious apples, each about 4 ¹/₂ ounces [125 grams]

2 ounces [60 grams] dried cranberries, soaked for 30 minutes in

10 tablespoons rum

a 5 ¹/₂ ounce [162 milliliter] can apricot nectar

a 5 ¹/₂ ounce [162 milliliter] can peach nectar

1 ¹/₂ teaspoons ground cinnamon mixed with

7 teaspoons sugar

Peel apples halfway down from stem end. Scoop out core, enough to remove all seeds. Divide cranberries and rum among apples, filling scooped out portion. Place apples in a baking dish large enough to hold them in one layer. Pour nectars around apples. Sprinkle cinnamon sugar mixture evenly over apples, about 1 teaspoon for each.

Bake apples in a preheated 375°F. [190°C.] oven for 1 hour to 1 ¹/₄ hours, basting with juices every 20 minutes, until apples are tender. If desired, the baked apples can be frozen.

Black Walnut Mandel Brot [p] [Biscotti]

When we lived in an old house on Cross Country Blvd., in Baltimore, MD, when my kids were growing up, we had a wonderful old black walnut tree. As the walnuts fell off the tree, the covering stained every thing but the walnuts were delicious. This is kind of an old fashioned taste, not too common anymore, but special in its way.

Makes about 70

³/₄ **cup [150 grams] sugar**

¹/₃ **cup [75 millilters] light vegetable oil [safflower]**

³/₄ **cup [175 milliliters] frozen egg substitute, thawed**

2 teaspoons baking powder

2 to 2 ¹/₂ cups [280 to 350 grams] all purpose unbleached flour

8 ounces [225 grams] shelled black walnuts, chopped

2 teaspoons vanilla

optional: vegetable cooking spray

1 ¹/₂ tablespoons ground cinnamon mixed with

4 tablespoons sugar

Combine all the ingredients, except spray and cinnamon sugar mixture, in a mixing bowl. Turn out dough onto a well floured surface. Knead until dough is well combined and no longer sticky, adding as much extra flour as needed.

Divide dough into 3 parts. Roll each part into a log about 12 inches [30 centimeters] long. Place logs well apart on a non-stick or lightly sprayed baking pan. Flatten logs slightly.

Bake in a preheated 350°F. [175°C.] oven for 30 to 35 minutes until lightly colored. Remove from oven and let cool on baking pan on a rack for 10 minutes. Leave oven on.

Cut logs diagonally into slices about ³/₄ inch [2 centimeters] thick. Place slices, cut side down, back on baking pan. Sprinkle slices with cinnamon sugar mixture. Return pan to oven to bake for 7 minutes. Turn slices to other side, sprinkle with cinnamon sugar mixture and bake an additional 7 minutes.

Transfer cookies to a rack to cool. Store in an airtight container for 2 weeks.

Brownies [p]

If you have a yen for brownies, the chewy, gooey kind with the least amount of fat, then this is your recipe. I make them ahead of time and freeze them in layers with waxed paper between. They are great.

Makes 24 to 40 squares

4 ounces [110 grams] apple sauce

³/₄ cup [50 grams] sifted cocoa, I prefer Dutch

2 cups [420 grams] sugar

4 egg whites

1 cup [140 grams] all purpose unbleached flour

4 teaspoons vanilla

8 ounces [220 grams] shelled pecans or walnuts, chopped, 2 cups heavy

pareve butter flavored cooking spray

Combine all the ingredients, except nuts, in a mixing bowl. [I use a hand mixer.] Add nuts and fold in. Spread dough in a well sprayed 9 x 13 inch [23 x 33 centimeter] baking pan. Bake in a preheated 300°F. [150°C.] oven for 40 minutes for chewy to 50 minutes for cake like.

Remove from oven and let cool in pan on a rack for 20 minutes.

Cut brownies into squares with a sharp knife dipped in water. Remove from pan carefully, with a water dipped small spatula to cool on a rack.

These freeze well. Place in a container in layers, divided by waxed paper.

Bread Pudding [d]

This recipe was a special challenge for me; to make a healthy low fat version of bread pudding appealed to me greatly. I love this pudding. Start this at least 1 day ahead of time. It can be frozen either before or after baking.

Serves 8

²/₃ cup [95 grams] white raisins
7 tablespoons rum
1 cup [225 milliliters] skim milk
¹/₂ whole vanilla bean
¹/₂ cup [100 grams] brown sugar
12 slices Italian bread, not sourdough, sliced diagonally ¹/₂ inch [1 ³/₄ centimeters] thick
butter-flavored cooking spray
1 ¹/₂ cups [350 milliliters] evaporated skim milk
1 ³/₄ cups [400 milliliters] frozen egg substitute, thawed
1 teaspoon vanilla
1 teaspoon ground cinnamon mixed with
1 tablespoon sugar

Macerate raisins in rum for 30 minutes. Scald skim milk with vanilla bean added. Let stand 15 minutes. Split vanilla bean and scrape inside seeds into milk and discard bean. Add sugar to milk and stir until sugar is dissolved.

Spray each side of each slice of bread with butter spray. Spray inside of a 1 ½ quart [1.4 liter] square, oblong or oval baking dish 2 inches [5 centimeters] deep. Lay bread slices in overlapping slices in baking dish.

In a bowl whisk together milk mixture, evaporated milk and egg substitute. Add raisins with rum. Add vanilla. Pour this mixture carefully over bread slices in baking dish. Press gently with a fork to help bread absorb egg milk mixture. Let sit, covered with plastic wrap, in the fridge overnight, [can be 2 days, if desired], pressing with fork several times. If desired, recipe can be completed up to this point and frozen. Thaw before continuing with recipe.

Sprinkle top of pudding with cinnamon sugar mixture. Place baking dish in a larger baking pan. Add boiling water to larger pan coming up ½ the depth of baking dish. Bake in a preheated 350° F. [175°C.] oven for 30 to 45 minutes, until custard tests done in the middle. [Don't let pudding be completely dry.]

Remove baking dish from water and serve warm or let cool on a rack.

The pudding can be baked ahead of time and reheated in a slow oven just before serving with low or no-fat whipped topping or frozen yogurt or no-fat yogurt, if desired. Or the pudding can be frozen after baking and cooling. Thaw before serving and/or reheating.

Carrot Cake [p]

This cake is delicious as is or frosted with Powdered Sugar Icing [see Index] if desired. I once had a dinner where every course used carrot as one of the ingredients. It was fun and everyone found the meal delicious. Freeze the extra loaf.

Makes 2 loaves

1 ¼ pounds [580 grams] carrots, peeled, shredded
¾ cup [175 milliliters] light vegetable oil [safflower]
2 cups [450 milliliters] sugar
1 teaspoon grated orange peel
½ cup [110 milliliters] water
¾ cup [175 milliliters] frozen egg substitute, thawed
2 ½ cups [350 grams] all purpose unbleached flour
pinch salt
1 tablespoon baking powder
1 teaspoon baking soda
1 tablespoon ground cinnamon
2 teaspoons ground cloves
½ teaspoon ground allspice
½ teaspoon ground nutmeg
3 ½ ounces [100 grams] raisins, dusted with
1 tablespoon flour
4 ounces [110 grams] shelled pecans, chopped
vegetable cooking spray
optional: powdered sugar, for dusting or Powdered Sugar Icing [see Index]

In a saucepan, combine carrots, oil, sugar, orange peel and water. Bring to a boil, stirring, and simmer for 5 minutes. Let cool.

In a large mixing bowl, place egg substitute. Combine dry ingredients and add to eggs along with carrot mixture. Stir just until combined. Fold in raisins and nuts. Pour batter into 2 sprayed loaf pans 5 x

9 inches [12 $\frac{1}{2}$ x 22 $\frac{1}{2}$ centimeters].

Bake in a preheated 350°F. [175°C.] oven for 50 minutes to 1 hour, until centers of cakes spring back when lightly touched.

Cool in pans for 30 minutes. Turn out onto racks to cool completely. Sprinkle with sifted powdered sugar or frost with Powdered Sugar Icing [see Index] if desired.

Store in the fridge until eaten.

The cake freezes well, wrapped in foil. Unwrap to thaw.

Graham Cracker or
Cookie Pie Crust (d or p)

This is a quickly made crust with lots of options. I particularly like this crust with Cheese Pie [see Index].

Makes a single 11 inch [28 centimeter] pie crust

8 ounces [225 grams] graham cracker or Petite Beurre or ginger snap or chocolate cookie crumbs
3 tablespoons sugar
6 tablespoons margarine, melted

Combine crumbs with sugar and margarine. Press evenly in bottom of pie pan, using your fingers. If your recipe calls for a baked crust, bake in a preheated 350°F. [175°C.] oven for 15 minutes, until lightly browned.

Cheese Pie [d]

This rich, moist, creamy, delicious pie is very low fat and yummy. This recipe makes a very large pie, serving a lot of people. I make this, serve half and freeze the rest for another party.

Makes an 11 inch [28 centimeter] pie, serving about 16

1 ¹/₂ pounds [675 grams] no-fat Philadelphia type cream cheese, softened
¹/₂ cup [110 milliliters] frozen egg substitute, thawed
³/₄ cup [160 grams] sugar
2 teaspoons grated lemon peel [see Note], about ¹/₂ lemon
1 ¹/₂ teaspoons vanilla
1 Nut Pie Crust [see Index] or Cookie or Graham cracker Pie Crust [see Index], unbaked

Topping

8 ounces [225 grams] no-fat sour cream
2 tablespoons sugar
¹/₂ teaspoon vanilla

In a large mixing bowl, place cream cheese, egg substitute, sugar, lemon peel and vanilla. Beat at low speed for about 20 minutes, until mixture is smooth and creamy. Pour onto prepared pie crust. Bake in a preheated 350°F. [175°C.] oven for 25 minutes. Cool on a rack.

Combine topping ingredients and spread evenly over cooled pie. Bake in a preheated 450°F. [230°C.] oven for 10 minutes.

Cool and refrigerate. Or freeze, well covered with foil.

Note: Peel lemon with a rotary vegetable peeler, taking only thin strips without any white pulp. In a food processor with the steel knife, run machine combining sugar and peel until peel is finely minced.

Chocolate-Peppermint Meringues [p]

A refreshing "after dinner mint." This different dessert is in honor of my friend, Brenda Brooks, who loves these treats.

Makes about 36

4 egg whites at room temperature
pinch cream of tartar
1 cup [210 grams] sugar
1 $^1/_2$ teaspoons vanilla
$^1/_4$ teaspoon essence of peppermint
1 tablespoon unsweetened cocoa, sifted
vegetable cooking spray
optional: chocolate sprinkles or jimmies

In a large mixing bowl [preferably copper] beat egg whites until foamy. Add cream of tartar and beat until stiff. While beating, start adding sugar, 1 tablespoon at a time, until all sugar has been added. Add vanilla and peppermint. Beat 1 more minute. Fold in cocoa carefully but thoroughly.

Spray 2 large baking sheets. Place meringue in a pastry bag, in batches, and pipe dollops of meringue onto sheets. You can place them fairly close together because they spread very little. Alternately, you can place meringues onto baking sheets by heaping tablespoons. I do find that the pastry bag is infinitely easier.

For more festive meringues, sprinkle tops with chocolate sprinkles or jimmies.

Bake meringues in a preheated 250°F. [120°C.] oven for 1 hour. Turn off oven and let them sit in oven, with door closed, for 4 hours to overnight.

Store in an airtight container.

Pie Crust [p]

This is a slight variation of a pie crust from the Joy Of Cooking cookbook. Follow directions carefully and I promise you the easiest pie crust ever.

For a double 9 inch [22 ¹/₂ centimeter] or a single 11 to 13 inch [27 1/2 to 32 ¹/₂ centimeter] crust

2 cups [280 grams] flour
1 teaspoon salt
¹/₄ cup [55 milliliters] cold water
5 ¹/₂ ounces [150 grams] margarine

For a double 11 to 13 inch [27 ¹/₂ to 32 ¹/₂ centimeter] crust

3 cups [420 grams] flour
1 ¹/₂ teaspoons salt
6 tablespoons cold water
8 ounces [225 grams] margarine

Sift flour and salt into a large mixing bowl. Remove 5 tablespoons [or 8 tablespoons for larger crust] flour to a small bowl. Mix this with water to make a flour paste and set aside.

With a pastry cutter, blend margarine with the rest of the flour until it resembles coarse meal, do this thoroughly. Add flour paste and toss with a fork. Knead in bowl with your hands until dough comes together in a ball. Cover dough with plastic wrap and chill for 30 minutes to 1 hour.

Roll out dough very thinly on a lightly floured surface. Place in a pie pan, without stretching, cutting off excess dough with a very sharp knife. Flute edge with your fingers or press edge with floured tines of a fork. Prick dough on bottom and sides with a fork.

To bake crust without filling, line crust with waxed paper. Place another pie pan [the same size] on top of waxed paper. Chill for 30 minutes.

Bake in a preheated 450°F. [230°C.] oven for 10 minutes. Remove top pie pan and carefully remove waxed paper. Bake an additional 5 to 10 minutes, until lightly browned. Cool on a rack.

This crust is excellent to use for Quiche [see Index] as well as for all kinds of pies.

Candied Grapefruit Peel [p]

Part of my feelings about recycling makes me enjoy making these no fat candies. I like to serve these and take them as a gift when I'm invited for dinner.

4 grapefruit
water
2 cups [425 grams] sugar
1 cup [225 milliliters] water
about 1 cup [210 grams] sugar

Carefully peel grapefruit in 4 sections. Reserve fruit for another use. Cut peel into thin strips. Do not remove white pith.

In a 4 quart [4 liter] saucepan, cover peel with cold water and bring to a boil. Boil for 10 minutes. Drain in a colander. Repeat this procedure 3 more times.

In same saucepan, place 2 cups [425 grams] sugar and 1 cup [225 milliliters] water. Bring to a boil, stirring until sugar is dissolved. Add grapefruit peel. Boil syrup and peel until almost all syrup has been absorbed by peel, about 45 minutes. Drain well and let cool slightly.

Place 1 cup [210 grams] sugar in a large paper bag. Place drained peel in bag and shake carefully to coat peel with sugar. Spread sugared peel on wax paper, to dry for 24 hours.

Store in plastic bags or pretty tins. Keeps for weeks in fridge, months in freezer.

Dried Fruit Struedel [p]

I resisted working with fillo dough for ages, but once you plunge in, it is not very difficult. Keep your leaves covered with a damp towel to prevent them drying out and you won't have a problem. I make the Apple Struedel [see Index] at the same time as I make these and freeze the portion that I don't use, for another time.

Makes 4 struedels, each cut into 7 or 8 portions

5 $^1/_2$ ounces [155 grams] pitted prunes
7 ounces [195 grams] dried apricots
7 ounces [195 grams] dried peaches
6 ounces [175 grams] dried apple chunks
3 $^1/_2$ ounces [100 grams] raisins
a 5 $^1/_2$ ounce [160 gram] can pineapple juice
a 5 $^1/_2$ ounce [160 gram] can peach nectar
8 ounces [225 grams] shelled pecans, chopped, 2 cups
12 sheets fillo leaves
pareve butter flavored cooking spray
1 $^1/_2$ to 2 ounces [40 to 60 grams] margarine, melted
about 3 tablespoons dried fine bread crumbs

Cut fruit with scissors into small pieces. Combine fruit with juices in a saucepan and simmer until fruit is reconstituted and soft, about 30 to 45 minutes. Cool and fold in nuts.

Lay 1 fillo leaf on a flat surface, keeping other leaves covered with a damp kitchen towel. Spray lightly and brush lightly with margarine. Repeat 2 more times making a pile of 3 fillo leaves. Sprinkle top fillo leaf with $^3/_4$ tablespoon bread crumbs. Leaving a wide border, spread about 1 $^1/_2$ cups of filling along long side of leaves. Carefully fold border over filling and roll up dough with filling, jelly roll style, as tightly as possible, folding in ends as you go. Place seam down on an ungreased baking sheet.

Repeat above 3 more times making 4 struedels. Score tops of struedel rolls with a serrated knife into 7 or 8 portions.

Bake struedels in a preheated 375°F. [190°C.] oven for 20 to 25 minutes, until nicely browned.

Immediately cut rolls into portions and serve; or cut into portions, cool on a rack, wrap carefully and freeze; or cut into portions and put aside until later, to reheat and recrisp in a 300°F. [150°C.] oven for 20 minutes before serving.

Grapenuts Pudding [d]

A friend, Marilyn Nicholas, let me read an old cook book of her mother's. It is a book written in the 1930s, by the wives of Union members from Boston. I loved reading it and this pudding recipe intrigued me. I adapted and adopted it for this book. It is made from simple and inexpensive ingredients, in keeping with the times. I like the velvety and crunchy tastes. I hope you enjoy it.

Serves 8 easily

3 cups [700 milliliters] evaporated skim milk
1 cup [225 milliliters] frozen egg substitute, thawed
1/2 cup [105 grams] sugar
1 cup [145 grams] Grapenuts cereal
3/4 cup [100 grams] dried cranberries, 3 1/2 ounces
1 teaspoon vanilla
butter flavored cooking spray
about 1 1/2 teaspoons ground cinnamon

Scald milk and let cool. In a mixing bowl, stir together eggs, sugar, Grapenuts, cranberries and vanilla. Gradually add cooled milk and mix until well combined. Pour mixture into a well sprayed 9 x 11 inch [22 x 27 centimeter] baking pan, suitable for serving. Sprinkle cinnamon evenly over top. [I use a small screen strainer.]

Bake pudding in a preheated 350°F. [175°C.] oven for about 25 minutes, until custard tests done with a clean knife. Cool on a rack and refrigerate until cold.

Cut into squares and serve from baking pan.

Kuchen, Aranka [d]

This is the tradional Weisgal "break the fast" cake served after Yom Kippur. It is a heavy, kind of bread-like, delicious coffee cake. This was my mother-in-law, Aranka Weisgal's recipe which was handed down to us after she died. It is surprisingly easy to make and has a long shelf life. Most people like this cake. It is also delicious toasted and buttered lightly.

Makes a 9 ½ inch [24 centimeter] cake

1 package dry yeast

¼ cup [55 milliliters] scalded skim milk, cooled to lukewarm

1 teaspoon sugar

5 cups [690 grams] all purpose unbleached flour, approximately

1 teaspoon salt

1 cup [225 milliliters] skim milk

3 ounces [90 grams] unsalted butter or margarine, cut up

⅞ cup [185 grams] sugar

1 tablespoon grated lemon rind, about 1 lemon [see Note]

3 egg whites

1 teaspoon vanilla

5 ½ ounces [150 grams] white raisins

butter flavored cooking spray

about 7 ounces [200 grams] whole almonds, unsalted, unpeeled

4 tablespoons sifted powdered sugar, for dusting

In a small bowl, proof yeast mixed with cooled ¼ cup [55 milliliters] milk and 1 teaspoon sugar, in a warm place for 10 minutes.

Place flour and salt in a large mixing bowl. Make a well in center of flour and pour in yeast mixture. Mix with a bit of flour. Cover this sponge with a kitchen towel and let sit in a warm place for 10 minutes.

Bring milk to scalding, remove from heat and add butter or margarine, stir until melted. Add sugar, lemon rind, vanilla, egg whites and raisins and mix well. Cool to lukewarm.

Add milk mixture to sponge and mix with flat beater of a mixer until well blended. The dough will be sticky. Lightly flour top of dough, cover with plastic wrap and a kitchen towel and let rise in a warm place until doubled, about 1 to 1 ½ hours.

Punch down dough and turn out onto a floured surface. Knead dough, adding a bit of extra flour, if necessary, until dough is smooth and elastic and no longer sticky.

In a well sprayed fluted tube pan [kugel form] decoratively place almonds in grooves, about 3 or 4 in each. Form dough into a cylinder and carefully place it in pan on top of almonds, pinching ends closed. Cover pan with a towel and let rise in a warm place until doubled, about ¾ to 1 hour.

Bake in a preheated 350°F. [175°C.] oven for 1 hour to 1 hour 10 minutes, until well browned.

Remove cake from pan immediately and cool completely on a rack. Dust with sifted powered sugar. Serve in thin slices.

Note: Peel lemon with a rotary type vegetable peeler, taking only thin strips of yellow without any white pith. Using the steel knife of a food processor, combine sugar and peel and run machine until peel is minced.

Dried Fruit Crisp [p]

Devising low fat or no fat recipes for dessert are a constant challenge for me. I like a crisp because it has very little fat. This is one that I think is very tasty, is full of fiber and has an interesting mixture of flavors.

Serves 8 easily

an 11 ounce [330 gram] package of mixed dried fruits [prunes, pears, apples, apricots]
a 6 ounce [175 gram] package dried apricots
a 7 ounce [200 gram] package dried peaches
3 ounces [90 grams] dried cranberries
3 ounces [90 grams] golden raisins
6 ounces [175 grams] pitted prunes
1 lemon, sliced thinly crosswise, seeded
2 - 5 ½ ounce [160 milliliter] cans peach nectar
2 - 5 ½ ounce [160 milliliter] cans apricot nectar
vegetable cooking spray
¼ cup [55 milliliters] light vegetable oil [safflower]
4 ounces [110 grams] shelled pecans, chopped
½ cup [105 grams] packed brown sugar
½ cup [46 grams] oatmeal, ground in blender or processor
½ cup [75 grams] all purpose unbleached flour

Combine fruits and nectars in a saucepan and bring to a simmer. Simmer uncovered for 20 to 25 minutes, until fruits have plumped and most of the juice has been absorbed. Cool slightly. Place fruit mixture in a sprayed 10 inch [25 centimeter] deep dish pie plate.

Mix vegetable oil, pecans, sugar, oatmeal and flour with a fork until well combined and crumbly. Sprinkle topping evenly over fruits. Bake in a preheated 375°F. [190°C.] oven for 40 minutes until topping is browned.

The crisp can be made 2 or 3 days ahead of time. Serve warm or at room temperature.

Lime-Tequila Sorbet [p]

Delicious, refreshing and very tart, add more sugar if it is to your taste. It is such fun to serve sorbet before the main course, to refresh the palate and before continuing dinner.

Makes about 28 ounces [800 grams]

1 ½ cups [315 grams] sugar
rind of 1 lime, minced [see Note]
¾ cup [175 milliliters] water
6 tablespoons tequila
2 cups [450 milliliters] lime juice

In a small saucepan, combine sugar, rind and water. Bring to a boil, stirring until sugar is dissolved. Simmer for 3 minutes.

Remove from heat, add tequila and lime juice. Cool. Strain into a plastic container and chill until cold. Place container in freezer and freeze until firm but not hard, about 2 hours. Place sorbet in a food processor or a mixer and process or beat until smooth. Repeat freezing and beating process 2 more times. Freeze until hard.

If necessary, about 30 minutes before serving, place sorbet in the fridge to soften enough to scoop.

The sorbet can be prepared up to 4 days ahead of time.

Note: If you have a food processor, peel lime with a rotary type vegetable peeler, taking only a thin strip without white pith. With the steel knife, combine sugar and peel and run machine until peel is minced.

Almond Mandel Brot [p] *Twice-Baked Cookies*

These are great to have on hand for unexpected guests or as a lovely gift for a host or hostess. They are nice to serve with fresh fruit after dinner. My father-in-law, Abba Weisgal, loved to dunk these in coffee or wine. [I think his teeth weren't too great.]

Makes about 70

¾ cup [150 grams] sugar
⅓ cup [75 milliliters] light vegetable oil [safflower]
¾ cup [175 milliliters] frozen egg substitute, thawed
2 teaspoons baking powder
2 ½ to 3 cups [350 to 410 grams] all purpose unbleached flour
8 ounces [225 grams] almonds, peeled, slivered, lightly toasted
½ cup [110 milliliters] Apple Sauce [see Index] or canned
2 teaspoons vanilla
2 teaspoons Frangelico liqueur
vegetable cooking spray
1 ½ tablespoons ground cinnamon mixed with
4 tablespoons sugar

Combine all the ingredients, except spray and cinnamon sugar mixture, in a mixing bowl. Turn out dough onto a well floured surface. Knead until dough is well combined and no longer sticky, adding as much extra flour as needed.

Divide dough into 3 parts. Roll each part into a log about 12 inches [30 centimeters] long. Place logs well apart on a lightly sprayed nonstick baking sheet. Flatten logs slightly.

Bake in a preheated 350°F. [175°C.] oven for 30 to 35 minutes until lightly colored. Remove from oven and let cool on baking sheet on a rack for 10 minutes. Leave oven on.

Cut logs, on the diagonal, into slices about ¾ inch [2 centimeters] thick. Place slices, cut side down, back on baking sheet, sprinkle each with some cinnamon sugar mixture and return to oven to bake for 7 minutes. Turn cookies to other side, sprinkle with cinnamon sugar and bake a further 7 minutes. Transfer cookies to racks to cool.

Store in an airtight container for about 2 weeks.

Meringues [p]

This is one of my favorite desserts. It is universally liked, is non-fat and is easy to make ahead, even a week ahead. I dedicate these to Marc Eiselsberg, who loves these and flatters me by cooking from my first book a lot and I trust will do the same with this one. Thank you, Marc.

There are some rules to follow to make fool proof meringues.

Egg whites must be at room temperature. Bowl and beaters must be clean and grease free.

Allow ¼ cup [55 grams] sugar for each egg white. Sugar must be added gradually.

If I am going away for a time and have some eggs in my fridge, I separate the whites from the yolks [which I toss out] and freeze the whites in small containers, noting how many whites in each container.

To make 15 large 3 inch [7 ½ centimeter] or
24 medium size 2 inch [5 centimeter] meringues

6 egg whites

a good pinch cream of tartar

1 ¼ cups [260 grams] sugar

1 ½ teaspoons vanilla extract

vegetable cooking spray

Beat egg whites in an elecric mixer on medium high speed until foamy. Add cream of tartar and continue beating until fairly stiff. At this point, while beating, start adding sugar, 1 tablespoon at a time, every 30 seconds. After all sugar is added, add vanilla and continue beating until well combined.

Spray 2 large non-stick baking sheets. Place meringue in a pastry bag, in batches, and pipe dollops of meringue onto sheets, a method I find very easy and quick. If desired, you can scoop up a bit of meringue in a large serving spoon, smooth it with a rubber spatula and push it onto baking sheets with the spatula. They spread very little so you can place them fairly close together.

Bake in a preheated 250°F. [120°C.] oven for 1 hour. Turn off oven and let meringues sit in oven, with door closed, to dry for 4 hours to overnight. Store in an airtight container.

Palachinka - Dessert Crepes [p]

There was a wonderful Hungarian restaurant, The Europa, very close to our home in Jerusalem. Many nights we would walk the block and a half and have dinner there. I was introduced to Palachinka and went home and made it to serve at my own dinners. You can make this easy dessert early in the day and re-heat just before serving. Everyone seems to like Palachinka.

Makes about 24 crepes

1 ¼ cups [175 grams] all purpose unbleached flour
1 cup [225 milliliters] frozen egg substitute, thawed
³⁄₄ cup [175 milliliters] orange juice
³⁄₄ cup [175 milliliters] water
¹⁄₂ teaspoon salt
1 tablespoon sugar
1 ¹⁄₂ tablespoons light vegetable oil [Safflower or Canola]
vegetable cooking spray
a bit of light vegetable oil, for frying
about ¹⁄₂ cup [110 milliliters] favorite fruit spread
powdered sugar, sifted, for sprinkling

Combine and mix flour, egg substitute, orange juice, water, salt, sugar and 1 ¹⁄₂ tablespoons oil in a blender until smooth. Transfer batter to a bowl, cover and let sit for 1 hour. Whisk well before using.

   In a sprayed, non-stick 6 to 7 inch [15 to 17 centimeter] fry pan with sloping sides, or a crepe pan, heat ¹⁄₂ teaspoon of oil until hot. When oil is hot, remove from heat and pour half of a ¹⁄₄ cup measure [about 2 tablespoons] of batter into center of pan. Tilt pan quickly so that batter covers bottom of pan, forming a thin pancake. Return pan to heat. When crepe edge begins to pull away from sides of pan, loosen crepe with a broad, flat knife and turn it to the other side to brown, just a few seconds. Transfer crepe to a kitchen towel. Continue making crepes in the same way, adding a bit of oil and respraying if needed, until all batter is used. Watch and adjust heat as necessary so crepes don't burn. Keep crepes covered with towel until all crepes are cooked. Let crepes cool.

Unwrap crepes and spread a bit of fruit, about 1 teaspoon, on each crepe and roll up. Place seam side down on a microwave safe or oven proof serving plate.

Just before serving, reheat Palachinka covered with film, in a microwave or in a medium oven until warm.

Sprinkle with a bit of powdered sugar and serve, 2 or 3 per person.

Nut Pie Crust [p]

This is one of the crusts that I use when I make Cheese Pie [see Index]. It is simple, quickly made and has very little fat. The flavor is terrific.

Makes an 11 to 13 inch [27 $^1/_2$ to 32 $^1/_2$ centimeter] pie crust

1 $^1/_4$ to 1 $^1/_2$ cups [175 to 210 grams] all purpose unbleached flour
$^1/_2$ cup [105 grams] sugar
4 $^1/_2$ ounces [125 grams] almonds, ground finely
1 teaspoon grated lemon peel, about $^1/_4$ lemon
$^1/_4$ teaspoon almond extract or $^1/_4$ teaspoon vanilla or $^1/_4$ teaspoon ground nutmeg
$^1/_8$ teaspoon salt
$^1/_2$ cup [110 milliliters] frozen egg substitute, thawed
vegetable cooking spray

Combine flour, sugar, almonds, lemon, flavoring and salt in a mixing bowl. Gradually add egg, mixing well as you add, until dough comes together in a ball. Roll out on a well floured surface with a rolling pin into a round large enough to fit a well sprayed pie pan. Chill for 1 hour to overnight.

To prebake pie crust, bake in a preheated 325°F. [165°C.] oven for 15 to 20 minutes, until lightly browned. Do not prebake for Cheese Pie [see Index].

Peach Crisp *[p]*

This is an easy and tasty dessert to make with frozen sliced or fresh peaches. I devised this recipe when I saw some gorgeous frozen peaches at the market and couldn't resist buying them.

Serves 8

3 pounds [1.35 kilos] sliced frozen peaches or peeled fresh
3 tablespoons lemon juice
1 tablespoon ground cinnamon
$^1/_2$ teaspoon ground nutmeg
$^1/_8$ teaspoon ground ginger
pareve butter flavor cooking spray
$^1/_2$ cup [100 grams] brown sugar
$^1/_2$ cup [75 grams] all purpose unbleached flour
$^1/_2$ cup [75 grams] oatmeal
4 ounces [110 grams] shelled walnuts, chopped
2 ounces [55 grams] margarine, melted

Mix together peaches, lemon juice, cinnamon, nutmeg and ginger. Pile mixture into a sprayed 9 $^1/_2$ inch [24 centimeter] deep dish pie dish.

Combine sugar, flour, oatmeal, walnuts and margarine until crumbly. Spread sugar mixture evenly over top of peaches.

Bake in a preheated 375°F. [190°C.] oven for about 1 hour, until nicely browned and bubbly.

Serve hot or at room temperature.

Pumpkin - Apple Loaf [p]

A dense, flavorful cake, easily made and very moist. The cake lasts for a few days. Pumpkin is one of those versatile ingredients that I like to use, either fresh or canned. I like it in sweet and savory dishes. Freeze the extra loaf for another time.

Makes 2 loaves

2 ¹/₂ cups [350 grams] all purpose unbleached flour
2 cups [405 grams] sugar
1 tablespoon pumpkin pie spice
1 tablespoon ground cinnamon
1 tablespoon baking powder
1 teaspoon baking soda
¹/₂ teaspoon salt
¹/₂ cup [110 milliliters] frozen egg substitute, thawed
8 ounces [225 grams] cooked pumpkin puree, canned or fresh, 2 cups
¹/₃ cup [75 milliliters] orange juice
¹/₃ cup [75 milliliters] light vegetable oil [safflower]
2 cups [450 milliliters] homemade Spiced Apple Sauce [see Index] or canned
8 ounces [225 grams] shelled pecans, chopped
vegetable cooking spray

Combine flour, sugar, pie spice, cinnamon, baking powder, baking soda and salt in a mixing bowl. In another bowl, combine egg substitute, pumpkin, orange juice, oil and apple sauce.

Add egg mixture to flour mixture and mix until moistened. Stir in pecans and mix just until combined.

Pour batter into 2 sprayed non-stick loaf pans or into 2 greased and floured loaf pans 4 x 8 inches [10 x 20 centimeters].

Bake in a preheated 350°F. [175°C.] oven for 50 minutes to 1 hour until a tooth pick stuck in the center comes out clean. Turn out onto a rack to cool.

The cakes freeze well, wrapped in foil.

Rhubarb - Strawberry Pie *[p]*

I love the combination of rhubarb and strawberries. This is a delicious pie, a nice sweet and sour flavor, well appreciated by everyone. "Easy as pie."

Makes an 11 inch [27 ¹/₂ centimeter] pie or
    2 - 9 inch [22 ¹/₂ centimeter] pies

1 pound [450 grams] frozen rhubarb, thawed

1 pound [450 grams] frozen strawberries, thawed

1 cup [210 grams] sugar

6 tablespoons cornstarch

2 tablespoons quick Tapioca

1 single 11 inch [27 ¹/₂ centimeter] Pie Crust [see Index],
    unbaked or 2 - 9 inch [22 ¹/₂ centemeter] unbaked

Combine all the ingredients, except pie crust and pour into unbaked pie crust. With pie crust scraps, make a latticed top. Bake pie in a pre-heated 450°F. [230°C.] oven for 15 minutes. Lower heat to 375°F. [190°C.] and bake an additional 45 to 50 minutes. Cool on a rack.

The pie can be baked several days ahead of time and stored in the fridge. The pie can also be frozen, tightly wrapped with foil.

Rice Pudding #1 [d]

It was amazing to me how many people requested that I make rice pudding and everyone has a different idea of how it should taste. As a result this is one of three versions that I like. [See Index for the other versions.] This is an easy, very dense rice pudding.

Serves 8

³/₄ **cup [110 grams] white raisins**
³/₄ **cup [175 milliliters] dark rum**
1 cup [175 grams] long grain rice, rinsed and drained
3 cans evaporated skim milk, 36 ounces [1 liter]
16 ounces [450 milliliters] skim milk
¹/₂ cup [105 grams] white sugar
¹/₂ cup [100 grams] brown sugar
pinch ground nutmeg
pinch ground allspice
1 teaspoon vanilla
vegetable cooking spray
optional: low or no-fat whipped topping

Macerate raisins in rum for 30 minutes.

Combine all the ingredients, including rum, in a saucepan. Bring to a simmer on top of stove. Transfer to a sprayed 3 quart [2 ¹/₂ liter] oven safe casserole dish, suitable for serving. Place casserole in a pre-heated 300°F. [150°C.] oven, cover and bake, for 2 hours and 45 minutes, stirring very occasionally. This part can be done ahead. If baked the day before, refrigerate overnight.

About 30 minutes before serving, place pudding in a preheated 300°F. [150°C.] oven for 20 minutes, covered.

Serve with the whipped topping, if desired.

Rice Pudding #2 [d]

This version of rice pudding is delicious and creamy and kind of soupy, also easy to make ahead of time, but completely different from the other versions.

Serves 8

²/₃ cup [125 grams] white raisins	
²/₃ cup [150 milliliters] rum	
1 cup [6 ounces - 175 grams] long grain white rice	
2 cups [450 milliliters] water	
3 cans evaporated skim milk, 36 ounces [1 liter]	
¹/₂ cup [100 grams] brown sugar	
1 ¹/₂ teaspoons vanilla	
1 cinnamon stick	
¹/₄ teaspoon ground nutmeg	

Macerate raisins in rum for 30 minutes.

Combine rice and water in a 4 quart [3 ¹/₂ liter] saucepan and bring to a boil, uncovered. Let boil for 2 minutes. Drain well. Set aside in a bowl.

In same saucepan, bring milk, sugar, vanilla, cinnamon stick, nutmeg, raisins and rum slowly to a boil. Add rice. Reduce heat to very low and simmer, partly covered for about 1 hour, stirring occasionally, to keep rice from sticking. The rice will absorb most of the liquid but will still be creamy. Remove and discard cinnamon stick.

Pour mixture into a 3 quart [2 ¹/₂ to 3 liter] microwave safe or oven safe serving bowl and let cool.

The pudding can be made up to 2 days ahead of time. Refrigerate covered until about 30 minutes before serving time.

The pudding can be served cold or if desired, the pudding can be heated in a microwave or in a preheated 300°F. [150°C.] oven for 20 minutes.

Rice Pudding #3 *[d]*

This versiion of rice pudding is a custardy pudding. It is easy to make and can be made ahead of time. I think this is my personal favorite.

Serves 8 easily

1 cup [175 grams] long grain white rice
2 cups [450 milliliters] water
3 cans evaporated skim milk, 36 ounces [1 liter]
¹/₂ cup [100 grams] brown sugar
3 ounces [90 grams] white raisins
²/₃ cup [150 milliliters] rum
³/₄ cup [175 milliliters] frozen egg substitute, thawed
2 teaspoons vanilla
¹/₄ teaspoon ground nutmeg
butter flavored cooking spray

Combine rice and water in a small saucepan. Bring to a boil and boil for 2 minutes. Turn off heat and drain rice.

In a large saucepan bring milk to a simmer, turn off heat and add sugar and rice. Stir well and let sit for 30 minutes, stirring occasionally.

Combine raisins and rum in a small saucepan. Bring to a simmer and turn off heat. Let sit for 30 minutes.

Combine eggs, vanilla and nutmeg. Add mixture to rice mixture together with raisins and rum. Pour into a sprayed 2 ¹/₂ quart [2 ¹/₄ liter] casserole, suitable for serving. Place casserole in a larger pot and fill larger pot half way up sides of casserole with hot water.

Preheat oven to 350°F. [175°C.]. Place casserole and larger pot in oven and turn down heat to 325°F. [165°C.]. Bake for 25 minutes. Stir pudding and turn heat to 300°F. [150°C.] and bake for 25 minutes. Stir pudding and bake for about 35 minutes more, until a knife inserted into center comes out clean. Let pudding cool on a rack with a piece of pastic wrap placed directly on top of pudding to prevent formation of a skin.

Serve pudding at room temperature or slightly warmed.

The pudding can be made up to 3 days ahead of time. Store in the fridge until ready to serve.

GO WITHS

For Salads, Vegetables, Main Dishes & Desserts

Aioli [p]

I make this garlicky mayonaisse to "go with" the Fish Stew - Bouilla-baisse [see Index]. It is very rich so a little bit goes a long way. If you have any left over, it is a good addition to Tuna Salad [see Index] and is delicious on a baked or boiled potato. This very easy "go with" lasts almost indefinitely.

Makes about 1 cup [225 milliliters]

¹/₂ cup [110 milliliters] no-fat mayonaisse
¹/₂ cup [110 milliliters] reduced fat mayonaisse
2 tablespoons [¹/₈ cup] snipped chives or garlic chives
2 to 3 tablespoons chopped garlic, to taste
dash salt

Mix all the ingredients together thoroughly. Let sit, refrigerated, for an hour to develop the flavors. Store in a covered jar in the fridge almost indefinitely.

Spiced Apple Sauce [p]

This is the applesauce I use as an ingredient in cakes and as a side dish to go with meats and poultry. It is delicious and easy to prepare. If I have apples that are no longer crisp, I make spiced apple sauce, and either eat it immediately or freeze for a later time.

Makes about 4 cups [1 liter]

2 ¹/₂ pounds [1.15 kilos] tart apples, peeled, cored, sliced [Granny Smith is good]
1 lemon, unpeeled, sliced thinly, seeds removed
2 to 3 pieces whole cinnamon stick
1 tablespoon ground cinnamon
¹/₂ teaspoon ground nutmeg
1 teaspoon ground allspice
¹/₂ teaspoon ground cloves
1 cup [225 milliliters] water, approximately
brown sugar or brown sugar "Twin", to taste

Place all the ingredients, except sugar in a 2 ¹/₂ quart [2 liter] saucepan and bring to a simmer. Simmer, over very low heat, until apples are very tender, adding water as needed, about 2 hours. Taste and add sugar, if needed.

Remove and discard cinnamon sticks. Cool and store covered in the fridge.

The apple sauce lasts at least a week and can be frozen.

Beet Horseradish [p]

This is a lethal, delicious horseradish. Use it with Gefilte Fish, Brisket [see Index] and other meats and poultry. This is easy to make and much better than the commercial kind.

Makes about 3 cups [700 milliliters]

14 ounces [400 grams] fresh horseradish root.

a 16 ounce [450 gram] jar pickled beets with juice

Peel horseradish and cut into $^1/_2$ inch [1 $^3/_4$ centimeter] pieces. Drop horseradish pieces, one at a time, through feed tube of a running food processor. CAREFUL the fumes are extremely strong. [If you have goggles, wear them.] When horseradish is chopped very finely, add beets and juices, and pulse until beets are chopped and mixture is combined.

Store in an airtight container with a tight lid, in the fridge. Keeps for about 2 months. It gradually loses its strength.

Bohemian Bread Dumplings [m or p]

My friend Maria Picard, who was a fabulous cook, made these dumplings every time she came from Connecticut to visit her children, the Rosens, my friends for 30 years, in San Francisco. I was lucky enough to watch her make them and also lucky enough to receive a copy of her recipe. I hope you like them too. I serve them as a side dish with anything that has a gravy. We miss you, Maria.

Serves 8, generously

14 ounces [400 grams] dried baguette or left over bread, toasted, chopped into crumbs [I chop them in a food processor]

2 $^1/_2$ cups [560 milliliters] Chicken Broth [see Index] or pareve chicken soup, from the mix

½ cup [110 milliliters] frozen egg substitute, thawed

olive oil cooking spray

2 teaspoons margarine or extra virgin olive oil

5 ½ ounces [150 grams] shallots, chopped, about 3 large

5 ounces [135 grams] carrots, chopped, 1 large or 2 medium

7 ounces [200 grams] celery, chopped, 2 large ribs

½ pound [225 grams] fresh mushrooms, coarsely chopped

2 tablespoons snipped fresh chives or dill or parsley leaves, chopped

salt, to taste

fresh black pepper, to taste

½ to 1 cup [75 to 140 grams] all purpose unbleached flour

Place bread crumbs in a bowl and add broth and eggs. Let sit until most of liquid is absorbed.

In a sprayed fry pan, in margarine or oil, saute shallots, carrots, celery and mushrooms until tender, 15 to 20 minutes. Add herbs, salt and pepper. Add mixture to bread crumb mixture. Add enough flour to bind mixture.

Form a test dumpling by dropping a 1 ½ inch [3 ¾ centimeter] dumpling into a pot of salted water. Let simmer for 10 minutes. If it falls apart, add more flour to mixture. Retest.

Bring a large kettle of salted water to a boil. Form dumplings with wet hands into 1 ½ inch [3 ¾ centimeter] balls and drop balls into water, in batches. [Dumplings will rise to surface while they cook.] Cook for 10 to 15 minutes. As they are done, remove with a slotted spoon to a bowl and serve hot.

The dumplings can be made ahead of time and reheated in an oven or microwave just before serving.

Save all your leftover bread to make these dumplings, they are great.

Bread Turkey Stuffing [p]

This is one of several stuffings that I make to go with Roast Turkey [see Index]. It is simple and easy to make.

Enough for an 11 pound [5 kilo] turkey [can be doubled]

vegetable cooking spray

1 ½ tablespoons Nyafat or margarine

8 ounces [225 grams] onions, diced

8 ounces [225 grams] green peppers, seeded, membranes removed, diced

8 ounces [225 grams] celery, with leaves, diced

8 ounces [225 grams] fresh mushrooms, sliced

5 to 6 cups, 1 ⅓ pounds [625 grams] bread cubes, from stale bread

1 ½ cups [350 milliliters] cold pareve chicken flavored soup, from the mix

½ cup [110 milliliters] frozen egg substitute, thawed

1 tablespoon poultry seasoning

2 teaspoons salt

1 teaspoon fresh white pepper

In a sprayed Dutch oven, heat fat and saute onions, green peppers and celery until well wilted. Add mushrooms and saute until mushrooms have softened, about 5 minutes. Set aside.

In a large bowl, lightly toss bread cubes with soup and eggs. Add vegetable saute and toss well to mix. Add poultry seasoning, salt and pepper and mix. Chill thoroughly before stuffing turkey.

Or place stuffing in a well sprayed baking dish, suitable for serving, and cover with foil. Bake in a preheated 375°F. [190°C.] oven for 1 hour. Remove foil and bake an additional 15 minutes, to brown top.

Bake stuffing early in the day and refrigerate. Bake for 20 minutes, uncovered, to rewarm.

How to Prepare and Sterilize Jars for Canning and Preserving

Wash jars in hot soapy water and rinse in very hot water. Put jars in a kettle on a folded kitchen towel or in a canner and cover with hot water. Bring water to a boil, covered, and boil jars for 15 minutes from time water comes to a boil. Turn off heat and let jars stand in hot water. Just before filling with hot food, invert hot jars onto a kitchen towel to drain. Sterilize lids for 5 minutes.

Fill jars while still hot and seal with lids. Lightly screw on gaskets. Put back in water bath with tongs, cover with 2 inches [5 centimeters] of water and bring back to a boil and boil for 10 to 20 minutes according to recipe instructions.

Transfer jars with tongs to racks to cool. Tighten gaskets. Label with contents and date. Store in a cool dark place.

Horseradish Sauce [d or p]

This is a simple sauce with a little bite and a little sweetness. I give you two different sauces, both equally good, one pareve, one dairy. This is a good "go with" for the Tomato Aspic [see Index].

Makes 1 ¹/₂ cups [350 milliliters]

³/₄ cup [175 milliliters] Horseradish [see Index] or store bought

³/₄ cup [175 milliliters] Dijon Mustard or no-fat sour cream substitute

Combine horseradish with mustard or sour cream and mix thoroughly. Place in a jar and refrigerate. Lasts for about a month.

Cranberry Relish *[p]*

This recipe for a very special cranberry side dish makes enough for several meals. It can be frozen or preserved in jars to store in your pantry. It is wonderful with Roast Turkey [see Index] for holiday meals, or with chicken dishes or even with fish. It has a mellow flavor that melts in your mouth. Margit Weisgal gave me this recipe.

Makes 8 cups [1.8 liters]

8 ounces [225 grams] dried cranberries
1 large apple, peeled, cored, chopped finely
1 orange, unpeeled, seeded, minced finely
1 lemon, unpeeled, seeded, minced finely
³/₄ cup [160 grams] sugar
¹/₂ teaspoon ground cinnamon
¹/₄ teaspoon ground cloves
¹/₄ teaspoon ground allspice
¹/₄ teaspoon ground nutmeg
2 to 3 cups water
1 bag cranberries, fresh or frozen, 12 ounces [340 grams]

Combine dried cranberries, apple, orange, lemon, sugar, cinnamon, cloves, allspice, nutmeg and water in a large saucepan. Bring to a boil and simmer, uncovered, for 30 to 40 minutes, stirring frequently, until apple is very soft. Add bag of cranberries and continue simmering until cranberries have popped and are very soft, an additional 30 to 40 minutes, adding more water as needed and stirring frequently.

Divide relish into serving portions and freeze or process in jars in a water bath for 15 minutes. See Index for Canning and Preserving instructions.

Corn Meal Dumplings [p]

I love anything made with corn meal. These assertive dumplings "go with" fricassees, stews and soups. I would eat these any time.

Makes 18 to 20 dumplings

1 ¹/₂ cups [210 grams] all purpose unbleached flour
1 ¹/₂ cups [225 grams] yellow corn meal
2 teaspoons baking powder
1 ¹/₂ teaspoons salt
3 tablespoons sugar
³/₄ cup [175 milliliters] frozen egg substitute, thawed
³/₄ cup [175 milliliters] water
2 ounces [55 grams] margarine, melted, cooled
2 tablespoons snipped fresh chives
2 tablespoons chopped fresh parsley leaves

Place flour, corn meal, baking powder, salt and sugar in a mixing bowl. Add egg substitute and water and mix until well combined. Add margarine, chives and parsley and mix well.

Dip a tablespoon in a glass of cold water, scoop up a spoon full of dough and drop onto simmering fricassee, soup, stew or gravy. Cover pot and steam dumplings for 20 minutes without lifting the lid. Do NOT peek.

Remove dumplings with a slotted spoon and set aside, if making these ahead of time. Cover until ready to rewarm in a microwave or over simmering liquid.

Corn Bread Turkey Stuffing *[m or p]*

I love corn bread and so favor this stuffing over the others in my book [see Index]. I sometimes make it easier by using one of the dried prepared corn bread stuffing crumbs in a box or bag. Or I bake my own Corn Bread [see Index].

Enough for an 11 pound [5 kilo] turkey [can be doubled]

---

2 cups [450 milliliters] hot Chicken Broth [see Index] or canned or pareve chicken flavored soup, from the mix

10 ¹/₂ ounces [300 grams] onions, chopped

10 ¹/₂ ounces [300 grams] celery with leaves, chopped

9 ounces [250 grams] sweet red peppers, cut up small

8 ounces [225 grams] fresh mushrooms, sliced

a 9 x 11 inch [22 ¹/₂ x 27 ¹/₂ centimeter] Corn Bread [see Index], baked, crumbled, or 6 cups [330 grams] toasted corn bread stuffing crumbs

¹/₂ cup [110 milliliters] frozen egg substitute, thawed

1 ¹/₂ tablespoons poultry seasoning

1 teaspoon rubbed sage

salt, to taste

fresh white pepper, to taste

2 tablespoons sugar, if using prepared crumbs or to taste

2 tablespoons chopped fresh parsley leaves

vegetable cooking spray

In a large mixing bowl, pour hot broth over onions, celery, peppers, mushrooms and corn bread crumbs. Toss well and let cool.

Add eggs, poultry seasoning, sage, salt, pepper, sugar, if using, and parsley. Toss well to mix. Chill thoroughly, covered, before stuffing turkey.

Or place stuffing in a well sprayed baking pan, suitable for serving, and cover with foil. Bake in a preheated 375°F. [190°C.] oven for 45 minutes. Uncover and bake an additional 15 minutes.

Bake stuffing early in the day and refrigerate. Bake for 20 minutes, uncovered, to rewarm.

270

Spicy Dry Rub for Poultry & Ribs *[p]*

This seasoning rub is delicious for spicy chicken or ribs. It keeps well and the recipe makes enough for several rubbings.

Makes about ¹/₃ cup [75 milliliters]

6 tablespoons chili powder
3 tablespoons ground cumin
1 tablespoon brown sugar
1 ¹/₂ teaspoons granulated garlic
1 ¹/₂ teaspoons onion powder
1 ¹/₂ teaspoons ground ginger
¹/₄ teaspoon ground cayenne pepper

Mix all the ingredients together and store in an airtight jar.

"Sun" Dried Tomatoes *[p]*

This "go with" ingredient is easy to make and takes almost no effort. I make them when plum tomatoes are on sale and store them in my pantry almost indefinitely. If you grow tomatoes, put in at least one plant of plum tomatoes and towards the end of the season, make some of these dried tomatoes.

Wash tomatoes well and core. Halve tomatoes lengthwise through core end. Sprinkle lightly with kosher salt and place them on a rack in an open baking pan. Preheat electric oven to 140°F. [60°C.]. If you have a gas oven, your pilot light will be enough heat. Place baking pan with tomatoes in oven for 12 to 24 hours, until tomatoes are dry and leathery.

Store tomatoes in a jar and fill with extra virgin olive oil, or store in a zip lock plastic bag. If you store in olive oil, the oil will become flavored and can be used in salads and in cooking.

Fudge Sauce [d or p]

This rich fudgy sauce is not exactly diet fare, but it isn't terribly high in fat and I know it will be reserved for very special occasions. This is the kind that gets chewy when drizzled hot on frozen yogurt. It is thick and delicious and good over Meringues [see Index].

Makes about 2 cups [450 milliliters]

4 ounces [110 grams] bitter-sweet chocolate, broken into bits, NOT semi-sweet or unsweetened

1 ¹/₂ tablespoons Coffee Flavored Liqueur [Kahlua] [see Index]

2 ounces [55 grams] butter or margarine

²/₃ cup [150 milliliters] boiling water

1 ³/₄ cups [350 grams] sugar

4 tablespoons corn syrup

2 teaspoons vanilla extract

In a 2 ¹/₂ quart [2 ¹/₂ liter] saucepan, over very low heat, melt chocolate together with liqueur and butter or margarine. Add water, sugar and corn syrup and combine well. Bring mixture to a boil, stirring, and boil rapidly over medium heat, without stirring, for 8 minutes exactly. Remove from heat, add vanilla and mix. Serve warm.

Store in a covered jar in the fridge almost indefinitely. Reheat sauce by placing jar, uncovered, in a pan of simmering water, stirring occasionally.

Giblet Gravy [m]

This is our regular gravy to go with all the poultry that we make. It is simple, tasty and full of character. Save the leftovers for Turkey Gumbo [see Index].

Makes about 5 cups [1.2 liters]

giblets, neck and wing tips from ducks, chickens or turkeys
2 cups [450 milliliters] water
2 cups [450 milliliters] defatted Chicken Broth [see Index] or canned or from the mix
3 ounces [100 grams] celery, diced finely
3 ounces [100 grams] shallots, peeled, diced finely
optional: liver
salt, to taste
fresh white pepper, to taste

In a medium saucepan, combine giblets, neck, wing tips, water and broth. Bring to a boil, skimming the froth as it rises. Add celery and shallots and simmer until giblets are tender, about 1 $1/2$ hours. Add liver, if using, and salt and pepper, to taste.

Remove giblets and neck from gravy with a slotted spoon. Dice giblets finely. Pull meat from neck and dice finely. Remove liver from hot gravy and dice finely. Add diced meats to gravy. Discard wing tips. Add defatted juices from cooked poultry.

Reheat and serve in a sauceboat.

The gravy can be made ahead of time and refrigerated or frozen.

Lemon - Lime Chutney [p]

This recipe is based on a recipe from the late Laurie Colwin from Gourmet Magazine. I have varied it somewhat. I find this chutney positively addictive. It should ripen at least 1 month and is still great [maybe better] after 4 or 5 months. I preserve this for myself and for gifts. It is great with Roast Chicken [see Index] or fish or even Brisket [see Index]. I serve it often.

Makes 22 to 24 - 4 ounce [110 gram] jars

2 ¹/₂ pounds [1.125 kilos] lemons

2 ¹/₂ pounds [1.125 kilos] limes

4 tablespoons salt

8 garlic cloves, minced

5 ounces [135 grams] shallots, chopped finely

3 ¹/₂ ounces [100 grams] dried currants

12 ounces [325 grams] dried cranberries

¹/₂ cup [110 milliliters] lemon juice

¹/₂ cup [110 milliliters] lime juice

1 cup [225 milliliters] cider vinegar

2 tablespoons minced fresh ginger root

1 teaspoon ground cayenne pepper

1 teaspoon dried hot red pepper flakes

2 teaspoons ground cardamon

2 teaspoons ground coriander

2 pounds [900 grams] brown sugar

Remove peel from lemons and limes with a swivel bladed vegetable peeler, being careful not to include white pith, which is very bitter. Cut away pith from lemons and limes and discard it. Remove seeds. Chop peel and flesh of lemons and limes in a food processor until finely chopped. Transfer fruit to a glass or plastic bowl and sprinkle with salt. Refrigerate overnight.

   Place lemon lime mixture in a kettle and add the rest of the ingredients. Bring to a boil, stirring. Simmer mixture until it is very thick, stirring frequently, about 1 to 1 ¹/₂ hours.

Wash 2 dozen 4 ounce [110 gram] jars and tops in hot suds and rinse them in scalding water. Put jars in a kettle on a folded kitchen towel, or in a canning kettle, and cover with hot water. Bring water to a boil and boil jars for 15 minutes and lids for 5 minutes. Leave jars in water until chutney is done.

Just before filling hot jars with hot chutney, turn jars upside down onto a towel to drain briefly. Fill jars while still hot and place tops on and lightly screw on gaskets. Place jars back in water with tongs and bring water to a boil. [Be sure water covers jars by about 2 inches [5 centimeters].] Boil jars for 10 minutes. Remove jars with tongs to racks to cool.

Tighten gaskets and label jars with contents and date. Place jars in your pantry to be eaten in a month or two, not before.

Enjoy!

Lemon Icing [p]

This simple tart icing is the one I use for the Nut Torte [see Index] for Pesach. It is a perfect marriage of flavors.

Enough for 1 cake [can be doubled]

grated lemon rind from ¹/₂ lemon
1 tablespoon lemon juice
1 tablespoon boiling water
1 cup [210 grams] powdered sugar, sifted

Combine lemon rind, lemon juice and water. Add to sugar, gradually, until icing is smooth and creamy. If it is too thick to spread, add a drop or two of water. Double for a layer cake.

Mango Chutney [p]

Chutney is delicious with meats and poultry. Placed in small attractive jars, it makes a lovely gift for a host or hostess. Mango chutney is an ingredient used in other dishes. I always have some on hand, preserved. How to is at the end of the recipe.

Makes about 1 ½ quarts [1 ½ liters]

¾ cup [150 grams] brown sugar
1 cup [225 milliliters] white vinegar
2 ¼ pounds [1 kilo] mangos, well ripened, peeled, sliced
1 tablespoon minced fresh ginger root
7 ounces [200 grams] onions, chopped finely
1 lemon, unpeeled, sliced thinly, seeded
3 ounces [90 grams] raisins
5 ounces [150 grams] dried cranberries
2 garlic cloves, chopped
1 tablespoon Worcestershire sauce
2 ounces [60 grams] green peppers, seeded, diced
1 fresh hot pepper, about 2 inches [5 centimeters] long, seeds and membranes removed, diced finely
1 teaspoon dry mustard
2 ounces [60 grams] almonds, unpeeled, chopped
1 teaspoon salt, to taste

In a 4 quart [4 liter] saucepan, bring sugar and vinegar to a boil, stirring. Add the rest of the ingredients and bring mixture to a simmer, mixing well. Simmer, covered, over low heat, for 3 hours, stirring occasionally. Cool.

Store in covered jars, in the fridge.

Or, wash about 8 - 8 ounce [225 milliliter] jars and tops in hot suds and rinse in scalding water. Put jars in a kettle on a folded kitchen towel, or in a canning kettle, and cover with hot water. Bring water to a boil and boil jars for 15 minutes and lids for 5 minutes. Leave jars in hot water until chutney is finished.

Just before filling hot jars with hot chutney, turn jars upside down onto a towel to drain briefly. Fill jars while still hot and put on tops and lightly screw on gaskets. Place jars back in water, with tongs, making sure jars are covered by 2 inches [5 centimeters] of water and bring water to a boil. Boil jars for 10 minutes. Remove jars with tongs to racks to cool.

Tighten gaskets and label jars with contents and date. Place jars in your pantry to be enjoyed or given as gifts.

Horseradish [p]

My father-in-law, Abba Weisgal, invented this horseradish. It is delicious and a sinus clearer upper. It is very hot but deceptive because of the touch of sweetness. Watch the fumes, they are lethal. This is delicious served with Gefilte Fish and Brisket [see Index] etc.

Makes about 3 cups [700 milliliters]

6 ounces [175 grams] fresh horseradish root

1 ¹/₃ pounds [600 grams] fresh apples, peeled, cored, cut into chunks

2 tablespoons cider vinegar

Carefully peel horseradish with a swivel bladed peeler. Cut into ¹/₂ inch [1 ³/₄ centimeter] chunks. While a food processor is running, drop horseradish pieces through feed tube. CAREFUL the fumes are extremely strong, I wear goggles. Run machine until horseradish is finely ground. Add apple pieces and chop until apples are finely ground and blended with horseradish. Add vinegar and pulse until blended.

Store, covered tightly, in a screw top or canning jar in the fridge for a couple of months. It will gradually lose its strength, but still be delicious.

Nuckerl [p]

I used to watch my mother-in-law, Aranka Weisgal, sit with a bowl in her lap, filled with the ingredients for nuckerl and a wooden spoon in her hand, whipping up these delicious doughy dumplings. Today I make these dumpling with a mixer, much easier and quicker. I like them with Veal Goulash and with Tomato Soup [see Index]. I am sure they are great with anything that has a gravy.

Serves 8

3 cups [410 grams] all purpose unbleached flour, approximately

4 egg whites

$1/_4$ teaspoon salt

1 cup [225 milliliters] water

Using a mixer with the flat or K beater, beat all the ingredients together, adding more flour, if needed, to make a slightly sticky, very elastic dough, about 5 minutes.

Bring an 8 quart [8 liter] kettle half full of salted water to a boil. Dip a spoon in cold water, scoop a bit of dough and let it slide into boiling water. Continue making nuckerl until all dough is used. They swell as they cook so judge the size of the spoon you use by the size of nuckerl you want.

Carefully release nuckerl from bottom of pot with a wooden spoon, after 1 minute. Let nuckerl cook for 5 minutes. Drain nuckerl, and rinse with cold water. Lay on kichen towels to dry a bit and refrigerate, covered, until needed.

Onion Marmelade *[p]*

A delicious "go with" for meat and poultry with a touch of sweetness. We like onions in any form, raw or cooked, and lots of them.

Makes 3 cups [³/₄ liter]

1 pound [450 grams] onions, halved lengthwise, sliced crosswise ¹/₂ inch [1 ³/₄ centimeters] thick
1 ¹/₂ tablespoons extra virgin olive oil
3 tablespoons brown sugar
3 garlic cloves, chopped
1 cup [450 milliliters] water
3 tablespoons balsamic vinegar
3 tablespoons red wine
3 ¹/₂ ounces [100 grams] tomato paste
salt, to taste
fresh black pepper, to taste

Saute onions in oil in a Dutch oven or a large non-stick fry pan until browning, about 10 minutes. Add sugar and saute until onions begin to caramelize, an additional 10 minutes or so. Add garlic and the rest of the ingredients. Bring to a boil, cover and simmer over low heat for 1 hour, stirring occasionally.

Uncover and simmer until onion mixture is very thick, stirring frequently, about 30 to 40 minutes.

Serve at room temperature.

Store covered in the fridge.

The marmelade can be frozen or processed in a water bath for 15 minutes. See Index for How to Prepare and Sterilize Jars for Canning and Preserving.

Pesto *[d] [Basil Sauce]*

Pesto is a flavorful condiment that marries particularly well with pasta, either hot or cold, as in Pasta Salad [see Index] or as a Topping For Pizza [see Index]. Pesto will keep for ages in the fridge and it can be frozen. This version is very low fat and just as good as any that I've tasted. Serve it with a tomato, Mozzarella and anchovy salad. Lovely.

Makes about 2 cups [440 grams]

6 garlic cloves, peeled
4 ounces [110 grams] fresh basil leaves, measured without stalks
3 ounces [90 grams] fresh parsley leaves, measured without stalks
4 ounces [110 grams] pine nuts
¹/₂ cup [55 grams] grated Parmesan cheese
4 tablespoons extra virgin olive oil
salt, to taste
fresh black pepper, to taste

In a blender or a food processor, chop garlic finely. Add basil, parsley, pine nuts and Parmesan. Run machine until mixture is pureed. While machine is running, add olive oil in a stream through feed tube or opening in blender top. Run machine until mixture is well combined. Add salt and pepper to taste.

Freeze in small containers, about 4 ounces [110 grams] each.

Try adding a small amount of pesto to any vegetable soup. Delicious!

Pickled Carrots *[p]*

Since tiny carrots have become so available, I like to make these pickles. They can be made with large carrots cut into carrot sticks but the little carrots are much more attractive. I like the ones that come in a bunch so that I can use the tops in a vegetable soup, they are delicious.

For each 1 quart [1 liter] jar

18 ounces [500 grams] tiny carrots, peeled, or carrot sticks
boiling water
5 sprigs fresh dill
5 garlic cloves, peeled
1 small hot pepper, fresh or dried, pricked
1 teaspoon mustard seeds
1 teaspoon black peppercorns
1 ¹/₂ cups [350 milliliters] water
1 ¹/₂ tablespoons white vinegar
1 ¹/₂ tablespoons salt

Pour boiling water over carrots and let stand, covered, for 3 minutes. Drain.

Pack carrots tightly in a very clean glass jar. Add dill, garlic, pepper, mustard seeds and peppercorns.

In a saucepan bring water, vinegar and salt to a boil, stirring until salt is dissolved. Pour hot brine over carrots in jar. Cover loosely and set in the sun for 2 days to 1 week until done. Taste to test.

Keeps for months in the fridge.

Pickled Onions [p]

These little piquant morsels are a good addition to our pickle collection. They take some time so plan ahead. They are nice on an Antipasto [see Index] platter.

Makes a 26 ounce [730 milliliter] jar

1 pound [450 grams] peeled white pearl onions [see Note]	
1 ¹/₂ cups [350 milliliters] water	
3 tablespoons salt	
2 to 3 sprigs fresh dill	
5 garlic cloves, peeled	
1 ¹/₂ cups [350 milliliters] white vinegar	

In a small bowl stir together water and salt, until salt is dissolved. Add peeled onions and let sit at room temperature for 24 hours.

Drain onions, rinse well and drain again. Transfer onions to a sterilized jar, together with dill and garlic.

In a small saucepan, bring vinegar to a boil. Immediately pour hot vinegar over onions in jar. Cover, let cool and let marinate in fridge for 4 days before using.

Onions keep in fridge for about a month or 2.

Note: If you can't buy peeled pearl onions, prepare as follows. In a large saucepan bring 2 ¹/₂ quarts [2 liters] water to a boil. Add onions and boil 1 minute. Remove from heat and let cool 'til they can be handled. Carefully trim root end and peel onions.

Potato - Chestnut Stuffing [m]

This is the stuffing I like to go with Roast Goose [see Index]. It is very delicious. If there are any leftovers, they are wonderful made into potato cakes and lightly sauteed. See Note.

Enough for an 11 pound [5 kilo] goose or turkey [can be doubled]

2 ¼ pounds [1 kilo] potatoes, peeled

2 tablespoons Nyafat or margarine

1 ½ pounds [680 grams] onions, chopped finely

2 garlic cloves, minced

5 ½ ounces [150 grams] celery, diced finely, 1 large rib

9 brine cured black olives, seeded, cut up [Calamata]

½ pound [225 grams] fresh mushrooms, halved, sliced

giblets from turkey or goose, cooked, diced [from the gravy]

1 pound [450 grams] chestnuts, boiled 15 minutes, peeled, cut up

2 to 3 teaspoons salt, to taste

¼ to ½ teaspoon fresh black pepper, to taste

½ teaspoon sweet paprika

pinch cayenne pepper

4 tablespoons minced fresh parsley leaves

vegetable cooking spray

In a saucepan, cover potatoes with cold water and boil until barely tender. Drain. Put potatoes through a ricer into a large mixing bowl and let cool as riced, do NOT mash them.

In a Dutch oven, heat fat until hot. Saute, stirring, onions, garlic, celery, olives and mushrooms until lightly colored, about 15 to 20 minutes. Remove from heat and add giblets, chestnuts, salt, pepper, paprika and parsley. Let cool.

Add onion mixture to cold potatoes and mix lightly so as not to mash or pack potatoes. Taste and correct the seasoning. Chill thoroughly before stuffing goose or turkey.

Or place mixture in a well sprayed baking dish, suitable for serving, cover with foil, and bake in a preheated 375°F. [190°C.] oven, for 45 minutes. Remove foil and bake an additional 15 to 20 minutes, until nicely browned.

Bake stuffing early in the day and refrigerate. Bake for 20 minutes, uncovered, to rewarm.

Note: If there are any leftovers, Mix with some thawed frozen egg substitute or egg whites, make into patties and saute lightly in a sprayed fry pan until browned on each side. They make a wonderful side dish.

Powdered Sugar Icing *[p or d]*

This is an all purpose icing with several variations in flavor. Pick the most suitable for your purpose and taste.

Enough for 2 to 3 loaves

2 tablespoons hot water or
1 tablespoon hot water and
1 tablespoon lemon juice or rum or strong instant coffee
1 cup [150 grams] powdered sugar, sifted
³/₄ teaspoon vanilla

Slowly add liquid to sifted sugar, mixing constantly. If icing is too stiff, add more water, a few drops at a time until of spreading consistency. Add vanilla.

The icing can be doubled for a 2 layer cake.

Parsley Dumplings *[p]*

This substitute for potatoes, rice or pasta is light, doughy and delicious. A perfect "go with" for Chicken Fricassee [see Index]. They are a natural with any dish that has a gravy. If you make them tiny they are great with soup.

Makes about 18 large sized dumplings

2 cups [280 grams] all purpose unbleached flour
4 teaspoons baking powder
1 teaspoon salt
1 teaspoon sugar
2 ounces [55 grams] margarine
5 tablespoons chopped fresh parsley leaves
¹/₂ cup [110 milliliters] frozen egg substitute, thawed

¹/₂ to ²/₃ cup [110 to 150 milliliters] water

Place flour, baking powder, salt and sugar in a mixing bowl. Add margarine and cut into dry ingredients with a pastry cutter or with two knives. Add the rest of the ingredients and mix just until dough is moistened, adding water gradually.

Dip a tablespoon in cold water and scoop up some dough and drop onto simmering gravy, soup, broth or water. Cover pot and steam for exactly 20 minutes without lifting the lid. No peeking.

Remove from pot with a slotted spoon if making this ahead of time. Keep covered until ready to rewarm in a microwave or on top of simmering liquid.

Preserved Lemons [p]

These lemons are fabulous. I use them in many ways. Chopped up and added to salads, they give a most unusual taste. When lemons are plentiful and cheap, I buy them and preserve them for future use. They'll keep for at least a year, if they last that long. You can double or triple the recipe. The lemons are a Moroccan specialty, that I learned from my son-in-law, Haim Mimran.

6 lemons

coarse [Kosher] salt

1 cinnamon stick

5 black peppercorns

5 whole cloves

bottled or fresh lemon juice

Quarter lemons lengthwise but don't cut all the way to the bottom. Spread lemons open carefully and salt them well. Close them up. Place a sprinkling of salt in bottom of a glass jar, just large enough to hold lemons. Place lemons in jar in layers and sprinkle each layer with some salt. Add cinnamon, pepper and cloves to jar. Fill jar with lemon juice and close tightly. Label top with the date. Let lemons stand for 30 days, turning jar every day or so. Refrigerate after 30 days.

Remove whatever portion of lemon needed and rinse lightly with water before using.

Roasted Garlic [p]

Roasted garlic pulp is delicious spread on toast or crackers. I use it as a seasoning on Rib Roast and Rack of Lamb [see Index], etc.

Each head of garlic yields about 2 to 2 ½ tablespoons of pulp.

With a scissors snip off papery top of garlic head without exposing garlic cloves. Place whole heads of garlic in a small baking pan root side down. Spray olive oil cooking spray lightly over heads of garlic. If desired, sprinkle lightly with salt. Cover baking pan with foil.

Roast garlic in a preheated 350°F. [175°C.] oven for 1 hour to 1 hour 15 minutes, until very soft. Let cool.

Cut heads in half crosswise. With a small knife, scoop out pulp onto a cutting board. Mash with a fork. Transfer to a small jar. Drizzle a bit of extra virgin olive oil over top. Keeps for months, covered, in the fridge.

Hot Sauce for Enchiladas [p]

This is a simple tomato based sauce, with a nice bite. It will perk up any Enchilada dish [see Index].

Makes about 5 ½ cups [1.3 liters]

1 tablespoon minced garlic

2 teaspoons extra virgin olive oil

8 to 12 tablespoons chili powder, to taste

a 28 ounce [800 gram] can tomatoes, chopped coarsely

a 6 ounce [170 gram] can tomato paste

2 cups [450 milliliters] pareve chicken flavored soup, from the mix

2 teaspoons dried thyme

2 teaspoons dried basil

1 teaspoon ground cumin

2 teaspoons sugar, to taste
½ teaspoon salt
½ teaspoon fresh black pepper
3 ounces [85 grams] fresh parsley leaves, chopped [about 1 cup]

Saute garlic in oil for 30 seconds. Add chili powder and saute over very low heat, stirring constantly, for a minute or two, CAREFUL, do not burn chili. Add the rest of the ingredients, except parsley. Simmer sauce, uncovered, for 30 minutes, until sauce is thickened. Add parsley and remove from heat.

The sauce can be made 3 days ahead and can be frozen.

Spaetzle [p]

Spaetzles are wonderful tiny dumplings, suitable for any dish that has a gravy. They are made with a spaetzle machine, an inexpensive gadget similar to a ricer. Spaetzles are an excellent "go with" in Goulash Soup [see Index].

Serves 8

2 cups [280 grams] all purpose unbleached flour
½ teaspoon salt
2 ounces [60 grams] margarine
½ cup [110 milliliters] frozen egg substitute, thawed
about ½ cup [110 milliliters] water

Place flour and salt in a bowl. Add margarine and cut into flour with a pastry cutter, until dough resembles meal. Add egg and enough water to make a sticky but stiff dough.

Bring a large kettle half full of salted water to a boil. Place dough in spaetzle maker in batches and drop dough into boiling water. Cook until spaetzles come up to top of water. Remove with a slotted spoon to a colander as they are cooked. Rinse spaetzles in cold water, drain well and spread out to dry on towels.

Refrigerate until ready to serve with gravy or soup. Rewarm by rinsing or dipping into hot water.

Summer Kosher Dills [p]

When my daughter, Margit Weisgal, ran the wildly successful Goliath Bar in Jerusalem, ["a stone's throw from the King David"], we served sandwich platters for a light supper or for lunch. I made these pickles for the platters on my front patio. They are not as salty as the barrel pickles that you buy in the U.S. and their taste is wonderful. Plan ahead because they can take as long as 1 week depending on how much sun you have. I don't have a patio any more but I do have some good western sun every day that the sun is out so I let these "cook" on my window sill. Serve with sandwiches or with meat or chicken, etc.

For each 1 quart [1 liter] glass jar

20 ounces [580 grams] Kirby cucumbers, about 5
4 sprigs fresh dill
4 garlic cloves, peeled
1 $^{1}/_{2}$ teaspoons mustard seed
1 $^{1}/_{2}$ teaspoons whole black peppercorns
1 small hot pepper, pricked
2 cups [450 milliliters] water
1 tablespoon salt
1 tablespoon white vinegar

Pack cucumbers tightly in a very clean screw top or gasket top glass jar, [plastic jars melt from boiling brine]. Add dill, garlic, mustard seed, peppercorns and hot pepper to jar. In a small saucepan, bring water, salt and vinegar to a boil, stirring until salt is dissolved. Immediately pour hot brine into jar. Cover loosely and place jar in sun, either on a porch, patio or window sill, for 2 days to 1 week.

When pickles are done they will have lost their bright green color and brine will be cloudy. Screw on tops and refrigerate. The pickles keep for weeks, maybe months.

"Sun" Dried Tomato Catsup [p]

My son-in-law, Haim Mimran, runs the lovely Cafe Liliane in San Francisco. He loves to cook and is always coming up with innovative ideas. We are constantly exchanging recipes and ideas on how to improve the ones we have. He gave me this very interesting "go with", which has a tart-sweet taste and is almost like a chutney. It is delicious at a cookout with all the foods that one enjoys in summer.

Makes about 4 cups [900 milliliters]

1 ounce [28 grams] chopped "Sun" Dried Tomatoes [see Index] soaked in
¹/₂ cup [110 milliliters] hot water for 20 minutes
2 -14 ¹/₂ ounce [410 grams] cans diced tomatoes with juice
9 ¹/₂ ounces [270 grams] onions, chopped
2 garlic cloves, chopped
2 tablespoons brown sugar
2 tablespoons cider vinegar
1 tablespoon light vegetable oil [safflower]

Combine all the ingredients, including soaking water, in a medium saucepan. Bring to a simmer, and simmer until mixture is thick, about 2 hours, stirring occasionally. Let catsup cool slightly and puree in a food processor or blender.

Store covered in the fridge for weeks.

Tartar Sauce [d]

This simple sauce is the perfect "go with" for the Poached Salmon [see Index]. This recipe was suggested to me by my friend, Marjorie Moch. It is very tasty and is good with other fish dishes.

Makes about 4 ½ cups [1 liter]

2 cups [450 grams] no-fat yogurt

2 cups [450 grams] low fat mayonaisse

6 ounces [175 grams] sweet onions, chopped, Vidalia is nice

2 large handfuls fresh Italian parsley leaves, chopped

2 tablespoons chopped garlic

salt, to taste

fresh white pepper, to taste

Combine all the ingredients and mix well. Refrigerate for several hours, to develop the flavor, before serving. The sauce keeps for months.

Tartar Sauce #2 [p]

This is another tartar sauce, that is a great "go with" for cold artichokes or aspapagus. It makes a nice dip with crudities and is good with all kinds of fish.

Makes about 2 ½ cups [½ liter]

½ cup [50 grams] minced green onions

½ cup [30 grams] minced fresh parsley leaves

4 ½ ounces [125 grams] minced Dill Pickles [see Index]

2 tablespoons minced drained capers

1 tablespoon Dijon mustard

1 teaspoon Worcestershire sauce

| 1 tablespoons minced garlic |
| salt, to taste |
| fresh white pepper, to taste |
| 16 ounces [450 grams] low fat mayonaisse |

Combine all the ingredients and mix well. Place in a jar, cover and refrigerate at least 1 hour before using. The sauce keeps almost indefinitely in the fridge.

Tomato Sauce For Pizza [p]

This delicious sauce especially formulated for the Pita Pizzas [see Index] is simple, easy to make and quick.

Makes 3 ½ cups [800 milliliters]

| olive oil cooking spray |
| 1 teaspoon extra virgin olive oil |
| 4 ounces [115 grams] onions, chopped finely |
| 2 large garlic cloves, chopped finely |
| a 28 ounce [800 gram] can tomatoes, chopped |
| 3 ½ ounces [100 grams] tomato paste |
| 1 ½ teaspoons dried oregano |
| 1 ½ teaspoons dried basil |
| 1 teaspoon dried thyme |
| ½ teaspoon salt |
| fresh black pepper, to taste |
| 1 teaspoon sugar |

In a sprayed medium saucepan, heat olive oil until hot. Add onions and garlic and saute, over medium heat, until well softened. Add the rest of the ingredients and simmer, uncovered, over low heat, stirring frequently, for 35 minutes, until thickened. Let cool.

Tonnato Sauce [p]

This is my version of a delicious sauce that is a perfect accompaniment for sliced cold turkey, sliced cold veal or sliced cold roast beef. Make the sauce a day ahead of time.

Enough for 2 pounds [900 grams] sliced meat

2 -6 ½ ounce [185 gram] cans tuna, packed in oil, drained
6 to 8 anchovy filets, not rinsed
½ cup [110 milliliters] frozen egg substitute, thawed
2 tablespoons lemon juice
¼ cup [55 milliliters] extra virgin olive oil
2 tablespoons capers

Puree tuna and anchovies in a food processor. Add and puree egg substitute and lemon juice. While machine is running, slowly add olive oil through feed tube in a stream and run until smooth. Add capers and puree.

Spread sauce over meat slices thickly and chill for several hours or overnight, covered. The sauce thickens as it chills.

Watermelon Pickles [p]

These sweet pickles are easy to make and use up that watermelon rind that we are left with each summer.

Makes 9 - 8 ounce [225 milliliter] jars

3 ³/₄ pounds [1.7 kilos] watermelon rind
4 cups [900 milliliters] water
¹/₄ cup [55 grams] coarse [kosher] salt
water, for boiling
4 cups [900 milliliters] water
4 cups [900 milliliters] cider vinegar
2 cups [425 grams] sugar
following tied in a piece of cheesecloth
1 teaspoon whole allspice
1 teaspoon whole cloves
2 to 3 sticks cinnamon
2 to 3 pieces preserved ginger
1 large lemon, unpeeled, sliced thinly, seeded

Peel green skin and discard from watermelon rind. Cut rind into small cubes. Place in a bowl. Mix together water and salt and stir until salt is dissolved. Add mixture to cubes in bowl, cover and let sit in fridge overnight. Drain.

Cover cubes with cold water in a saucepan. Bring to a boil and boil until tender, 10 to 15 minutes. Drain.

In same saucepan, combine the rest of the ingredients and bring to a boil, stirring until sugar is dissolved. Add watermelon cubes and boil until watermelon is translucent, about 1 hour.

Pour into sterilized preserving jars and process in a water bath for 10 minutes. See Index for How to Prepare and Sterilize Jars for Canning and Preserving.

A Few Words About Making and Serving a Chinese Meal

1. Chinese food requires more last minute cooking than other food because the crispness of the vegetables must be preserved. Plan ahead because all slicing and chopping and some of the preparation can be done in advance, as indicated in the recipes.

2. All recipes serve 8 people. Choose a variety from the soups, meats, vegetables and barbeque recipes. Rice or noodles are a must at every Chinese meal.

3. A little meat goes a long way.

4. Test and taste your soy sauce. I only use light soy sauce.

5. Homemade Chicken Broth [see Index] or canned or pareve chicken flavored soup, from the mix, can be used in the recipes calling for this ingredient.

6. If you are serving finger food, serve paper napkins along with your cloth napkins. Your guests will be more comfortable using these.

7. Cut most ingredients into bite size pieces so they will be easy to pick up with chopsticks.

8. Dried black Chinese mushrooms must be soaked in hot water for 30 minutes before using. The stems are always discarded. I prefer dried Shitake to fresh, as the flavor is more intense. Store dried mushrooms in a covered container in the fridge or freezer to prevent bugs.

9. I prefer a non-stick Dutch oven to a wok, when cooking Chinese food.

10. Store fresh ginger root in a covered jar filled with vodka, in the fridge. It will last almost forever.

11. Over the years, I've collected various Chinese dishes, many both inexpensive and attractive. I have rice bowls for rice and/or soup, tiny tea cups and a tea pot, tiny plates for sauces and of course, bamboo chopsticks, sake cups, and sake carafes for individual serving. Any large platters and covered bowls are suitable for serving.

CHINESE

Chinese Barbeque Ribs [m]

I love these ribs. They are great and delicious and a terrific part of any Chinese meal.

Serves 8

2 tablespoons chopped garlic
1 ¹/₂ cups [350 milliliters] lite soy sauce
1 cup [210 grams] sugar
³/₄ teaspoon fresh black pepper
1 teaspoon grated fresh ginger root
grated peel of 1 orange
³/₄ teaspoon 5 Spice Powder [see Index]
16 to 20 beef back ribs, about 10 pounds [4.5 kilos]

Combine all the ingredients, except ribs, in a small saucepan. Heat just until sugar is dissolved, stirring. Cool.

Place ribs in a large pan. Pour cooled marinade over ribs, turning and covering ribs with marinade. Marinate ribs at least overnight and up to 2 days, turning frequently. Drain and discard marinade.

Place ribs on a rack in a foil lined baking pan and bake in a pre-heated 300°F. [150°C.] oven for 2 hours. Discard fat.

The ribs can be prepared ahead of time and reheated in a 300°F. [150°C.] oven for 15 to 20 minutes.

5 Spice Powder [p]

If you can't buy this already mixed, make your own.

Makes about ½ cup [110 milliliters]

2 tablespoons black peppercorns
2 tablespoons whole cloves
2 tablespoons fennel seeds
1 tablespoon broken cinnamon stick
1 tablespoon broken star anise

Combine ingredients in a blender or clean coffee grinder to pulverize. Store in an airtight container.

Steamed Bok Choy [p]

This lovely side dish is a good addition to a Chinese meal. It is tasty and easy and quick to make.

Serves 8

2 teaspoons sesame oil
2 tablespoons minced garlic
3 ounces [90 grams] green onions, about 1 bunch, sliced
2 tablespoons lite soy sauce
3 pounds [1.36 kilos] bok choy, stalks halved lengthwise, sliced crosswise or baby bok choy, whole
1 tablespoon cornstarch mixed with
½ cup [110 milliliters] cold pareve chicken flavored soup, from the mix

In a Dutch oven or a wok, heat oil until hot. Add garlic and onions and stir fry for 30 seconds. Add soy sauce and bok choy, cover pot and cook until steaming. Uncover and toss well. Add cornstarch mixture and combine well. Cover and steam 2 minutes. Serve.

Cauliflower in Black Bean Sauce [p]

This tangy dish is an interesting and different way to serve cauliflower. I like this as part of a vegetarian dinner.

Serves 8

3 ¹/₃ pounds [1 ¹/₂ kilos] fresh white cauliflower
2 tablespoons fermented black beans, soaked 10 minutes, drained
2 to 4 garlic cloves, to taste
1 tablespoon lite soy sauce
1 teaspoon sugar
1 teaspoon dry sherry
1 ¹/₂ cups [350 milliliters] cold pareve chicken flavored soup, from the mix
1 tablespoon cornstarch
1 teaspoon lite soy sauce
olive oil cooking spray
salt, to taste
fresh black pepper, to taste
2 ounces [60 grams] green onions, sliced, ¹/₂ cup, to garnish

Remove cauliflower leaves and cut out core. Separate cauliflower into florets and slice florets into bite size. Half fill a kettle with salted water and bring to a boil. Add cauliflower slices and cook over high heat for 5 minutes ONLY. Drain, rinse under running cold water, drain and set aside.

In a mortar and pestle or mini food processor, mash black beans, garlic, soy, sugar and sherry together to make a paste and set aside. Combine soup, cornstarch and soy sauce and set aside.

Add cauliflower slices to a well sprayed Dutch oven or wok and stir fry for 3 minutes. Add black bean paste and broth mixture, mixing to combine well. This part can be prepared ahead.

Just before serving, heat cauliflower mixture, stirring until sauce is thickened and cauliflower is hot. Add salt and pepper to taste. Sprinkle with green onions and serve.

Chicken Won Tons *[m]*

I buy won ton skins fresh from our Oriental grocery store. They are tender and very delicate. I love working with them. The skins are also available in most supermarkets.

Enough for 54 to 60 won ton skins

1 large dried black Chinese mushroom
7 ounces [200 grams] raw boneless, skinless chicken, trimmed of fat
1 large green onion
2 egg whites
1 1/2 teaspoons lite soy sauce
1 1/4 teaspoons salt
couple grinds fresh white pepper
1 package won ton skins
cornstarch

Cover mushroom with hot water and let soften for 30 minutes. Drain, remove and discard stem.

In a food processor or meat grinder, mince chicken, mushroom and green onion. Add the rest of the ingredients, except cornstarch, and combine well.

Place a teaspoon of filling on each skin. Fold over to form a triangle. Wet edges with water to stick. Fold over again, making a double fold. Wetting each corner with water, fold over each corner to meet in the middle, forming a little nurses cap. Lay won tons in one layer, not touching, on a corn starch sprinkled baking sheet, [I use a small screen strainer] until all won tons are made. Cover and refrigerate until ready to cook and freeze the extras.

Place won tons, still on baking sheet, in freezer for about 1 hour until frozen. Remove from pan and store in a zip lock plastic bag until needed. Do not thaw before cooking.

Celery Cabbage Salad [p]

My friend Marjorie Moch says this is the best Chinese Caesar salad she's ever eaten, allbeit tongue in cheek. This crisp, simple salad is a refreshing addition to a Chinese meal.

Serves 8

2 ³/₄ pounds [3.37 kilos] Napa or Chinese celery cabbage

7 ounces [200 grams] green onions, sliced, about 2 bunches

fresh black pepper, to taste

¹/₂ recipe Caesar Salad Dressing [see Index]

Divide each cabbage leaf in half lengthwise. Slice cabbage leaves crosswise into thin slices. Place cabbage and onions in a large salad bowl. Sprinkle with freshly ground pepper, to taste.

Just before serving, dress the salad and serve.

Chinese Roasted Chicken [m]

This might be the best and easiest way to roast chickens or game hens. The complete dish can be finished ahead of time. Rewarm just before serving.

Serves 8

4 cups [900 milliliters] lite soy sauce
³/₄ cup [175 milliliters] dry sherry
3 green onions, including green, sliced
1 teaspoon grated fresh ginger
1 ¹/₂ tablespoons brown sugar
1 ¹/₂ teaspoons salt
couple grinds fresh black pepper
¹/₂ teaspoon 5 Spice Powder [see Index]
1 tablespoon grated orange peel, about ¹/₂ orange
2 whole chickens, each about 3 ¹/₂ pounds [1.66 kilos] OR
4 Cornish game hens, each 1 ¹/₂ pounds [680 grams]
3 green onions, including green, sliced, to garnish

In a large wide pot, large enough to hold poultry side by side, place all the ingredients, except poultry. Bring to a boil, stirring occasionally. Add chickens or hens and simmer uncovered, for 45 minutes, turning chickens or hens once.

Drain chickens or hens [see Note] and place them on a rack in a foil lined baking pan, containing about 1 ¹/₂ inches [4 centimeters] water. [Poultry should not touch water.] Roast in a preheated 400°F. [205° C.] oven for 15 to 20 minutes for hens or 20 to 25 minutes for chickens until well browned and crisped. Cool.

Cut up chickens into serving size pieces. Cut hens in half on either side of back bone, removing and discarding back bone. Cut down center of breast, dividing hens in half. I use a scissors. Cut out little rib bones with the scissors.

About 20 to 30 minutes before serving, place poultry pieces on a rack in a foil lined baking pan and rewarm in a preheated 300°F. [150°

C.] oven for 15 to 20 minutes.

Transfer poultry to a platter, sprinkle with green onions and serve.

Note: Reserve and freeze liquid, skimmed of fat, to make this dish another time. Add ¹/₂ measure of onion, ginger and spices to liquid.

Chinese Mushroom Soup [m]

This simple soup is easy to make and is delicious enough to serve at any meal, not just a Chinese dinner.

Makes 9 cups

1 ounce [28 grams] dried black Chinese mushrooms, about 20

18 ounces [500 grams] fresh mushrooms, sliced

9 cups [2 liters] Beef Stock [see Index] or canned

1 tablespoon lite soy sauce

¹/₄ teaspoon fresh white pepper

¹/₂ cup [60 grams] green onions, including green, sliced, to garnish

Soak dried mushrooms in very hot water to cover for 30 minutes, until soft and pliable. Cut off and discard stems. Cut caps into thin strips and set aside.

In a 5 quart [5 liter] kettle, combine fresh mushrooms, stock, soy sauce and pepper. Bring to a boil and simmer uncovered for 1 hour. Strain soup through a double thickness of cheese cloth placed in a large strainer. Discard mushrooms [or make an omelet]. This part can be made ahead.

Just before serving, add dried mushrooms and return soup to a boil. Simmer for 15 minutes.

Add green onions and serve.

Egg Rolls [m or p]

These are small crispy rolls, either fried in a small amount of vegetable oil and drained well on paper towels, or baked crisp in the oven. They freeze very well before cooking, and are a nice hors' d'oeuvre to serve at any kind of dinner party.

Makes 20 to 25

Filling

3 or 4 large dried black Chinese mushrooms

vegetable cooking spray

2 teaspoons peanut oil

1 teaspoon grated fresh ginger

1 tablespoon chopped garlic

optional; 8 ounces [225 grams] boneless, skinless raw chicken, diced finely

4 ½ ounces [125 grams] celery, chopped

3 ½ ounces [100 grams] green onions, including green, chopped

½ a 2 ½ ounce [75 gram] can sliced bamboo shoots, chopped

½ a 2 ½ ounce [75 gram] can sliced water chestnuts, chopped

8 ounces [225 grams] Chinese celery cabbage, chopped finely

½ teaspoon salt

¼ teaspoon fresh black pepper

2 tablespoons cornstarch

2 tablespoons plus 1 teaspoon soy sauce

cornstarch, for sprinkling

1 package egg roll skins, thawed, if frozen

flour paste: 1 tablespoon flour mixed with 1 tablespoon water

optional: peanut oil, for frying

vegetable cooking spray

Cover mushrooms with very hot water and let soften for 30 minutes. Drain, reserve 2 tablespoons liquid, reserve the rest for another use. Cut off and discard stems, chop caps finely.

In a sprayed Dutch oven, heat oil until hot. Add ginger, garlic and chicken, if used, and stir fry until chicken loses color. Add mushrooms, celery, onions, bamboo shoots, water chestnuts, cabbage, salt and pepper. Stir fry for 1 minute. Mix cornstarch with soy sauce and reserved mushroom liquid and add to mixture. Stir fry for 1 minute. Remove from heat and cool.

Sprinkle a flat baking pan with cornstarch [I use a small screen strainer] and set aside.

Working with 1 skin at a time, with 1 point towards you, place about 2 tablespoons [1/8 cup] filling across the lower middle. Fold up point to cover filling, fold in each side, roll up egg roll to enclose filling completely and seal with a bit of flour paste. Turn seam side down on prepared baking sheet. Continue making egg rolls in same manner until all filling is used.

At this point, if desired, egg rolls can be frozen. Place egg rolls in freezer, still on baking sheet, for about 1 1/2 hours. When rolls are frozen hard, store in a zip lock bag in freezer. No need to thaw to cook.

If frying egg rolls, place a small amount of oil in a sprayed fry pan and fry egg rolls until brown on each side, turning only once.

To oven crisp egg rolls: place egg rolls, seam side down, on a well sprayed baking pan, spray egg rolls lightly on each side and bake in a preheated 400°F. [205°C.] oven for 15 to 20 minutes, until brown and crispy turning only once.

Serve immediately, with Hot Mustard [see Index], sweet and sour sauce and soy sauce.

Hot and Sour Soup *[p]*

This is my favorite Chinese soup. It is full of vegetables with lots of dried black mushrooms [shitake] and other Chinese goodies and is definitely on the spicy side.

Makes about 15 cups [3.37 liters]

¹/₂ cup [110 milliliters] rice vinegar
1 teaspoon salt
1 tablespoon lite soy sauce
¹/₄ teaspoon fresh black pepper
1 to 2 teaspoons Tabasco sauce, to taste
2 teaspoons sesame oil
¹/₈ teaspoon chili paste with oil
30 dried black Chinese mushrooms, 1 ¹/₂ ounces [45 grams]
2 ounces [50 grams] cellophane noodles
8 cups [1.8 liters] pareve chicken flavored soup, from the mix
an 8 ounce [225 gram] can sliced bamboo shoots, drained
7 ¹/₂ ounces [210 grams] bean sprouts, rinsed in hot water, fresh or canned
1 pound [450 grams] tofu, cut into small dice
9 ¹/₂ ounces [275 grams] bok choy, ribs halved lengthwise, sliced crosswise
1 egg
2 egg whites
3 ¹/₂ ounces [100 grams] fresh snow peas, trimmed
lite soy sauce, to taste

In a screw top jar, place vinegar, salt, soy sauce, pepper, Tabasco, sesame oil and chili paste and set aside.

Place mushrooms in a bowl with hot water to cover and let sit until soft and spongy, about 30 minutes. Drain, reserving 2 cups [450 milliliters] soaking liquid. Remove and discard stems and slice caps into thin strips.

Place noodles in a bowl with hot water to cover and let sit until noodles are soft, about 15 minutes. Drain and cut with a scissors into 2 inch [5 centimeter] lengths.

In a 5 quart [5 liter] kettle, place soup, bamboo shoots, bean sprouts, tofu, bok choy, mushrooms, noodles and strained mushroom soaking liquid. Bring to a boil and simmer for 20 minutes. Shake ingredients in jar to mix and add to kettle. Mix and simmer for 3 minutes.

Beat egg and egg whites together and add to soup in a stream. Add snow peas, and soy to taste, bring to a simmer. Turn off heat.

Stir to mix and serve.

Hot Mustard [p]

This is very hot and spicy, so a little goes a long way.

Makes about $\frac{1}{3}$ cup [75 milliliters]

5 to 7 tablespoons boiled water, cooled

4 tablespoons dry mustard, sifted [Colemans]

Gradually add water to mustard, mashing and mixing until mixture is smooth and creamy. Let mustard sit for 10 minutes to develop flavor.

Scallion Mandarin Cakes [p]

These are a variation on 2 Chinese specialties, Mandarin pancakes that are used with Duck [see Index] and scallion cakes, a delicious side dish. Try these with Chinese Roast Duck [see Index] and other Chinese dishes.

Makes 24 cakes

about 2 ¼ cups [315 grams] all purpose unbleached flour
2 ½ ounces [80 grams] green onions, chopped finely
½ teaspoon salt
1 cup [225 milliliters] boiling water
1 tablespoon sesame oil
olive oil cooking spray

Place flour, green onions and salt in a mixing bowl. Add boiling water in a stream while mixing with a chop stick to thoroughly incorporate water with flour mixture. Turn out onto a well floured surface and knead until dough comes together in a ball, adding as much extra flour as needed.

Divide dough into 2 parts and roll each part into a log 12 inches [30 centimeters] long. Divide each log into 12 pieces. Press each piece, using your fingers, into a circle, 3 to 4 inches [7 ½ to 10 centimeters] round. Roll each round, with a floured rolling pin or using your fingers, into a 6 inch [15 centimeter] round. Brush one side of a round with a thin coat of sesame oil covering surface thoroughly. Immediately press a second round on top of oiled round to make a sandwich of two rounds with oil in middle, pressing edges together. Continue making sandwiches the same way with the rest of the rounds making 12 sandwiches and using all the oil.

Spray a non-stick fry pan and heat. Add one sandwich and lightly fry on one side until pancake puffs a bit. Turn cake over and lightly fry on second side. Don't let pancakes brown too much before turning. Remove pancake from pan and let cool slightly. When cool enough to handle, separate sandwiches into 2 pancakes, stacking them on a towel. Continue making pancakes until all sandwiches are done.

Let pancakes cool and wrap well with plastic wrap until ready to serve. Before serving, reheat pancakes in microwave oven or in a steamer until warm.

The pancakes can be frozen still wrapped in plastic wrap and well wrapped in foil. Thaw before reheating.

Chinese Roasted Duck [m]

If you like crispy tasty duck, you'll love this recipe. I borrowed from the Chinese Roast Chicken [see Index] to make ducks that contain almost no fat.

Serves 8

4 cups [900 milliliters] lite soy sauce
³/₄ cup [175 milliliters] dry sherry
3 green onions, including green, sliced
1 teaspoon grated fresh ginger
1 ¹/₂ tablespoons brown sugar
1 ¹/₂ teaspoons salt
couple grinds fresh black pepper
¹/₂ teaspoon 5 Spice Powder [see Index]
1 tablespoon grated orange peel, about ¹/₂ orange
2 whole ducks, each about 5 ¹/₂ pounds [2.5 kilos], well trimmed of fat, skin pricked all over on fatty parts

In a large wide pot, large enough to hold ducks side by side, place all the ingredients, except ducks. Bring to a boil, stirring occasionally. Add ducks and simmer uncovered, for 45 minutes, turning ducks once.

Drain ducks [see Note] and place them on a rack in a foil lined baking pan. Roast in a preheated 300°F. [150°C.] oven for 2 hours until well browned and crisped. Cool. Cut up ducks into serving size pieces.

About 30 minutes before serving, place duck pieces on a rack in a foil lined baking pan and reheat in a preheated 300°F. [150°C.] oven for 20 minutes.

Transfer duck to a platter and serve.

Note: Reserve and freeze liquid, skimmed of fat, to make duck another time. Add ¹/₂ measure of onions, ginger and spices to liquid.

Noodles with Chinese Vegetables [p]

This filling and varied dish contains everything that you would need as the vegetable course at a Chinese dinner. The soft and crunchy textures in this dish contrast nicely.

Serves 8

8 ounces [225 grams] fresh bean sprouts
1 ounce [28 grams] dried black Chinese mushrooms, about 20
a 3 ¾ ounce [105 gram] package cellophane noodles
2 teaspoons sesame oil
olive oil cooking spray
2 tablespoons chopped garlic
1 tablespoon grated fresh ginger root
5 ½ ounces [150 grams] green onions, including green, sliced
8 ounces [225 grams] leeks, white and light green parts, sliced
8 ounces [225 grams] Chinese celery cabbage, sliced thinly
8 ounces [225 grams] celery, sliced diagonally
8 ounces [225 grams] bok choy, ribs halved lengthwise, sliced thinly crosswise
5 ½ ounces [150 grams] snow peas [pea pods], trimmed
an 8 ounce [225 gram] can sliced bamboo shoots, drained
an 8 ounce [225 gram] can sliced water chestnuts, drained
1 teaspoon salt
1 teaspoon sugar

¹/₄ teaspoon fresh white pepper
3 tablespoons lite soy sauce
2 cups [450 milliliters] pareve chicken flavored soup, from the mix
2 tablespoons cornstarch mixed with
2 tablespoons water
2 cups [450 milliliters] pareve chicken flavored soup, from the mix
1 tablespoon lite soy sauce
2 teaspoons sesame oil

Pour boiling water over bean sprouts, drain and set aside.

Cover mushrooms with very hot water and let sit for 30 minutes until soft and pliable. Drain, cut off and discard stems, slice caps thinly and set aside.

Soak noodles in hot water to cover for 20 minutes. Drain, cut noodles with a scissors into 2 inch [5 centimeter] lengths and set aside.

Heat 2 teaspoons oil in a sprayed non-stick Dutch oven or wok until hot. Add garlic and ginger and stir fry for 30 seconds. Add green onions, leeks, cabbage, celery, pea pods, bok choy, bamboo shoots, water chestnuts, mushrooms, salt, sugar, pepper and soy sauce, toss well, and remove from heat. This part of recipe can be made ahead.

About 15 minutes before serving, add 2 cups [450 milliliters] soup and bring to a boil stirring. When boiling, add cornstarch mixture and stir until thickened.

In another pot, place bean sprouts and noodles. Add 2 cups [450 milliliters] soup, soy sauce and sesame oil. Heat until warmed through, tossing and mixing constantly.

Place noodle mixture on a platter, top with vegetable mixture and serve.

Pot Stickers *[m]*

My California grandkids love Chinese food and a particular favorite of theirs are pot stickers. Jonathan and Alix Mimran can eat these at any meal. I think they are fun to make.

Makes about 54

6 ½ ounces [185 grams] Chinese celery cabbage, minced finely, 1 ½ cups
3 ounces [90 grams] green onions, including green, minced finely
12 ounces [340 grams] ground turkey
2 tablespoons lite soy sauce
2 teaspoons chopped garlic
1 teaspoon grated fresh ginger
1 tablespoon Sake [rice wine] or dry sherry
1 tablespoon sesame oil
1 ½ tablespoons cornstarch
1 package pot sticker or dumpling round skins
cornstarch
olive oil cooking spray
1 tablespoon extra virgin olive oil, divided

³/₄ to 3 cups [175 to 700 milliliters] water

¹/₄ cup [55 milliliters] lite soy sauce mixed with

¹/₄ cup [55 milliliters] rice vinegar

1 large green onion, sliced

For the filling, combine celery cabbage, green onions, turkey, soy, garlic, ginger, sake, sesame oil and 1 tablespoon cornstarch and mix well. [If mixture seems too loose, add another ¹/₂ tablespoon cornstarch.]

On each skin, place 1 rounded teaspoon filling. Fold over skin to make a ¹/₂ moon shape. Using your fingers and water, seal dumpling closed. Place on a cornstarch sprinkled baking pan, flattening dumpling so that closure is on top, and dumplings sit on baking pan in one layer, not touching. Cover with plastic wrap and refrigerate until ready to cook, or freeze dumplings still on baking pan for 1 hour. Store in plastic zip lock bags. No need to thaw before cooking.

For each batch, add ³/₄ teaspoon oil to a well sprayed fry pan. Place in pan as many dumplings as will fit. Fry dumplings over medium high heat until browning on bottom. Add ³/₄ cup [175 milliliters] water to fry pan, cover, and steam until dumplings are cooked through, about 5 to 8 minutes.

Add green onions to soy vinegar mixture to make a dipping sauce for dumplings and serve, 3 to 6 pot stickers per person, or 8 to 10 for hungry grandchildren.

Sesame Noodles *[p]*

I usually make the components of this dish early in the day and warm them up for dinner. Or make the sesame dressing early in the day and make the noodles at the last minute, mix with the dressing and serve. I particularly like this dish with Chinese Roasted Chicken [see Index] or as a main dish at a vegetarian dinner.

Serves 8

1 tablespoon chopped garlic
3 tablespoons plus 1 teaspoon light soy sauce
1 ¹/₂ tablespoons rice vinegar
3 tablespoons sesame oil
¹/₂ to 1 teaspoon dried hot red pepper flakes, to taste
1 teaspoon sugar
¹/₄ cup [25 grams] toasted sesame seeds
¹/₃ cup [75 milliliters] water
salt, to taste
fresh black pepper, to taste
¹/₄ cup [25 grams] toasted sesame seeds
1 pound [450 grams] thin spaghetti
4 tablespoons sliced green onions, including green

In a blender, combine garlic, soy, vinegar, oil, hot peppers, sugar, water and ¹/₄ cup [25 grams] sesame seeds. Run blender until mixture is smooth. Transfer mixture to a small bowl and add salt and pepper to taste. Add ¹/₄ cup [25 grams] sesame seeds, mix and set aside.

In a large kettle cook spaghetti until al dente, about 9 minutes. If serving immediately, drain and mix spaghetti with sesame mixture, sprinkle with green onions and serve.

If making ahead of time, rinse spaghetti with cold water and set aside until just before serving. Reheat spaghetti over steaming water or in boiling water, drain and mix with sesame mixture, sprinkle with green onions and serve.

Spinach Won Tons [p]

I love working with fresh won ton skins from the Chinese grocery. They are tender and very delicate. The skins are also available in most supermarkets. It is very relaxing for me to spend an hour sitting on my stool, listening to music and rolling won tons. Benjamin Lavon, my grandson, loves Won Ton Soup [see Index] and I love to make it for him.

Enough for 65 to 80 won ton skins

4 dried black Chinese mushrooms
7 ounces [200 grams] frozen chopped spinach, cooked, squeezed dry
3 water chestnuts, blanched in boiling water, chopped finely
3 $^1/_2$ ounces [100 grams] bean sprouts, blanched in boiling water, chopped finely
1 large green onion, chopped finely
2 teaspoons lite soy sauce
1 $^1/_4$ teaspoons salt
couple grinds fresh white pepper
1 package won ton skins
cornstarch

Cover mushrooms with hot water and let soften for 30 minutes. Drain, remove and discard stems. Squeeze water from caps and chop finely. Add the rest of the ingredients and combine well.

Place a teaspoon of filling on each skin. Fold over to form a triangle. Wet edges with water to stick. Fold over again, making a double fold. Wetting each corner with water, fold over each corner to meet in the middle, forming a little nurses cap. Lay won tons in one layer, not touching, on a cornstarch sprinkled baking sheet, [I use a small screen strainer] until all won tons are made. Cover and refrigerate until ready to cook and freeze the extras.

Place won tons still on baking sheet in freezer for about 1 hour, until frozen. Remove from pan and store in a zip lock plastic bag until needed. Do not thaw before cooking.

Subgum Fried Rice [p]

This is an all purpose "fried" rice that is full of lovely Chinese and fresh vegetables, taking advantage of the accessibility of all manner of Chinese ingredients.

Serves 8 generously

vegetable cooking spray
2 teaspoons peanut oil
2 tablespoons chopped garlic
2 ¹/₂ ounces [75 grams] Chinese celery cabbage, chopped finely
10 to 12 dried black Chinese mushrooms, soaked 30 minutes in hot water, drained, stems removed, caps diced finely
3 ounces [90 grams] celery, diced finely
¹/₂ a 5 ounce [135 gram] can sliced water chestnuts, cut up
¹/₂ a 5 ounce [135 gram] can sliced bamboo shoots, cut up
8 ounces [225 grams] bean sprouts, rinsed in boiling water, drained, cut up
3 ¹/₂ ounces [100 grams] green onions, including green, sliced
³/₄ cup [175 milliliters] frozen egg substitute, thawed
6 cups [840 grams] cooked Rice [see Index] [2 cups raw]
2 ounces [50 grams] snow peas, trimmed, sliced
³/₄ cup [175 milliliters] pareve chicken flavored soup, from the mix
2 tablespoons lite soy sauce
¹/₂ teaspoon ground ginger
¹/₂ teaspoon salt
few grinds fresh white pepper, to taste
2 ounces [60 grams] green onions, including green, sliced, to garnish

In a sprayed large Dutch oven or wok, heat oil until hot. Add and stir fry garlic, cabbage, mushrooms, celery, water chestnuts, bamboo shoots, bean sprouts and onions over high heat for 2 or 3 minutes. Add eggs and mix quickly. Add rice and snow peas and mix well. Remove from heat and set aside until just before serving.

Add soup, soy, ginger, salt and pepper and mix well. Cover and steam for 5 minutes, stirring frequently. Turn out into a serving bowl, sprinkle with green onions and serve.

Won Ton Soup [m or p]

This soup is, by special request, for my grandson, Benjamin Lavon, who thinks his Grandma is a good cook. Thank you Ben.

Serves 8

24 to 32 filled Won Tons [see Index]

boiling salted water

6 cups [1.4 liters] Chicken Broth [see Index] or canned or pareve chicken flavored soup, from the mix

4 teaspoons lite soy sauce

8 ounces [225 grams] bok choy, leaves halved lengthwise, sliced ³/₄ inch [2 centimeters] thick crosswise

2 large green onions, including green, sliced

3 ounces [90 grams] snow peas, trimmed, halved

1 teaspoon sesame oil

Cook won tons in batches, about 6 at a time, in boiling water, about 2 minutes. [No need to thaw, if frozen.] Remove with a slotted spoon to a colander, to drain.

Bring soup to a boil, add soy and bok choy. Simmer for 15 minutes. Add won tons and simmer until won tons are hot. Add onions, snow peas and sesame oil.

Serve, allowing 3 or 4 won tons per person.

Chinese Vegetable Soup *[p]*

This soup contains an interesting mixture of Chinese vegetables. It is very low in fat, has wonderful flavors and textures and is suitable for many dinners.

Makes 16 cups [3.6 liters]

35 [75 grams] dried black Chinese mushrooms soaked in

2 cups [450 milliliters] hot water, for 30 minutes, reserve
    soaking liquid

½ a 3 ¾ ounce [105 gram] package cellophane noodles, soaked
    in hot water for 20 minutes, drained

2 packages Dashi soup stock mix [available in Oriental markets]

with 8 cups [1.8 liters] water or

8 cups [1.8 liters] pareve chicken flavored soup, from the mix

2 heaping tablespoons pareve chicken flavored soup mix

a 5 ounce [135 gram] can sliced water chestnuts, rinsed, drained

a 5 ounce [135 gram] can sliced bamboo shoots, rinsed, drained

a 14 ounce [400 gram] can bean sprouts, rinsed, drained, or fresh

9 ½ ounces [280 grams] bok choy, leaves halved lengthwise,
    sliced crosswise

5 $\frac{1}{2}$ ounces [155 grams] Chinese celery cabbage, leaves halved
   lengthwise, sliced crosswise

1 pound [450 grams] tofu, cut into $\frac{1}{2}$ inch [1 $\frac{3}{4}$ centimeter] dice

4 egg whites, beaten lightly

3 to 4 tablespoons lite soy sauce, to taste

$\frac{1}{2}$ teaspoon sesame oil

salt, to taste

fresh black pepper, to taste

3 ounces [90 grams] snow peas, trimmed, halved diagonally

3 large green onions, including green, sliced

Cut off and discard stems of soaked mushrooms. Slice caps and set aside. Cut soaked noodles, with a scissors, into 2 inch [5 centimeter] lengths and set aside.

Place Dashi and water or soup into a soup kettle and add dry soup mix. Add strained mushroom liquid. Bring to a simmer, stirring. Add mushrooms, noodles, water chestnuts, bamboo shoots, bean sprouts, bok choy, celery cabbage and tofu. Simmer soup for 20 minutes. Add egg whites, stirring vigorously. Add soy, sesame oil, salt and pepper.

Stir in snow peas and green onions and serve.

PESACH

Charosit - Mimran [p]

This Sefardic recipe is from the family of my son-in-law, Haim Mimran. It is so delicious that I've adopted it to join our traditional family Charosit [see Index]. I have introduced this charosit to many Seders and have found everyone intrigued with it.

4 ¹/₂ ounces [125 grams] filberts [hazelnuts], unroasted, unpeeled
4 ¹/₂ ounces [125 grams] almonds, unroasted, peeled
4 ¹/₂ ounces [125 grams] seeded dates, check for bits of seeds
4 ¹/₂ ounces [125 grams] raisins
1 ¹/₂ teaspoons ground cinnamon
3 to 4 ounces [75 to 100 milliliters] sweet red wine

Lightly toast filberts and almonds in a preheated 350°F. [175°C.] oven for 10 to 15 minutes.

In a food processor or food grinder, chop together nuts, dates and raisins, until finely minced. Transfer mixture to a bowl. Add cinnamon. Gradually add wine, mixing until ingredients hold together. Let the charosit sit for 15 minutes. With moistened hands, roll charosit into tiny ¹/₂ inch [1 centimeter] balls. Store in fridge until needed.

The charosit keeps at least 1 week, refrigerated, and can be frozen.

Charosit - Weisgal [p]

This is our traditional family recipe, handed down from my husband's family. This is the more familar charosit of most of the families that I know.

10 ¹/₂ ounces [300 grams] filberts [hazelnuts], unroasted, unpeeled
1 pound [450 grams] apples, peeled, cored
³/₄ cup [175 milliliters] sweet red wine
2 ¹/₂ teaspoons ground cinnamon
optional: sugar to taste

Lightly toast filberts in a preheated 350°F. [175°C.] oven for 10 to 15 minutes.

In a food processor or food grinder, grind finely nuts and apples. Don't run processor steadily or nut oils will be released. Transfer to a bowl and combine with the other ingredients. Cover loosely and chill for at least 1 hour to develop the flavor.

The charosit keeps at least 1 week, refrigerated.

Brown Eggs For Pesach [p]

These special eggs are traditional in the Weisgal family. We use them at the Seder table and for the week of Pesach. When peeled they are brown, creamy and delicious with almost a smoky flavor. Try them, you'll like them.

Allow 1 to 2 eggs per person

Wash egg shells thoroughly and carefully. Place in a large pot with a tight fitting lid and fill pot with cold water. Bring slowly to a boil and turn down to the lowest possible heat. [I use a diffuser.] Cover and simmer slowly for 24 hours, adding water as necessary.

The eggs keep in the fridge for a week or more.

Matzo Balls *[p]*

These feather light dumplings are a must for Pesach, but delicious any time of year. The secret to their lightness is ample rolling boiling water and as with any dumpling, no peeking while cooking. My sister in law, Nathalie Weisgall, showed me this method of making these matzo balls.

Makes about 35 to 40 small balls

1 cup [130 grams] matzo meal
1 teaspoon salt
$^{1}/_{2}$ cup [110 milliliters] frozen egg substitute, thawed
2 tablespoons ground ginger
3 tablespoons vegetarian Nayafat or margarine, softened
$^{2}/_{3}$ to $^{3}/_{4}$ cup [150 to175 milliliters] cold parve chicken flavored soup, from the mix

Combine all the ingredients in a mixing bowl, adding as much chicken soup as needed to make a fairly stiff dough, keeping in mind that dough will stiffen more as it sits. Chill covered for several hours to overnight.

With moistened hands, make small balls and drop them into a large kettle of boiling, salted water. Cover pot and boil for 30 to 40 minutes, without peeking.

Remove balls with a slotted spoon to a bowl. Keep covered until ready to serve in a bowl of hot Chicken Soup [see Index].

The balls can be frozen. Thaw before reheating in boiling, salted water.

Matzo - Turkey Stuffing for Pesach [p]

I might like this stuffing better than any other stuffing that I make [see Index]. It is hearty fare and a delicious side dish.

Enough for an 11 pound [5 kilo] turkey [can be doubled]

olive oil cooking spray
5 ¹/₂ ounces [150 grams] green pepper, seeded, diced finely
7 ounces [200 grams] onions, chopped
3 ¹/₂ ounces [100 grams] celery, with leaves, chopped
1 ¹/₂ tablespoons Nyafat or margarine
5 ounces [135 grams] fresh mushrooms, sliced
10 matzos
¹/₂ cup [110 milliliters] frozen egg substitute, thawed
¹/₂ cup [110 milliliters] cold pareve chicken flavored soup, from the mix
2 teaspoons poultry seasoning
2 teaspoons salt
¹/₂ teaspoon fresh white pepper
¹/₂ teaspoon ground ginger
1 tablespoon minced fresh parsley leaves

In a sprayed fry pan or Dutch oven, saute peppers, onions and celery in fat, until well wilted. Add mushrooms and saute an additional 5 minutes. Remove from heat and set aside.

Under lukewarm running water, rinse matzos on both sides, shaking off all excess water. In a large bowl, break matzos into bite size pieces. Add eggs, soup and vegetable saute and mix well to combine. Add poultry seasoning, salt, pepper, ginger and parsley. Toss to combine well.

Cover and chill thoroughly before stuffing turkey. Or place in a sprayed baking dish, suitable for serving, cover with foil, and bake in a preheated 350°F. [175°C.] oven for 1 hour. Uncover and bake an additional 15 minutes to brown top. Bake early in the day and refrigerate. Bake for 15 minutes, uncovered to reheat.

Nut Torte, Klari [p]

This fabulous, flourless cake, courtesy of our cousin Klari Kaufman is the best cake I ever tasted that is kosher for Pesach. This cake is great any time of the year, but we save it for Pesach. It contains a lot of eggs but serves 12 easily, so judge for your self.

Makes a 10 inch [25 centimeter] cake serving 12

9 egg yolks, room temperature
9 egg whites, room temperature
1 ¹/₂ cups [300 grams] sugar
1 teaspoon grated lemon peel, about 1/4 lemon. Note: Peel lemon with a rotary vegetable peeler, taking only thin strips without any white pulp. In a food processor with the steel knife, run machine combining sugar and peel until peel is finely minced.
10 ¹/₂ ounces [300 grams] filberts [hazelnuts], unsalted, unpeeled, ground finely
vegetable cooking spray
powdered sugar for sprinkling or Lemon Icing [see Index]

In a large mixing bowl, beat egg yolks 1 minute. Add sugar and lemon peel and continue beating until light and thick. Add ²/₃ of nuts and beat until combined.

In another mixing bowl, beat egg whites until stiff. Fold whites into yolk mixture, gently but thoroughly. Fold in the rest of the nuts. Pour batter into a sprayed 10 inch [25 centimeter] spring form pan.

Bake in a preheated 350°F. [175°C.] oven for 1 hour, until cake springs back when lightly touched. Make sure cake is done or it will fall out of pan when cooling.

Cool cake in pan, on a rack, completely, UPSIDE DOWN. Remove from pan.

Sprinkle with sifted powdered sugar, or ice top of cake and drizzle down sides with Lemon Icing [see Index].

Cut into thin slices and serve.

SUGGESTED MENUS

1.
Purchased Salsa   Tortilla Chips   Caponata
Gaspacho Soup
Greek Salad
BEEF ENCHILADA
Red Beans and Rice   Onion Marmelade   Mango Chutney
Warm Tortillas
Fresh Fruit Salad   Mandlel Brot of Choice

2.
Crostini   Tapenade
Tomato Consomme
Mixed Green Salad with Caesar Salad Dressing
MARINATED BEEF STEW with
Onions, Carrots, Potatoes, Parsnips, Mushrooms
Garlic Bread
Dried Fruit Crisp   Fresh Fruit Salad

3.
Eggplant Salad   Pita Toasts   Sardine Spread
Avgolemone Soup
Greek Salad
BRISKET with
Carrots, Potatoes, Mushrooms, Onions, Parsnips
Corn Bread
Palachinka   Fresh Strawberries and Blueberries

4.
Chopped Herring   Crostini
Tomato Celery Soup
Cucumber Salad
BRISKET ala SOPHIE with
Carrots, Potatoes, Mushrooms, Parsnips, Leeks, Shallots
Beer Bread
Meringues   Fresh Fruit Salad

5.

Sviha   Olive Salad
Onion Soup
Greek Salad
BRAZILIAN BLACK BEAN STEW with
Ribs and Sausages
Broccoli
Drop Biscuits
Dried Fruit Struedel   Fresh Pineapple

6.

Chicken Crepes
Green Pea Soup
Roasted Pepper Salad with Garlic Bread
STUFFED CABBAGE ROLLS
Farfel   Carrot Cakes
Brownies   Fresh Fruit Salad

7.

Avocado Salad   Crostini
Fresh Corn Soup
Mixed Green Salad with Greek Salad Dressing
CHICKEN CACCIATORE
Linguine   Broccoli
Garlic Bread
Peach Crisp   Fresh Fruit Salad

8.

Cold Artichokes with Tartar Sauce 2
Mock Oxtail Soup
Tomato Onion Salad
CHICKEN FRICASSEE with
Choice of Dumplings
Sweet and Sour Red Cabbage
Apple Struedel   Fresh Fruit Salad

9.

Eggplant Salad   Melba Toast   Roasted Pepper Salad
Tomato Consomme
Mixed Green Salad with Caesar Salad Dressing
GARLIC CHICKEN
Polenta   Hot Artichokes
Sour Dough Italian Bread
Palachinka   Fresh Pineapple and Strawberries

10.

Sviha   Olive Salad
Onion Soup
Mixed Green Salad with Rasberry Vinaigrette
LEMON PEPPER CHICKEN with
Mushrooms
Succotash   Stewed Tomatoes
Palachinka   Fresh Fruit Salad

11.

Tchina   Houmous   Eggplant Salad
Pita Toasts
Garlic Soup
Middle East Vegetable Salad
CHICKEN MUSAKHAN on Pita
Rice   Asparagus
Meringues   Fresh Pineapple and Strawberries

12.

Crostini   Caponata
Avocado Soup
Mixed Green Salad with Caesar Salad Dressing
CHICKEN PAPRIKASH with Nuckerl
Sauerkraut   Mushrooms and Peas
Sour Dough Italian Bread
Pumpkin Apple Cake   Fresh Fruit Salad

13.

Eggplant Salad   Melba Toast   Roasted Pepper Salad
Carrot Soup
Greek Salad
ROASTED CHICKEN with Giblet Gravy
Bohemian Bread Dumplings   Stewed Tomatoes
Scones
Pumpkin Apple Cake   Fresh Fruit Salad

14.

Chopped Herring with Pita Toasts
Green Pea Soup
Greek Salad
CHICKEN SESAME
Zucchini Cakes   Carrot Cakes
Corn Bread
Apple Crisp   Mandel Brot of Choice

15.

Chicken Crepes
Chinese Vegetable Soup
Mixed Green Salad with Rasberry Vinaigrette
SPICY CHICKEN
Roasted Corn   Sauerkraut
Whole Wheat Bread
Mandel Brot of Choice   Fresh Fruit Salad

16.

Tabouli   Pita Toasts   Tapenade
Broccoli Soup
Cucumber Salad
CHICKEN WITH TOMATOES AND CARROTS
Southern Green Beans   Twisted Noodles
Biscuits
Chocolate Peppermint Meringues   Melon and Watermelon

17.

Mushroom Pie
Onion Soup
Spinach Salad
BLACK BEAN CHILI
Red Pepper Salad
Irish Soda Bread
Rice Pudding of Choice   Fresh Fruit Salad

18.

Guacamole with Tortilla Chips   Sangria
Broccoli Soup
Mixed Green Salad with Rasberry Vinaigrette
CINCINNATI CHILI with Accompaniments
Bean Medley
Beer Bread with Sun Dried Tomatoes and Olives
Dried Fruit Crisp   Fresh Melon Cubes

19.

Turkish Salad with Pita Toasts
Carrot Soup
Middle East Vegetable Salad
TEXAS CHILI
Red Beans and Rice   Garlic Bread
Apple Crisp   Mandel Brot of Choice

20.

Guacamole with Tortilla Chips   Margaritas
Onion Soup
Cucumber Salad
TURKEY CHILI
Corn Pudding   Carrot Cakes
Biscuits
Palachinka   Fresh Fruit Salad

21.

Corn Cakes   Carrot Cakes
Turkey Barley Soup
Greek Salad
CHOUCROUT GARNI with
Smoked Meat, Sausages, Potatoes
Challa
Chocolate Peppermint Meringues   Fresh Fruit Salad

22.

Chicken Crepes
Asparagus Soup
Tomato Onion Salad
CORNED BEEF with
Cabbage, Potatoes, Carrots, Parsnips
3 Stage Rye Bread
Dried Fruit Struedel   Fresh Fruit Salad

23.

Sviha   Olive Salad
Lentil Split Pea Soup
Mixed Green Salad with Rasberry Vinaigrette
COUS COUS with SHORT RIB STEW with
7 Vegetables
Biscuits
Peach Crisp   Mandel Brot of Choice

24.

Crostini   Carrot Cakes
Vegetarian Minestrone
Mixed Green Salad with Caesar Salad Dressing
SHORT RIB DAUBE
Bohemian Bread Dumplings   Stewed Tomatoes
Rhubarb Strawberry Pie   Melon Cubes

25.

Purchased Salsa   Tortilla Chips   Avocado Salad
Corn Soup
Mixed Green Salad with Rasberry Vinaigrette
ROASTED DUCK
Red Cabbage   Wild Rice   Apple Sauce   Onion Marmelade
3 Stage Rye Bread
Carrot Cake   Fresh Fruit Salad

26.

Zucchini Pie   Spinach Rice Bake
Green Pea Soup
Cucumber Yogurt Salad
EGGPLANT PARMESAN
Polenta Polo   Vegetable Latkes
English Muffin Bread
Rice Pudding of Choice   Melon with Blueberries

27.

Quesadillas   Pita Pizzas
Mushroom Timbale
Cauliflower Yogurt Salad
FISH STEW BOUILLABAISSE
Spinach Rice Bake
Garlic Bread
Bread Pudding   Strawberries and Blueberries

28.

Tchina   Pita Toasts   Houmous
Cabbage Borscht
Middle East Vegetable Salad
FLANK STEAK
Yorkshire Pudding   Stewed Tomatoes
Sour Dough Italian Bread   or   Challa
Palachinka   Fresh Strawberries and Blueberries

29.

Antipasto with Bread Sticks
Onion Soup with Cheese
SPINACH GNOCCHI with MARINARA SAUCE
Mushroom Timbale
Garlic Bread
Cheese Pie   Fresh Fruit Salad

30.

Chopped Herring   Crackers   Tapenade
Cabbage Borscht
Mixed Green Salad with Rasberry Vinaigrette
RACK OF LAMB
Wild Rice   Southern Green Beans
3 Stage Rye Bread
Meringues   Mandel Brot of Choice

31.

Herring in Cream Sauce   Stuffed Mushrooms
Corn Soup
Greek Salad
SPINACH LASAGNE
Polenta Polo with Pesto
Sour Dough Italian Bread
Rice Pudding of Choice   Fresh Fruit Salad

32.

Sardine Spread   Crackers   Melba Toast   Smoked Salmon Mousse
Cold Zucchini Soup
Caesar Salad with Parmesan
LASAGNE
Spinach Timbale
Garlic Bread
Rice Pudding of Choice   Fresh Fruit Salad

33.

Mushroom Quiche   Herring in Cream Sauce
Pumpkin Soup
Caesar Salad
VEGETABLE LASAGNE
Cold Artichokes with Tartar Sauce   Onion Marmelade
Beer Bread
Rice Pudding of Choice   Melon and Peaches

34.

Cold Artichokes with Tartar Sauce 2
Bone Soup
Tomato Onion Salad
MEAT LOAF
Stuffed Potatoes   Sweet and Sour Red Cabbage
Corn Bread
Baked Apples   Mandel Brot of Choice

35.

Chopped Herring   Tortilla Chips   Avocado Salad
Black Bean Soup
MEAT LOAF ala ARAN KAY
Boiled Potatoes   Sauerkraut
3 Stage Rye Bread
Carrot Cake   Fresh Fruit Salad

36.

Cold Artichokes with Tartar Sauce 2
Mock Oxtail Soup
Cucumber Salad
MUFFALETTA on Round Sour Dough Italian Bread
Roasted Corn   Sauerkraut
Palachinka   Melon and Blueberries

37.

Chicken Crepes   Turkish Salad with Pita
Avgolemone Soup
Greek Salad
MOUSSAKA
Tomato Aspic with Green Bean Vinaigrette
Beer Bread
Brownies   Fresh Fruit Salad

38.

Turkish Salad   Pita Toasts   Eggplant Salad
Bean Soup
Mixed Green Salad with Rasberry Vinaigrette
OSSO BUCCO
Nuckerl   Cranberry Relish   Apple Sauce
Garlic Bread
Carrot Cake   Fresh or Frozen Peaches

39.

Tapenade   Crostini
Gaspacho
Roasted Pepper Salad
PAELLA
Sangria   Garlic Bread
Chocolate Peppermint Meringues   Melon Cubes

40.

Quiche David   Zucchini Pie
Asparagus Soup
Caesar Salad with Parmesan
PASTA WITH BELL PEPPER SAUCE
Tomato Aspic with Horseradish Sauce
Beer Bread
Bread Pudding   Fresh Fruit Salad

41.
Caponata   Pita Toasts   Olive Salad
Potato Leek Mushroom Soup
Cucumber Salad
PASTA with MEAT BALL SAUCE
Fresh Asparagus
Garlic Bread
Chocolate Peppermint Meringues   Melon Cubes

42.
Antipasto with Bread Sticks
Split Pea Soup
PASTA with SAUSAGE SAUCE
Cranberry Relish   Assorted Pickles
Garlic Bread
Apple Struedel   Fresh Pineapple and Blueberries

43.
Turkish Salad   Pita Toasts   Guacamole
Bean Soup
Mixed Green Salad with Caesar Salad Dressing
STUFFED PEPPERS
Polenta   Asparagus
Brownies   Melon Cubes and Peaches

44.
Pesto Pizza   Pita Pizza
Vegetable Minestrone
Cauliflower Salad
BAKED RIGATONI
Broccoli Spinach Bake
Garlic Bread
Grapenuts Pudding   Peaches and Blueberries

45.
Chicken Crepes
Goulash Soup
Mixed Green Salad with Rasberry Vinaigrette
ROAST BEEF HASH
Broccoli   Stewed Tomatoes
Garlic Bread
Carrot Cake   Fresh Fruit Salad

46.
Zucchini Cakes   Carrot Cakes
Tomato Consomme with Spaetzle
Mixed Green Salad with Rasberry Vinaigrette
ROASTED RIB OF BEEF
Potato Kugel   Peas and Mushrooms
Challa
Rhubarb Strawberry Pie   Melon Cubes

47.
Zviha   Eggplant Salad
Garlic Soup
Greek Salad
BARBEQUE RIBS
Roasted Corn   Carrot Cakes
Drop Biscuits
Dried Fruit Struedel   Melon and Strawberries

48.
Zucchini Cakes   Corn Cakes
Avgolemone Soup
Sweet Pepper Salad
RIBS in SOY BEER SAUCE
Asparagus   Sweet and Sour Red Cabbage
Scones
Baked Apples   Mandel Brot of Choice

49.
Tabouli   Pita Toasts   Avocado Salad
Bone Soup
Tomato Onion Salad
SPICY RIBS
Sauerkraut   Succotash
Corn Bread
Pumpkin Apple Cake   Fresh Fruit Salad

50.
Mushroom Crepes
Pumpkin Soup or Garlic Soup
Cole Slaw 2
COLD POACHED SALMON with Tartar Sauce
Pasta Salad   Sweet and Sour Red Cabbage
3 Stage Rye Bread
Rice Pudding of Choice   Frozen No Fat Yogurt

51.
Eggplant Salad   Pita Toasts   Tabouli
Goulash Soup
Greek Salad
TONGUE with Horseradish Sauce
Boiled Potatoes   Stewed Tomatoes
3 Stage Rye Bread
Carrot Cake   Fresh Fruit Salad

52.
Corn Cakes   Zucchini Cakes
Carrot Soup
Mixed Green Salad with Rasberry Vinaigrette
TURKEY GUMBO
Rice   Ratatouille
Sour Dough Italian Bread
Baked Apples   Mandel Brot of Choice

53.

Zviha   Pita Toasts   Olive Salad
Tomato Celery Soup
Celery Cabbage Salad
VEAL GOULASH with Nuckerl or Spaetzle
Broccoli
Biscuits
Baked Apples   Mandel Brot of Choice

54.

Vegetable Latkes
Garlic Soup
Mixed Green Salad with Rasberry Vinaigrette
VEAL SHANKS with Tomatoes, Carrots and White Beans
Garlic Bread
Brownies   Fresh Fruit Salad

55.

CHILI PARTY FOR A CROWD
Crostini   Sweet Pepper Salad
Mixed Green Salad with Caesar Salad Dressing
TEXAS CHILI   CINCINNATI CHILI
TURKEY CHILI   BLACK BEAN CHILI
Bean Medley   Spaghetti   Rice
Chopped Onions   Oyster Crackers
3 Stage Rye Bread   Biscuits   Corn Bread
Apple Struedel   Brownies   Meringues   Fresh Fruit

56.

LUNCH or BRUNCH
Quiche, David   Zucchini Pie
Bloody Marys   Whiskey Sours   Sangria
Cold Cucumber Yogurt Soup
TUNA SALAD   SMOKED FISH SALAD
Pasta Salad   Tomato Aspic   Broccoli Spinach Bake
English Muffin Bread   Irish Soda Bread
Bread Pudding   Fresh Fruit Salad

57.
HOLIDAY
Gefilte Fish with 2 Horseradishes
Chicken Soup with Matzo Balls
Tomato Onion Salad   or Tomato Aspic
ROASTED TURKEY
Stuffing of Choice   Giblet Gravy
Apple Sauce   Cranberry Relish
Potato Kugel   or   Stuffed Potatoes
Sweet and Sour Red Cabbage   or   Sauerkraut
Matzo   or   Challa
Nut Torte, Klari   Fresh Fruit Salad

58.
HOLIDAY
Gefilte Fish with 2 Horseradishes
Chicken Soup with Noodles
Mixed Green Salad with Rasberry Vinaigrette
ROASTED GOOSE with Giblet Gravy
Potato Chestnut Stuffing
Asparagus   Roasted Pepper Salad   Cranberry Relish
Challa
Rhubarb Strawberry Pie   Meringues

59.
YOM KIPPUR
Pita Pizza   Pesto Pizza
Herring in Cream Sauce
Zucchini Pie   Mushroom Pie
Avgolemone Soup
Cole Slaw 2   Tomato Mozzarella Anchovy Basil Salad
NOODLE KUGEL   LASAGNE
Stewed Tomatoes   Broccoli Spinach Bake
Challa
Kuchen, Aranka

60.

CHINESE
Egg Rolls with Hot Mustard and Chutneys
Won Ton Soup with Chicken Won Tons
Celery Cabbage Salad
CHINESE ROASTED CHICKEN
Steamed Bok Choy   Subgum Fried Rice
Jasmine Tea   Sake
Brownies   Canned Lychee Nuts

61.

CHINESE
Pot Stickers with Dipping Sauce
Chinese Mushroom Soup
Celery Cabbage Salad
CHINESE ROASTED DUCK
Mandarian Scallion Pancakes   Steamed Rice
Jasmine Tea   Sake
Meringues   Fresh Fruit Salad

62.

CHINESE
Egg Rolls   Pot Stickers   Hot Mustard   Chutneys
Hot and Sour Soup
NOODLES with CHINESE VEGETABLES
Cauliflower in Black Bean Sauce   Wild Rice
Jasmine Tea   Sake
Rice Pudding of Choice   Fresh Fruit Salad

63.

CHINESE
Egg Rolls with Hot Mustard and Chutneys
Chinese Vegetable Soup
Celery Cabbage Salad
CHINESE BARBEQUE RIBS
Sesame Noodles   Steamed Bok Choy
Jasmine Tea   Sake
Carrot Cake   Fresh Strawberries

EQUIVALENTS

TEMPERATURES

F.	C.
150°	65°
200°	90°
250°	120°
275°	135°
290°	145°
300°	150°
325°	165°
350°	175°
375°	190°
400°	205°
425°	220°
450°	230°
475°	245°
500°	260°

LINEAR MEASUREMENTS

1/2 inch	=	1 3/4 centimeters
3/4 inch	=	2 centimeters
1 inch	=	2 1/2 centimeters
1 1/2 inch	=	3 3/4 centimeters
2 inches	=	5 centimeters
2 1/2 inches	=	6 1/4 centimeters
3 inches	=	7 1/2 centimeters
4 inches	=	10 centimeters
5 inches	=	12 1/2 centimeters
6 inches	=	15 centimeters
7 inches	=	17 1/2 centimeters
8 inches	=	20 centimeters
9 inches	=	22 1/2 centimeters
10 inches	=	25 centimeters
11 inches	=	27 1/2 centimeters
12 inches	=	30 centimeters
13 inches	=	32 1/2 centimeters
14 inches	=	35 centimeters
15 inches	=	37 1/2 centimeters

WEIGHTS

1/2 ounce	=	15 grams	=	1 tablespoon
1 ounce	=	25 to 30 grams	=	2 tablespoons
2 ounces	=	55 to 60 grams	=	1/4 cup
2 1/2 ounces	=	75 grams		
3 ounces	=	90 grams		
3 1/2 ounces	=	100 grams		
4 ounces	=	110 grams		
4 1/2 ounces	=	125 grams		
5 ounces	=	135 to 140 grams		
5 1/2 ounces	=	150 grams		
6 ounces	=	175 grams		
6 1/2 ounces	=	185 grams		
7 ounces	=	200 grams		
8 ounces	=	225 grams		
9 ounces	=	250 grams		
9 1/2 ounces	=	275 grams		
10 1/2 ounces	=	300 grams		
11 1/2 ounces	=	325 grams		
12 ounces	=	340 grams		
12 1/2 ounces	=	350 grams		
13 1/2 ounces	=	380 grams		
14 ounces	=	400 grams		
1 pound	=	450 grams		
18 ounces	=	500 grams		
1 1/3 pounds	=	600 grams		
1 1/2 pounds	=	680 to 700 grams		
1 3/4 pounds	=	800 to 820 grams		
2 pounds	=	900 grams		
2 1/4 pounds	=	1 kilogram		
3 pounds	=	1.35 kilograms		
3 1/3 pounds	=	1 1/2 kilograms		
3 1/2 pounds	=	1.6 kilograms		
3 3/4 pounds	=	1.7 kilograms		
4 pounds	=	1.75 kilograms		
4 1/2 pounds	=	2 kilograms		
5 1/2 pounds	=	2.5 kilograms		
6 pounds	=	2.75 kilograms		
6 1/2 pounds	=	3 kilograms		

VOLUME MEASUREMENTS

1/8 cup	=	28 milliliters
1/4 cup	=	55 milliliters
1/3 cup	=	75 milliliters
1/2 cup	=	110 milliliters
2/3 cup	=	150 milliliters
3/4 cup	=	175 milliliters
7/8 cup	=	200 milliliters
1 cup	=	225 milliliters
9 ounces	=	250 milliliters
1 1/4 cups	=	300 milliliters
1 1/3 cups	=	325 milliliters
1 1/2 cups	=	350 milliliters
1 3/4 cups	=	400 milliliters
2 cups	=	450 milliliters
2 1/2 cups	=	560 milliliters
3 cups	=	700 milliliters
3 1/2 cups	=	820 milliliters
4 cups	=	900 milliliters
4 1/2 cups	=	1 liter
5 cups	=	1.2 liters
6 cups	=	1.4 liters
7 cups	=	1.6 liters
8 cups	=	1.8 liters
9 cups	=	2 liters
10 cups	=	2.25 liters
12 cups	=	2.7 liters
14 cups	=	3 liters
15 cups	=	3.37 liters
16 cups	=	3.6 liters
18 cups	=	4 liters
30 cups	=	5.75 liters

INDEX

"m" for meat, "d" for dairy, "p" for pareve.

351